FORGETTING ABORIGINES

CHRIS HEALY

UNSW
PRESS

A UNSW Press book

Published by
University of New South Wales Press Ltd
University of New South Wales
Sydney NSW 2052
AUSTRALIA
www.unswpress.com.au

National Library of Australia
Cataloguing-in-Publication entry

Healy, Chris.
Forgetting Aborigines/author, Chris Healy.
Sydney: University of New South Wales Press Ltd, 2008.
ISBN: 978 086840 884 2 (pbk.)
Includes index.
Aboriginal Australians – History.
Aboriginal Australians, Treatment of.

994.0049915

Design Di Quick: *cover image* F.D. Manley, *King George VI
Definitive Series 1950–57*, 19 March 1952, has been reproduced
with permission of the Australian Postal Corporation. Original
artwork held in the National Philatelic Collection.
Printer Ligare Press
Paper 100gsm woodfree using fibre supplied from Australian
plantation forests.

This book was produced with assistance from a University of
Melbourne publications grant.

*Indigenous readers are respectfully advised that some people
mentioned in writing or depicted in photographs in the following
pages have passed away.*

CONTENTS

1 FORGETTING ABORIGINES

Is it the fear of forgetting that triggers the desire to
remember, or is it perhaps the other way around?

Andreas Huyssen[1]

On the desk in front of me is *Corroboree*. It's a dice and token
game, like *Snakes and Ladders*, that my mother remembers playing in the late 1940s. The game consists of a journey around the
board that finishes at a watercolour image of indigenous men dancing by firelight for an audience of women, children and, of course,
the players of *Corroboree*. Along the route there are 25 small images of events that occur for the player who lands on the space: for
example, at 87 the instruction reads 'Lost Churinga Back to 71'; at
52, 'Bushfire Back to Mia-Mia'; at 41, 'Miss Two Decorate Shield'.
To look at *Corroboree* in the early 21st century is to both see and,
in a sense, to participate in a world of racist images of indigenous
people. The semi-naked primitives who 'Make Fire' and 'Dig for
Honey Ants' take us to a world in which non-indigenous people
confidently represented indigenous people as an archaic race who
did not belong to the world of modern Australia.

Jessie Mackintosh,
Corroboree, *c. 1940.*
(National Library of
Australia)

Today most cultural critics would regard this as a game of bad representations, full of those rubbish pictures that students are trained to spot and condemn, the kind of images that non-indigenous Australians disavow and disown. When showing *Corroboree* to friends, I have literally been asked to put it away. This reaction is entirely understandable, motivated perhaps by a sense that such images are disrespectful and that they may offend indigenous Australians, or that these kinds of representations connect non-indigenous Australians to a shameful past when not only image-making but government policies, social regulation and cultural norms impacted on indigenous Australians, often with terrible consequences for cultural and community sustainability, morbidity and mortality. The impulse to look away from *Corroboree* may also be motivated by a sense that leaving behind such clichéd images of indigenous people demonstrates a desire to make a better future for both indigenous and non-indigenous Australians. But to close the board and conceal its images is also to hide from the past in the present. It is to make Aborigines disappear. It is to forget.

As well as being a 'bad representation', *Corroboree* is also one artefact in a vast archive of entanglements between indigenous and non-indigenous Australians over more than two centuries. *Forgetting Aborigines* is a small cultural history of how, in the recent past, some of those entanglements have been remembered and forgotten.[2] My argument is not simply that non-indigenous Australia is amnesic in relation to indigenous people, although that's certainly sometimes the case. Nor am I proposing that if only non-indigenous Australians replaced their forgetting with remembering, then there would be real historical grounds for better settler–indigenous relationships today, attractive though that notion is. My memory metaphor is not that of the novel *The White Earth*, in which the bleached bones of massacred indigenous people lie forgotten at the bottom of the swimming hole waiting to be ethically recalled in the present.[3] Instead, I'm concerned with how remembering and forgetting work to produce indigenous and non-indigenous people in relation to each other. I want to consider the intercultural space of Aboriginality as constituted by strange and transient patterns of remembering and forgetting, where Aboriginal people and things appear and disappear as if by magic, where cultural memory is performed so as to invoke, revisit and transcend heterogeneous pasts. In these spaces, cultural memory is as real and as shifting as sand.

ABORIGINALITY

> The silence that envelops so much of the settler–indigenous
> past can often be understood without the help of accountants
> cataloguing names, relationships and violent deaths. The
> silence sometimes needs to be respected.
>
> Klaus Neumann[4]

Before turning to questions of cultural memory, I want to consider the intercultural space of 'Aboriginality', a term I've borrowed from anthropologist Marcia Langton. In her remarkable book *Well, I heard it on the radio and I saw it on the television* ... , Langton ranges widely from analysing the conditions of film production and distribution to subtle and provocative readings of image-making by a range of indigenous cultural producers, including the Warlpiri Media Association and Tracey Moffatt.[5] It is both an essay concerned with how images work and a policy document, explicitly aiming to 'guide and inform the Australian Film Commission and other readers and policy-makers in the development of policies and programs to encourage Aboriginal production and distribution'.[6] One of Langton's central concerns is with the disparity between the actual life circumstances of indigenous people and the 'cultural and textual construction of things "Aboriginal"'.[7] For Langton, these mismatches are produced by two forces often operating together, one historical and the other conventional. She writes of settler culture:

The most dense relationship is not between actual people, but between white Australians and the symbols created by their predecessors. They relate to stories told by former colonists [and] the constant stereotyping, iconising and mythologising of Aboriginal people by white people who have never had any substantial first-hand contact with Aboriginal people.[8]

Corroboree would be a good example of such a 'symbol'; a 'construction of things "Aboriginal"', which is animated by ideas and images from the colonial archive of indigenous people as primitives, entirely disconnected from indigenous life in the 1940s. Langton explores a number of possible alternatives to the production of familiar negative stereotypes, one of which might be the production of images 'generated when Aboriginal and non-Aboriginal people engage in actual dialogue ... [in which] the individuals involved will test imagined models of the other ... to find some satisfactory way of comprehending the other'.[9] Because Langton is, in part, concerned with the development of protocols for image-making involving indigenous people, it's this kind of negotiation and exchange that she recommends: a dialogic model that, arguably, has underpinned films such as *Two Laws* and *Ten Canoes*.[10]

Here I'm interested in how the term 'Aboriginality' can be used for thinking about cultural relationships between indigenous and non-indigenous people. Langton does not use Aboriginality to describe the Aboriginal-ness of a thing or an authentically Aboriginal quotient. On the contrary, she writes:

'Aboriginality' arises from the subjective experience of both Aboriginal people and non-Aboriginal people who engage in any intercultural dialogue, whether in actual lived experience or through a mediated experience such as a white person watching a program about Aboriginal people on television or reading a book.[11]

While I do not think that 'Aboriginality' is a term which provides a general theory of colonialism in Australia, it does offer a useful orientation to colonial culture. It conceptualises the indigenous and the non-indigenous as referring to both separate and connected domains. Like two overlapping elements in a Venn diagram and the colonial encounter itself, Aboriginality figures indigenous and non-indigenous as coming into existence for each other at points of intersection. In this sense, Aboriginality also presupposes 'Europeanality'. So for a non-indigenous writer such as me, this theory provides a productive way of thinking about the 'cultural and textual construction of things "Aboriginal"' as an intercultural activity. Rather than, as in the Federal Court case concerning the Native Title claim of the Yorta Yorta, referring to the memoirs of a colonial settler as providing an accurate account of indigenous people, such accounts would be thought of as concerned with Aboriginality, a product of what each side in a dialogue brought to their specific interactions.[12] It follows that Aboriginality is no more *about* actual Aboriginal people than it is *about* actual non-Aboriginal people. Instead of making pronouncements about 'Aborigines', Aboriginality directs me towards what happens interstitially, through what anthropologist Fred Myers has described as 'intercultural trafficking'.[13] To make this clear, except when I'm quoting the work of others, I'll use the terms 'Aborigine/s' and 'Aboriginal' only in relation to constructions (images, narratives and so on) in the domain of Aboriginality.

Following sociologist Émile Durkheim, Langton describes Aboriginality as 'a social thing', emphasising that she's not referring to abstract ideas or immaterial ideologies but actual engagements that produce real effects in the world. Without detracting from this emphasis, my preference is to consider Aboriginality in spatial terms, to think about Aboriginality as a zone in the concrete sense of describing places and moments in which indigenous and non-indigenous people observe, interact and experiment in ways that make each other in relation to the other. In this sense, it's closely related to historian Mary Louise Pratt's term 'contact zone' as describing:

the space of colonial encounters, the space in which peoples
geographically and historically separated come into contact
with each other and establish ongoing relations ... A 'contact'
perspective emphasizes how subjects are constituted in and
by their relations to each other. [It stresses] copresence,
interaction, interlocking understandings and practices, often
within radically asymmetrical relations of power.[14]

Far more than a moment of first contact or fatal impact, Aboriginality is a 'contact zone' in an extended field that's both colonial
and postcolonial.[15] It's a notion that allows me, in what follows,
to consider indigenous television in the 1960s and the art of Aboriginal kitsch. It takes me to heritage as contested terrain, to indigenous galleries in museums and to indigenous tourism.

REMEMBERING AND FORGETTING

He who has once begun to open the fan of memory never
comes to the end of its segments.

Walter Benjamin[16]

This is not the place for a general or theoretical account of memory studies as a burgeoning and unwieldy field of inquiry across
the humanities.[17] I do, however, need to provide some co-ordinates
for my discussion of forgetting and remembering. *Forgetting
Aborigines* is concerned with a wide range of ways in which 'the
past' is recalled and made present. My interest is not in memory as a thing but in remembering as a process, which can take
the form of personal testimony and witnessing, writing and film,
photography and television, painting and museum exhibitions,
teaching and celebration, mourning and commemoration. As
historian Greg Dening might have it, remembering as performance. Inasmuch as they are communicative, these performances
of memory by people and things are public. While many impor-

tant insights into cultural memory are influenced significantly by studies of and theories concerned with individual memory, particularly those that derive from psychoanalytic traditions, *Forgetting Aborigines* is predominately concerned with remembering as a communicative and shared cultural practice. Yet, unlike the influential tradition around collective memory associated with the work of sociologist Maurice Halbwachs, I do not regard memory as something that's possessed by a class of people or a nation as a point of collective identification.[18] Here I approach remembering not as something complete but as a shifting, heterogeneous, partial and repetitive assemblage of acts, utterances and artefacts. Finally, it's important to insist that *Forgetting Aborigines* is attempting to think about both remembering and forgetting, because there is never one without the other. At the most basic level, the selective recognition of some things rather than others, and the discerning organisation of those elements so that they can be made present, requires forgetting. So, while I will pay attention to the ethics of remembering, I am in no way wanting to regard memory as a cure for forgetting. Without forgetting there is only an endless present overwhelmed by the flow of everything all at once.

Forgetting Aborigines is concerned with the ways in which, in the recent past, Aboriginal people and things have been remembered and forgotten in Australia. At the broadest level, it refers to remembering and forgetting the occupation of the continent by indigenous people and the British colonisation of the same continent. 'Events' such as these are remembered through a variety of institutional and habitual practices, from property law to naming country, public rituals and language. In this sense, remembering and forgetting takes us directly to how historicity – a lived experience of being in history – is constitutive of everyday life. In this modest cultural history of Aboriginality over the last four decades, I'm concerned with a paradox that Murri scholar Philip Morrissey writes about as central to the 'dominant school of settler thought'. It consists of:

the rhetorical of 'doing away with' Aborigines – their erasure as subjectivities and intelligences from history and contemporary Australia ... Paradoxically, in spite of the success of this erasure, Aboriginal corporeality – the embodied being of Aborigines – remains a troubling and disturbing fact for settler Australia.[19]

Settler Australians have, since the beginning, too often thought of indigenous people, and hence Aboriginality, as either absent or present – imagining that they were once in place but are now gone, belong somewhere else or out of place, because they are out of time, finished and done for. This cultural imaginary suited colonial dispossession and the governance of a dying race. There was and is a:

sheer conflict between circumstance and rhetoric. In principle, Aborigines were savages, yet as individuals they might be recognised as dignified and estimable people. On the one hand, an Aboriginal presence was real, and it had to be reckoned with; on the other hand it had to be imagined away.[20]

As Morrissey reminds us, the rhetorical erasure of Aborigines has flourished at the same time as it has been flatly contradicted by the persistence of indigenous being. Indigenous people and Aborigines just keep on appearing, often in the eyes of settler Australians as if for the first time. From Bungaree at Sydney Cove to Catherine Freeman at Stadium Australia, indigenous people have been called upon to perform Aboriginal presence. My conceptualisation of this paradox is that in the domain of Aboriginality, Aboriginal people and things appear in and disappear from public culture in strange but definite ways. Aborigines are recognised and identified, then they are overlooked and disregarded. The argument of *Forgetting Aborigines* is that the performance and organisation of social memory provides one way of thinking about why Aborigines keep on disappearing. But to get to those questions we need to take a detour through history.

FROM MEMORY BACK TO HISTORY

> The traumatised, we might say, carry an impossible history within them, or they become themselves the symptom of a history that they cannot entirely possess.
>
> Cathy Caruth[21]

The pre-eminent mode in which indigenous people are remembered in Australia is as absent. The evidence of this trope and its dominance is ubiquitous. We can find it in continental metaphors – a silent country with a dead heart – more broadly in the poetic and visual imagining of Australian space; and most powerfully in the founding faith of colonisation in Australia, that land was there for the taking. Real historical experiences and fantasies grounded these acts of imagination. Ideas about and practices in relation to the rights and status of indigenous people varied considerably, from ruthless cruelty to humanitarian and religiously inflected racism, and these were adapted and elaborated again and again through colonial encounters. Compared with Europe and many lands colonised by Europeans before 1788, much of the Australian continent was sparsely settled by indigenous people, although this was less true of resource-rich regions along the coasts and inland waterways. Also, diseases brought to Australia by non-indigenous people most likely travelled ahead of the physical occupation of country with significant and deadly consequences.[22] As a result, when Europeans saw the country for the first time, the numbers of indigenous people in place were already substantially lower than historical population numbers. The devastation of diseases was also exacerbated by the ways in which European-settler disruptions of relatively stable patterns of land occupation in one place produced rapid knock-on effects in places at a distance. So, the movements of people forced out of their traditional country created conflict and loss of life in neighbouring country in advance of white settlement. And there is little doubt, except among the most vehement of revisionists, that the violent seizure of land in many places across the continent actually destroyed indigenous communities.

Although the actual historical experience of settler–indigenous relations varied enormously over the century and a half after 1788 in which the Australian continent was effectively colonised, we know that indigenous people continued to be actually present throughout occupied country. This was clearly the case in many rural and remote regions where, more recently, indigenous property rights have been enshrined under land rights legislation and native title processes, precisely because indigenous people can demonstrate the maintenance of so-called traditional relationships to country. The continuity of historical relationships to country is the basic pattern across much of settled Australia where, for most of the last 200-odd years, Aboriginal people have been integral to economic and social life. A more marginal Aboriginal presence was maintained by the palimpsest of town camps, missions and reserves over the Australian landscape. The situation was different in some larger towns and cities where, because of a range of features – the scale and anonymity of city life, the extent of disruption of relatively autonomous indigenous communities, the levels of interconnection between indigenous and non-indigenous communities – it can more plausibly be suggested that indigenous people seemed to be absent. And after all, these were the places where most non-indigenous Australians have lived from the second half of the 19th century. Even so, we know that Aboriginal people and communities have always lived and worked in Australian cities and towns. To mention only the most obvious examples from Australia's two biggest cities, indigenous communities in Fitzroy, La Perouse and Redfern have deep historical roots.

So we are faced with an immediate paradox: Aborigines are remembered as absent in the face of a continuing and actual indigenous historical presence. It has been the work of many historians over the past two decades to try to make sense of the historical dimensions of this paradox. The historian Ann Curthoys has drawn attention to the significant presence of Aborigines in 19th-century historical accounts in contrast to an absence in much 20th-century historiography.[23] Similarly, Henry Reynolds has argued that the 20th century was Australia's forgetful century. There are persuasive contrasts between 19th-century colonial historians who 'exoticised the drama of colonial encounters with Indigenous peoples, adding excitement and tragedy to a narrative about a strange land' and 20th-century historians concerned 'to create a respectable story of progress and evolution towards self-government'.[24] Yet this compelling argument is essentially one concerned with nationalism and nationalist historiography. It's an account of non-indigenous historical consciousness that seems to break down at the level of local historical knowledge.

Take, for example, the local articulations of being-in-history in Mark McKenna's evocative book *Looking for Blackfellas' Point*, which explores the imbrication of white and black historical experiences on the far south coast of New South Wales.[25] In reflecting on 'the story of a battle between the Monaro and Bega tribes, witnessed by one of the first British settlers to enter the Bega Valley, W.D. Tarlington', McKenna writes of Aborigines being absent from the very earliest historical accounts:

> The white man discovered the land and the 'Aborigines'
> dutifully destroyed one another the very next day. Like the
> 'empty land' myths in the Afrikaner histories of South Africa,
> the first wave of pioneer histories of European settlement of
> the south coast of New South Wales told the story of a land
> left for the taking.[26]

One thing that makes *Looking for Blackfellas' Point* so forceful is its attention to the particularities of colonisation and how specific local dynamics mattered, not just in terms of shaping actual historical experiences but equally in terms of forming social memory. The relative isolation of the south coast from Sydney mattered, as did initial encounters on the beaches. The marauding sealers and the development of a local whaling industry were important, as were the particular individuals involved. Also significant were the patterns of land grabs and the sheer barbarism of early white settlements; the variable reliance on indigenous labour and ongoing patterns of indigenous occupation; the presence of missions, philanthropic and government-run institutions, and so on. While there was a general amnesia in relation to the historical and contemporary presence of indigenous people in this region from about the 1860s to the 1960s, it was a forgetting that was neither total nor unchanging. Aboriginal people were periodically wheeled onto the stage of theatrical history to perform as 'the last of their tribe' (a characterisation which I return to in chapter 5) or to embody the miracles that the Lord could work on our 'sable brothers'. McKenna also demonstrates that the spaces of exchange and dialogue between indigenous and non-indigenous people, the space of interaction that I'm calling Aboriginality, did not disappear entirely. He makes it clear that indigenous people were always there and that they certainly were not waiting quietly for a time in the 20th century when history would grant them a new part to play.

On the basis of recent historical scholarship, it's clear that, in general, late 19th- and early 20th-century histories were blighted by an aporia in relation to the historical and contemporary presence of indigenous people. At the same time, local or popular historical knowledge does not conform to this template. These propositions should, and no doubt will, be pursued further down through the archives; however, my interest here lies, in a sense, at the other end of those histories, in the present past – in how 'the past', historical knowledge, social memory, historical consciousness and senses of being in history shape contemporary culture. How might we understand remembering and forgetting as part of the contemporary legacy of the historical paradox of presence and absence?

WHY WEREN'T WE TOLD?

Since the election of John Howard's government in 1996,
disavowal and sheer ignorance about Australian culture
and history have acquired a respectability that was
unthinkable only three years before his election; there is a
renewed fervour for 'roping off' the past and pulling rowdy
Aborigines into line; there is, once again, white debate about
assimilating Aborigines, and a growing disinclination to hear
stories about mothers and the children parted or thrown
together by policy in the past.

We are being asked to forget about the past few years of
remembering.

Meaghan Morris[27]

The second half of the 20th century offers us, at first glance, a
radically different milieu. From at least the mid-century, indigenous people and things began assuming a central place in Australian public culture. Writing about the 1950s, when important
shifts in governance were then being set in train, historian Anna
Haebich notes: 'Quite simply, Aboriginal affairs was now a matter
of national and international importance which could no longer
be left to "bumbling" parochial state administrations.'[28] Thus the
1951 Commonwealth and state ministers' Native Welfare Council might mark a new moment in the long and tortuous history of
the governance of indigenous people with its many and varied
legislative, administrative, juridical and bureaucratic outcomes.
More broadly, this coincided with a wider public prominence for
certain individuals who were recognised as Aborigines: Harold
Blair was a headlining presence in the ABC's 1951 *Jubilee Concert Tour*; Albert Namatjira was at the height of his popularity
in the late 1940s and 1950s; there was a long list of Aboriginal
boxers in the golden years of professional fighting stretching from
George Sands's 1946 championships to George Bracken's 1956

lightweight triumph; and Sir Douglas Nicholls was awarded an MBE in 1957.[29]

Yet, just as indigenous people and Aboriginal affairs began to take a more prominent place in public culture, some of the ways in which Aboriginality was discussed took a very different form. In the late 1960s, anthropologist WEH Stanner famously condemned 'the great Australian silence' and chastised historians for perpetuating a 'cult of forgetfulness practised on a national scale'.[30] Stanner predicted that scholarship would fill up the silence. In 1984, Henry Reynolds pronounced that:

> many scholars in numerous disciplines have transformed our knowledge and understanding of Aboriginal Australia in the past and present ... In giving up their cult of forgetfulness, white Australians have accepted a less flattering image of their past but a much more realistic one. In coming face to face with black Australians they have at last come face to face with themselves.[31]

It seemed that the forgetfulness had come to an end. Yet a mere 15 years later, in 1999, Reynolds began his book *Why Weren't We Told?* with these words:

> Why were we never told? Why didn't we know? I have been asked these questions by many people, over many years, in all parts of Australia ... Why didn't we know? Why were we never told? ... Why do so many people ask the same questions of themselves, of me, of their education, their heritage, of the whole of Australian society?[32]

At the end of the 20th century, after even more scholarship, why had the filling up of the silence not banished the cult of forgetfulness?

One possibility is the lack of fit between history and the present past. There is no doubt that Stanner was right to identify a forgetting of indigenous people in historical writing. Yet, paradoxically, he was writing at a time of considerable non-indigenous babble about Aboriginal people and things. To take only the two most obvious examples: the walk-off at Wave Hill generated significant national media and political attention for many months in 1966, and the 1967 referendum saw a zealous campaign result in the polity speaking loudly and (almost) as one in favour of what were couched as full citizen rights for Aborigines.[33] In other words, while there was silence and absence in some domains, there was clamour and presence in others. Yet, three decades on, the same question returns in a different form, 'Why weren't we told?' At one level, we might regard this as entirely predictable. Contemporary media culture is, after all, both profoundly amnesic and completely obsessed with remembering. Similar patterns can be identified in relation to non-indigenous people and things. In this sense, the forgetting and remembering of the stolen generations might be regarded as similar to the ways in which say, sexual abuse perpetrated by Catholic clergy has been forgotten and remembered. Or perhaps the appearance of figures such as Catherine Freeman or Michael Dodson might be said to follow the same patterns of media management and massage that magically produce figures such as Ian Thorpe or Pauline Hansen as media-culture icons.

There is certainly some truth in this proposition. The media studies work of Alan McKee and John Hartley has made a strong case for thinking about the indigenous public sphere as a significant and distinctive part of what they call the 'Australian semiosphere'.[34] However, to account for a media sphere of indigeneity without considering questions of historical articulation simply reverses Stanner's attention to history at the expense of contemporary indigenous presence. Both arguments forget Aborigines in different ways. In a rich discussion of Tracey Moffatt's film *Night Cries* (1989) and other matters, cultural critic Meaghan Morris provides the outlines of a very different answer to Reynolds's question 'Why didn't we know?', a question that largely concerns the stolen generations:

But we cannot not know now that the policy's application in Australia to Aboriginal people had a calculatedly ethnocidal and a systematically racist purpose; and we cannot not know that the taking of Aboriginal children was practised on a horrifically large scale.

Only in recent years, however, has some notion of the scale of the trauma and disruption that this policy created begun to filter through to the *white* Australians in whose idealised name it was practised. Or, rather than speaking of an 'idea' filtering through, I should say that only recently have we begun to develop a collective capacity to comprehend, to empathise, to imagine that trauma and disruption. This is also a matter of a politics of remembering. It is important to clarify that many (I would guess most) white Australians 'were not "aware" of what was happening' *not* because we did not *know* it was happening (we did) but because we were unable or did not care to *understand* what we knew; we could not imagine how Aboriginal people felt. So we whites have not, 'just found out' about the lost children; rather, we are beginning to remember differently, to understand and care about what we knew.[35]

Forgetting Aborigines is centrally concerned with the politics of memory that Morris describes here. It's attentive to the roles of remembering and forgetting in making the past appear and disappear in the present and in making sense of the force of the past in the present. I want to think of remembering and forgetting as in a state of dynamic tension. This notion is partly inspired by another film, Ivan Sen's tough and poetic *Dust* (1999). Through the use of various techniques – mise en scène, sound, editing and diagesis – this entire film feels incredibly tense, unresolved and haunted. Not until its final chaotic scenes when a dust storm uncovers bones in the area where the characters have been working is there some sense of the energy that's produced the 'nervous system' on screen. The country itself might be disclosing or concealing, but the force of memory is ever present. To ask the question 'Why weren't we told?' after a screening of *Dust* invites one simple response, 'How can you forget a past that's present?'

STILL NOT SORRY

> Such facts as were known were used to vindicate historicist fabrications, not to illuminate a way of life seen as having interest and importance in its own right ... much inexact, often spurious, information about the Aborigines found its way into print, and more damagingly, into the unexamined assumptions of scholars and public alike.
>
> WEH Stanner[36]

The writing of *Forgetting Aborigines* has been dominated by the tenure of a conservative federal government led by John Howard. Between 1996, when it came to power, and 2000 the new government brought the process of reconciliation to a grinding halt and began to systematically dismantle many of the institutions produced under policies of indigenous self-determination. 'Reconciliation' was regarded as one of a grab bag of feel-good gestures beloved by those guilt-ridden Labor supporters who chatter away over chardonnay. They were in the thrall of a culture cult simultaneously ignorant of 'real Aborigines' and overinvested in a myth of nobility at Nhulunbuy. As Peter Howson, former Minister for Aboriginal Affairs (1971–72), put it in an article on Michael Long's Long Walk, the endeavour was wrongheaded, 'pursuing the same futile symbolic objectives of treaties and apologies as those who walked across the Sydney Harbour Bridge in 2000'.[37] Symbolic reconciliation was to be replaced by practical reconciliation. At the same time, the Howard government set about repudiating more than a quarter of a century of government policies based on self-determination, instead promoting indigenous integration as the future for black Australians. Particularly between 2000 and 2007, the years of the Howard government were a time when an indigenous political presence disappeared from the national political agenda. Indeed, Howard himself argued as much in 2007 when he had his 'conversion' just before he was voted out of office.[38]

These were the years of the culture wars and the history wars, when in the pages of *Quadrant*, *The Australian*, *Herald Sun* and beyond culture warriors sought to defeat the abysmal legacy of economist and public servant HC Coombs and many other meddlers. In terms of my concerns here, I'm ambivalent about the significance of these wars. Much of what passed as 'public debate' was uninteresting, tendentious, self-serving or moralistic. More importantly, as political scientist Murray Goot and historian Tim Rowse have demonstrated, these debates were often wildly at odds with the broadly acknowledged and widely understood consequences for indigenous people of dispossession.[39] Yet there was an attempt to reclaim history from those who, it was said, had promulgated the nation as stained by a shameful genocide. In this project, Keith Windschuttle was pivotal. His decisive gesture was attempting to settle the past once and for all with *The Fabrication of Aboriginal History*.[40] The historian Klaus Neumann has provided a concise outline:

> Windschuttle's argument is deceptively simple. He says
> that historians ... have grossly overestimated the number
> of Tasmanian Aborigines killed by settlers in the first half
> of the nineteenth century. According to his calculations,
> 'only' 120 Aborigines were killed by whites – 'mostly in self-
> defence or in hot pursuit of Aborigines who had assaulted
> white households'. Windschuttle argues that the historians
> of colonial Tasmania have produced histories to further
> a political agenda. They got away with it because nobody
> checked their sources.[41]

But on the basis of these claims, Windschuttle makes a much broader argument:

The British colonization of this continent was the least violent
of all Europe's encounters with the New World. It did not
meet organized resistance. Conflicts were sporadic rather
than systematic. Some mass killings were committed by
both sides but they were rare and isolated events where the
numbers of dead were in the tens rather than the hundreds.
The notion of 'sustained warfare' is fictional.[42]

Australian settlement thus becomes a commendable achievement
of civilisation brought to 'the most primitive human society ever
discovered'.[43]

Neumann has argued persuasively that Windschuttle's most
insidious sleight of hand was that, in counting the dead, he avoid-
ed accounting for dispossession: 'It is the initial act of dispossession, more so than settler–indigenous conflict, that had a lasting
impact on settler-colonial society and keeps haunting Australia to
the present day.'[44] More broadly, Neumann has written against the
tendency of history to disconnect past and present, to think about
a past as 'done with'. Instead, he is interested in moving:

away from a debate about historical evidence and towards
one about the production of histories; away from a discussion
about the past and towards one about how we live with, talk
about and keep silent about that past; ... towards a proactive
imagining of histories beyond prevailing orthodoxy.[45]

In these kinds of projects, remembering and forgetting are central
processes. The early years of a new century were good times to
be writing *Forgetting Aborigines*, not so much because of the
history wars but because there was a lot of forgetting around.
In these years, it was entirely clear that there is never an end to
remembering and forgetting.

THE WORK OF REMEMBERING

> The emergence of anti-colonial and 'independent' nation-
> states after colonialism is frequently accompanied by a
> desire to forget the colonial past. This 'will-to-forget' takes
> a number of historical forms, and is impelled by a variety of
> cultural and political motivations. Principally, postcolonial
> amnesia is symptomatic of the urge for historical self-
> invention or the need to make a new start – to erase painful
> memories of colonial subordination.
>
> Leela Gandhi[46]

This book is part of a long cultural tradition of, as Philip Morrissey writes, non-indigenous people 'addressing Aboriginal–settler issues specifically for settlers'.[47] It emerges out of an intellectual and cultural milieu that, in many cases, also supplies me with the material to think with. *Forgetting Aborigines* could not have been written without the political, administrative and institutional innovation in relation to indigenous affairs that has occurred since the 1960s; what Goot and Rowse describe as the politics of inclusion and non-discrimination that was shadowed by social exclusion. It also depends on the extraordinary volume and quality of cultural production emerging from the domain of Aboriginality in painting, film, photography, exhibition, performance, poetry, fiction and much more. The art of Gordon Bennett, Destiny Deacon and Fiona Foley, the films of Tracey Moffatt, the fiction of Tony Birch, Kim Scott and Alexis Wright, as well as the songs of Paul Kelly and Yothu Yindi, are testimony to the energy around rendering postcolonial Australia differently over the last two decades. This book also comes out of an intellectual world and has been enabled by the work of journalists, historians and archaeologists, art historians and anthropologists, social scientists and cultural theorists, some of whom you'll encounter in these pages. But there are two other kinds of intellectual work that I want to mention specifically.

I've already discussed here the work of Marcia Langton and Philip Morrissey, two indigenous intellectuals among a cohort of indigenous scholars – Larissa Behrendt, Tony Birch, Aileen Moreton-Robinson, Hetti Perkins, Mandawuy Yunupingu and others – who, across a number of disciplines, have made creative and transformative contributions to intellectual debates.[48] These postcolonial critics have not only been theoretically innovative but have encouraged their readers 'to revise our inherited stories intimately, to remember our own childhood or "maternal" experiences differently, and to do this *inter*-subjectively, in a collective or public way'.[49] The work of these indigenous scholars seems to me connected to that of a number of non-indigenous scholars who have tried to think about a very simple but profoundly unsettling condition: that 'Aboriginal presence was real, and it had to be reckoned with'. For a long time, the history of indigenous and non-indigenous cultural interaction has, in a sense, been read off a political/juridical history in which the achievement of civic rights is haunted by dispossession and genocide. So, indigenous people have been thought of as having been gently conquered with the unfortunate result that many are now 'homeless'. They have been thought of as having survived and as now asserting their rights, rights which were not extinguished despite that dark history. It seems to me more persuasive to say that, in addition to a history of dispossession and domination, relationships between indigenous and non-indigenous people have also been ones of mutually transformative co-habitation.

The historian Nicholas Thomas provides us with a significant account of such an alternative conceptualisation in *Possession: Indigenous art/colonial culture*. Rather than imagining that settler colonialism in Australia has, through genocide, produced a pure white Australia, Thomas, borrowing the title of a Rover Thomas (no relation) painting, wants to think of colonial and postcolonial culture as a 'meeting place'. For too long, he argues, colonial relationships have been thought of either from the European perspective, in which Europe both dominated and stole from distant and subjugated lands, or from the (newer) perspective of a cosmopolitan globalisation in which flows between many nodes reigned supreme as if 'old relations between centres and peripheries had been superseded'. Instead, he is interested, as I am, in the virtues of a local optic. Such a perspective reminds us that 'the distinctive feature of settler colonialism was the sustained and direct character of engagement between indigenous and European cultures', one in which an 'uncertain combination of acknowledgement and denial ... has characterized the settler–indigenous relation in general'.[50] My argument in *Forgetting Aborigines* is that remembering and forgetting constitute some of the ambivalence of postcolonialism 'viewed from a distinctive local vantage point'. In her elegant introduction to postcolonial thought, literary scholar Leela Gandhi puts memory at the heart of the postcolonial criticism. She notes that the 'will-to-forget' of 'postcolonial amnesia is symptomatic of the urge for historical self-invention or the need to make a new start – to erase painful memories of colonial subordination'. For Gandhi, postcolonialism is a response to the 'mystifying amnesia of the colonial aftermath ... a disciplinary project devoted to the academic task of revisiting, remembering and, crucially, interrogating the colonial past'.[51] One way of describing the unresolved aspects of postcolonialism in Australia is to imagine remembering and forgetting as haunting 'those places where one's discourse is only made possible by its relation to the Other'.[52]

Forgetting Aborigines is a modest contribution to a cultural history of Aboriginality in Australia since the 1960s. It's a minor history in the sense that it shadows many of the well-known political and social landmarks of indigenous affairs. I begin in the 1960s, a decade remembered as when indigenous people were admitted to 'citizenship'. It's well known that the 1967 referendum did not confer any such legal rights; that it was a proposal 'to alter the Constitution so as to omit certain words relating to the People of the Aboriginal Race in any State and so that Aboriginals are to be counted in reckoning the Population.'[53] Nonetheless, in both history and memory the referendum is accurately associated with new forms of public and political recognition for indigenous Australians. My study of the 1960s in chapter 2 also concerns the public sphere in the form of a television series, *Alcheringa*, that brought images of indigenous people into homes and schools. It's a useful starting point because it deals with the basic question of indigenous presence and non-indigenous knowledge. Chapter 3 is concerned with indigenous art. It focuses on how a painting movement at the remote settlement of Papunya has been remembered in ways that disconnect contemporary Aboriginal art from a longer artistic entanglement between indigenous and non-indigenous people in the form of Abo art. Together, these chapters enable me to tell stories about how culturally significant examples of Aboriginality in the 1960s and 1970s have been remembered.

Throughout the 1980s and 1990s across a number of different cultural institutions, Aboriginality assumed new and distinctive roles in public culture. In chapter 4, my interest in these examples – the bicentennial celebrations, judicial inquiries and rulings – is focused on how they transformed notions of heritage and opened up spaces for vernacular histories. Chapter 5 is concerned with museums and how intercultural objects, and the ways in which they are institutionally located and exhibited, rework colonial inheritances. These and many other initiatives were part of a process of creating what Tim Rowse has called the indigenous public sphere. My analysis is focused on the ways in which remembering is central to the new presence of Aboriginality. The decade or so straddling the new millennium might be remembered as posing questions about intimacy in the domain of Aboriginality: from the kiss between Ernie Dingo and Cate Blanchett in *Heartland* (1994) to the double act of Nikki Webster and Djakapurra Munyarryun at the opening ceremony of the Sydney Olympic Games (2000). In chapter 6, my minor history of this turn to intimacy concerns Lurujarri, a tourist walking trail in Western Australia. In chapter 7, I return to the broad questions of remembering and forgetting in order to ask whether, in addition to the ethical gains of remembering Aborigines, there might also be

George Lacy,
Aboriginal Camp by a
Stream, *c. 1855–60.*

things to be said in support of forgetting Aborigines.

On the wall in front of me is an image of a land full of Aborigines. It's a watercolour painting by George Lacy, *Aboriginal Camp by a Stream*, painted some time between 1855 and 1860 near Bendigo. The painting is part of a series described in a 1970 auc-

tion catalogue as 'Depicting the historical gold rush days around
Bendigo and events of that time, they display the wonderful lyric
of the early colonial days, its history and rich humour ... unique
and lovely paintings of our colourful past.'[54] The camp is occupied
by about 40 Aboriginal men, women and children, sitting under

shelters, climbing trees, diving into the river, carrying children, making implements and going about their everyday life. It's an ordinary camp site not unlike those I've made with friends and family on the Murray River at Easter or at Wilsons Promontory. I like this image of Aboriginality because of its fullness and because it seems able to grant indigenous people a place entirely appropriate for 'dignified and estimable people'. Its romanticism doesn't appeal, nor does it invoke a sense of melancholic loss. The painting simply takes indigenous people in place to be part of public culture. There's no massed and menacing ceremony, no spectacle of primitive difference, no abject fourth world mendicants, no degenerate savages. It's simple in the complex modes of those 'documentary' images of William Hogarth, except the sun shines from the north, the bodies are black and there's no gin in sight. Like the board game *Corroboree*, it poses a difficult question: what kinds of remembering and forgetting might enable us to live with these artefacts of colonial culture, both to tell different and enabling stories and to mourn?

2 ABORIGINES ON TELEVISION

And yet, indigenous Australians remained politically invisible. Indeed, for most Australians, including me, they were physically invisible as well. I cannot explain this collective blindness, let alone my personal ignorance. Of course I knew Aborigines existed: one of my favourite childhood books was *The Way of the Whirlwind*, by Mary and Elizabeth Durack. By the time I was sixteen I knew my way around Sydney and had explored suburbs a long way from the leafy communities of the east. On holidays I had visited the Blue Mountains, and, more significantly, had spent many weeks at Uncle Neville's property at Leadville near Coolah, home of the fabled Black Stump. On these stays I had travelled around the Mid-West to Coonabarabran, Mudgee, and Warren, not to mention numerous smaller settlements. Yet I have no conscious memory of ever seeing a black Australian, let alone actually meeting one. I was vaguely aware that they existed somewhere out there in the bush in squalid and primitive conditions and that they were to be pitied as a Stone Age race clearly unable to adapt to Australian civilization. Yet I remained completely uninterested. I was able to take up the distant cause of American Negroes and South African Bantu (as they were known then) with genuine passion and indignation. But I didn't give a stuff about the Australians whose lands had been stolen, whose children had been stolen, whose very existence had been stolen by my ancestors and was still being stolen by my contemporaries. Okay, so none of this was taught at school and not much of it was known even to historians at the time. But sheer commonsense and logic should have made it obvious to all but the cretinous that something terrible had happened. And yet it didn't. I can only assume that we were all in a state of denial, that we simply were not ready to face the shame and the guilt of our history. Of course, some of us still aren't; but they no longer have the excuse of claiming that they weren't told.

Mungo MacCallum[1]

Non-indigenous people often remember their relationship to Aboriginality as belated. In this passage from his autobiography penned in a new millennium, Mungo MacCallum, a journalist born in 1941, is attempting to make sense of what he imagines as the political invisibility of indigenous people in the mid-1950s. His resources, unsurprisingly, are memory and his biographical relationship with Aboriginality. As a historical explanation, his memories are troubling to him; he had visited parts of New South Wales where significant indigenous communities lived, yet he claims to have 'no conscious memory of ever seeing a black Australian'. Instead, he knew 'they existed somewhere out there in the bush' but he was 'completely uninterested'. He claims not to have been taught about the 'Australians whose lands ... children [and] very existence had been stolen' – things which *even historians* knew not – yet he knew 'that they [Aboriginal people] were to be pitied as a Stone Age race'. These memory-fuelled reflections are a strange mix of blindness and insight, recollection and forgetfulness. At their core is a seemingly deeply felt and genuine combination of guilt and self-recrimination – 'I can only assume that we were all in a state of denial' – and a strong sense that his current knowledge about, and disposition towards, indigenous people is different. Read in the register of politics as therapy, we could say, once MacCallum was unconscious but now he is conscious of Aborigines' disadvantage and committed to taking up their cause. It is an account that tells of the invisible becoming visible, of ignorance being replaced by knowledge: in short, it's a story of progress.

I first read an excerpt from this passage in Germaine Greer's essay *Whitefella Jump Up*, in which she too was puzzling over her 'condition of unknowing'.[2] Both are politically inflected stories: MacCallum's told with an eye on the transformative years of the Whitlam government and Greer's told to anticipate her departure for the United Kingdom where, after 'living in the genuinely multicultural society of postgraduate students in Cambridge', she began to see Australia for what it really was. In a similar vein, historian Ann Curthoys's account of the 1965 NSW Freedom Ride quotes many of the participants as concluding that the key achievement of the ride was to put race relations on the political agenda.[3] These autobiographically inflected accounts of how indigenous people became politically visible also resonate with more broadly cultural accounts such as Sally Morgan's *My Place*, which could be described as a story about how an indigenous woman came to see herself as such for the first time.[4] Together, I think these examples suggest a now commonplace characterisation of the period after the Second World War and prior to the 1967 referendum as a time when Aborigines were invisible. Subsequently, in this narrative, indigenous people achieve new public and political visibility, perhaps at some time in the 1960s, or during the Whitlam government, or even later still, following the passage of the first federal Land Rights Act under the Fraser government in 1976. It is certainly true that political activity by indigenous people and their supporters achieved a new public prominence from the 1960s and that the referendum was followed by an unprecedented wave of federal governmental initiatives. Even so, I want to take issue with these stories of remembering and forgetting because it seems to me that these stories fit within a pattern of remembering and forgetting, of making Aborigines appear and disappear, that stretches across Australia's colonial and postcolonial history.

How might I approach MacCallum's autobiographical excerpt in this light? If I wanted to argue historically, I would assert that MacCallum's is a faulty memory: images and talk about Aborigines circulated widely as significant components of public culture in the postwar period. In his first 20-odd years, MacCallum would have been exposed to endless newspaper images of and stories about Aboriginal people. He probably licked the 2/6d stamp of One Pound Jimmy Tjungurrayi, of which over 99 million were sold between 1950 and 1966.[5] He might have munched on Jaffas while watching the work of actors Rosalie Kunoth-Monks and Robert Tudawali in *Jedda* (1955). An Albert Namatjira painting, or a reproduction, might have hung on the walls of MacCallum's comfortable middle-class home, given that the years of his youth stretch from Namatjira's first sell-out show in Sydney in 1945 to his death in 1959. As for political visibility, during this period all of the key 'Aboriginal Advancement' leagues were in place and, by the early 1960s, the Yirrkala Bark Petition marked both a continuity with 19th-century indigenous activism and the beginnings of a new politics. In one way or another, it's almost certain that in the domain of Aboriginality, Mungo saw plenty of 'black Australians' in his youth.

However, to dismiss MacCallum's autobiographical recall, his memories, as merely wrong, tells us little about the significance of memory's culture. Part of my argument in this book is that individuals don't only remember as individuals. Instead, the rules and forms of memory, and the significance and value accorded to particular memories, are the products of, and in turn part of, shared culture. When we say 'I remember', or write about our memories, we do so in ways not only of our own invention. To think about memory in this way does not make MacCallum's autobiography unimportant or a mere cipher, but it does direct us to different questions. Instead of asking 'Are MacCallum's memories historically accurate?', we might ask 'How did a particular memory-making culture enable MacCallum's recollections?' In other words, we can both acknowledge the actual historical record that attests to Aboriginal presence in public culture and consider the remarkable absence of Aborigines in the records of remembering. We can begin to think about these two processes through the clues in the very words MacCallum uses to substantiate Aboriginal invisibility.

Aborigines were part of MacCallum's personal experience. Aboriginal people and things were part of his horizons of experience. *The Way of the Whirlwind*, MacCallum's favourite childhood book, featured an elaborate story about Nungaree and Jungaree searching for their baby brother who has been stolen by the whirlwind.[6] He knew Aboriginal people lived beyond the boundaries of Sydney and he remembers thinking of Aborigines as a 'squalid', 'primitive' and 'Stone Age' race 'to be pitied'. To rewrite this in historical terms, we could say that as a child and young adult, MacCallum knew that Australia was a colonial nation made by a superior race, that its indigenous peoples had been dispossessed and, as a result, suffered enormous material disadvantage, an inevitable predicament that, nevertheless, white Australians should view with sympathy. In addition to remembering Aborigines as politically invisible, these recollections also rehearse the dominant liberal understanding of race relations in Australia for most of the 20th century. This is not an absence of knowledge but a specifically colonial understanding of the effects of Australian history on indigenous people. MacCallum's autobiography could then be recast as a historical account of the shift in memory cultures brought about by the replacement of an enduring colonial historical consciousness by a postcolonial historical consciousness.

There are, however, some significant limitations in explaining MacCallum's remembrance as emblematic of changes in historical circumstances. In the first place, it tells us very little about the question I posed earlier, 'How did memory's cultures enable Mac-Callum's recollections?' The answer posed by this history of memory would seem to be that in postwar Australia, the actual historical presence of Aborigines was forgotten as part of the colonial historical imagination. Indigenous Australians came into view only for particular (white) purposes, principally, in this instance and at this time more generally, as a focus of pity. Yet this conclusion provides little insight into forgetting, the perennial twin of remembrance. Effectively, it argues that once white Australians forgot Aborigines and now they don't; once there was a culture of forgetting and now, presumptively, there is a fully conscious and adequate culture of remembering. Thus it mirrors MacCallum's account of his own coming to awareness – the story of an unconscious or disinterested white observer who becomes conscious and committed – and the positivism of so much historical writing and thinking. Historians tell us that existing accounts are inadequate and then demonstrate the extent of the shortcomings and persuade us to a better account. This confident replacement of one story with a 'better' story is itself forgetful. In other words, if MacCallum's current historical consciousness – postcolonial and politically committed – is so much better, how is it that it has forgotten its own forgetting of Aboriginal presence in his childhood and implicitly veiled any contemporary forgetting?

At this point, I don't think it's possible to resolve these questions in relation to a brief aside in an autobiography. Even so, it can provide us with some useful starting points for this inquiry into forgetting Aborigines. In the first place, I've indicated that here my interest is principally in memory as a cultural artefact rather than memory as an individual psychic process. Second, I've insisted that I want to think about memory historically, and about history as a contribution to memory's cultures. Rather than playing history and memory off against each other to decide which is wrong and which is right, historical thinking and remembering can be thought of as interrelated but distinct modes of calling on the past. Just as different historical moments enable different kinds of memories, so different memory cultures enable various kinds of historical thinking. Third, I've called on the truism that there is no remembering without forgetting to suggest that remembering differently is only half the battle, that in both colonial and postcolonial Australia it might be equally important to consider the routines and habits of forgetting that shadow both memory and history. There'll be no end to these patterns unless we begin to remember our forgetting.

ALCHERINGA

My memories are different from MacCallum's; not better or worse, simply different memories of different times and places. In the late 1960s at my Melbourne school, Manningham Primary, films were screened during the holidays, presumably to keep us off the street in those brief respites from formal instruction. The format, as I remember it, was a feature such as *Born Free* – a film that never failed to bring forth a flood of tears – preceded by a 'short'.[7] More than once, that short came from the television series *Alcheringa*, a prize-winning 1962 ABC program of 12 quarter-hour episodes, initially broadcast weekly, that recreated, romantically and anthropologically, an imagined world of everyday indigenous practices 'before the coming of the white man'.[8] The series was written and directed by Frank Few, an American-born director who also made some of the first wildlife or nature documentaries in Australia, and hosted by Bill Onus, a Yorta Yorta man. The cast members were all indigenous.[9]

In each episode, Bill Onus appears after the opening sequence and provides specific commentary that serves to frame the action. At the end of each episode, Onus reflects on what has been shown and anticipates the next week's program. The series consists of dramatic re-creations of the life of indigenous people of 'long ago'. For the most part, these re-creations focus on Aborigines acquiring the means of physical subsistence. Programs include 'Making a stone axe' (episode 3), 'Fishing' (episode 5), 'Women gathering food' (episode 6) and 'Hunting an emu' (episode 8), as well as two more socio-cultural episodes, 'Trading' (episode 2) and 'Walkabout' (episode 10). The various activities are dramatised as the life of an Aboriginal family group – a man, woman, young girl and boy – who, we are told, are spending the hot summer months in an 'allocated area', after which they will be 'reunited with the tribe in the autumn' (episode 1).[10]

The series was shot on 16 millimetre black-and-white film, all of it filmed in outdoor locations under natural light without synchronised sound, with the exception of the Onus commentary which frames each episode. For the most part, the camera is static, using medium shots and medium close-ups. Occasional tracking and following shots of characters walking through the bush are intercut with close-ups of faces and manufacturing activity. There are a few panoramic sequences, particularly in the 'Walkabout' episode, and the editing is, in general, leisurely, as is the pace of the dramatisation. Exceptions are the hunting scenes in the episodes 'Hunting a kangaroo' (episode 7) and 'Hunting an emu' (episode 8), in which relatively fast cuts are used to dramatise the chase and the kill.

The soundtrack consists of occasional diagetic sound such as scraping and axe blows on a tree that were recorded separately, an orchestral score played for mood and feel, and an omniscient narration by the actor John Morgan. This narration performs a number of roles. It explains some of the on-screen action; for example, telling us in episode 1, 'Upon the return of mother and daughter from their food gathering, the boy tells them what he and his father have achieved during their absence.' It provides contextual information elaborating on the on-screen action, much of it couched as authoritative anthropological knowledge:

Trading performed an important function in spreading the culture of the Aboriginal people across Australia. Various articles, corroboree, ritual cults, art designs and material culture of all kinds were passed on directly or indirectly through trade, bringing to the varied cultures scattered across the continent a degree of unity.[11]

Occasionally, the commentary becomes explicitly didactic. At other times, the narration borders on the bizarre and mysterious; for example, in an episode on gathering shellfish (episode 11), the narrator informs the viewer that 'The Australian Aborigine had extremely good teeth.'

These are the basic elements of *Alcheringa*, which is but one example fished from a very large reservoir of cultural products – images, newspaper accounts, books, public displays, films, television programs, theatrical events, and much else besides – in which non-indigenous people have told each other stories about 'things Aboriginal'. I hope it's already abundantly clear that, in important ways, *Alcheringa* produces 'bad' representations of indigenous people. In the first instance, however, I want to insist on thinking about such representations in specific rather than moralistic terms. In other words, I want to avoid such general observations as '*Alcheringa* offers only a partial sense of everyday indigenous life in precolonial Australia', as this is a charge that could be levelled at any such representation that will, by definition, always be inadequate. I am more interested in the consequences of particular representational and televisual choices; for example, that the 'historical' Aboriginal people are silent, their actions and minds only explicable because of the omniscient narrator. At the same time, I want to acknowledge what *Alcheringa* actually achieves: given its scale and audience, it provided a reasonably nuanced account of some aspects of 'traditional' indigenous everyday life and material culture for the students at Manningham Primary.

I want to examine *Alcheringa* here, not to judge it as producing good or bad representations, but because it exemplifies some of the central tensions between 'archaic Aboriginal being' and 'pure white modernity' that seem to overflow from, or produce a surplus in, this televisual restaging of an imagined precolonial Aboriginal world. To put it another way, I want to think about how such programs work in a paradoxical memory culture haunted by strange patterns of amnesia in the contact zones between indigenous and non-indigenous Australians. Here, I want first to simply recall the existence of *Alcheringa* (and the presence of indigenous people in other early Australian television programs such as *Whiplash*) neither as a breakthrough example of popular representations of Aborigines nor as racist rubbish, but as an example of how Aboriginality – in stories, images, objects and relationships – has been a variegated but constant presence in Australian public culture.[12] I want to explore how *Alcheringa* deploys and relies on characterisations of indigenous people that are primitivist, condescending and disrespectful; how it understands indigenous people as colonised; and how, in some ways, it is a relatively open and complex television series that produces Aboriginality as a postcolonial space of exchange that looks forward to more recent examples of television.

STONE AGE PRIMITIVES

The primitive does what we ask it to do. Voiceless, it lets us speak for it. It is our ventriloquist's dummy – or so we like to think.

Marianna Torgovnick[13]

Each episode of *Alcheringa* begins with the same fixed camera shot of a flat, empty landscape punctuated by a small dead tree in the middle distance. As the opening narration begins, two Aboriginal men enter the frame from behind the camera and walk towards the tree. John Morgan's sonorous and theatrical, mid-century English-Australian voice intones:

Theirs was a timeless land unmarked or divided by the wheels of science. Before the first half-formed words of recorded history, these people made peace with an unchanging world. These were the people of the dreaming time, of a world now dying. A world of ages past. A world of Alcheringa.

As the narration closes, a powerful and insistent indigenous song reaches a crescendo as the word 'Alcheringa' appears on screen in a script constructed out of boomerang shapes. The screen then fades to black, before Bill Onus appears to introduce the weekly component part. If the intensity of the opening sequence helped lodge this series in my memory, it certainly did so by insisting, from the very beginning, on the primitivism of the people about whom I was to learn. Through image, narration and diagesis, *Alcheringa* is relentless in producing a vision of Aborigines as primitives.

The first move in guaranteeing the primitiveness of indigenous people is to establish them as a distinctive group defined by race. This is achieved in both the opening shot of two black men carrying spears in an arid landscape, and the first lines of the narration: 'The Australian Aborigine is an Australoid, one of the four basic races of mankind. He lives in close harmony with nature and is dependent upon her for his existence' (episode 1). While the narration tells the listener that the 'origins' of the indigenous people are scientifically inconclusive, the real origins of Aborigines are made entirely clear: Aborigines are part of nature, and definitely of another time. The notion that 'He lives in close harmony with nature' is the strongest single theme that structures the series, organised as it is around the variety of ways in which Aborigines acquire the means of subsistence – men fishing and hunting, and women gathering food – and the technical means that enabled this mode of life – fire, boomerangs, stone axes and bark canoes. But this version of 'harmony with nature' is not a proto-environmentalist insistence that all human societies exist in a mutually interdependent relationship with nature. In this case, it is predominantly an account of 'harmony with nature' – and indeed a form of existence – that is 'of another time', in the sense that the anthropologist Johannes Fabian and many others have argued is so central to evolutionist thinking.[14] Aborigines are a distinct and separate race of people who are both ancient and underdeveloped in comparison to 'Europeans' who are both the paradigm for, and pinnacle of, human biological and social development. Aborigines were

Production shot from Alcheringa. *Doris Simpson.*
Photo: John Pearson. (With the permission of the ABC)

superstitious and cunning people whose cultural barbarism was
marked by polygamy. And the viewers of *Alcheringa* know this
because they are told so by the omniscient narration, which confidently instructs the viewer on all aspects of the lives and minds of
these silent, naked black people.

The primitivism of indigenous people is secured most emphatically in *Alcheringa* through images of Aboriginal bodies that ground and guarantee otherness. This is clear from the first episode through the use of close-ups of near-naked black bodies, and the prosthetic scarification applied to the skin of Harry Williams and Doris Simpson, the male and female leads. In later episodes, particularly the episode on collecting shellfish, the camera lingers fetishistically on Doris Simpson's body to produce an eroticised primitive woman. Certainly John B Murray, the series producer, understood how important it was for Simpson to appear topless, and spent some time convincing her that, in his words, *Alcheringa* was not 'just more exploitation'. While I am sure that Murray's aims concerned his sense of verisimilitude, in some respects it was more exploitation, and not only of Simpson's body.

But perhaps it's not all so neat in *Alcheringa*. In the first place, 'primitives' take many forms, especially in the Pacific. We know this because indigenous people across the Pacific (including Australia) have, at various times for Europeans, appeared both noble and beastlike. More broadly, primitives can be evil enemies or loyal companions, wily tricksters or childlike simpletons, lazy or labour power, and much else besides. Nor are these categories necessarily fixed: the capacity to control the name of the other is a fundamental part of the power of colonial attribution. If we stay, for a moment, with the critic Marianna Torgovnick's notion of the primitive as 'our ventriloquist's dummy', then the mobility of the category suggests that indigenous people are figured as primitives not simply to produce racist representations but in order to fulfil particular functions for non-indigenous people. So, what roles were these primitives playing for non-indigenous viewers who were, after all, the majority audience for the television series? In addition to being primitives, I want to suggest that in *Alcheringa* Aborigines are both decent primitives, and they are 'our primitives', Australian primitives. Despite living at a low level of material development, being superstitious and possibly polygamous, they are a people who are resourceful and strong, family-centred and networked by trade, who possess culture and spirituality, great ingenuity and skill. These ambiguities are made clear in episode 3 of the series, 'Making a stone axe'.

On the face of it, this episode is about the processes involved in making a stone axe. The lesson for the viewer is that 'the stone axe raised his standard of existence'. But these aspects of the program are intercut with a series of close-ups and wide shots of the two happy children of the family, swimming at the waterhole, playing with a koala and just generally mucking around. The narration didactically informs the viewer that children were 'treated affectionately' and given 'considerable freedom', but 'as in most primitive nomadic tribes, infant mortality among the Australian Aborigines was high. Disease, hunger and unavoidable lack of care were the main causes.' Whatever we might make of the odd phrase 'unavoidable lack of care', this vision of indigenous people is, in part, underpinned by a strongly humanist sense of the primitive possessing particular premodern virtues. In this sense, not only is family strong, attachment to place rich and meaningful, and childhood a space of play rather than instrumental training; Aboriginal society itself becomes momentarily utopian. These premodern virtues of the world of *Alcheringa* are also articulated as lessons for the present. In other episodes, the narrator tells us that 'time had not yet become man's master'; notes with some appreciation the 'remarkable ability [of indigenous people] to take advantage of his natural environment'; and evokes an explicit moralism in commentary such as: 'Unlike modern men, the Aboriginal hunter killed game for food alone.'[15] We can hear in these small, melancholic laments a refrain that is common in appraisals of modernity from Goethe to Joni Mitchell. But what's important in *Alcheringa* are the human connections made between the values of their world and 'our' world.

These claims about Aborigines are clearly addressed to nonindigenous people as lessons that can be learnt from 'our' primitives about 'our' society, and I do not mean this in any generic sense but as a specifically Australian injunction. These lessons are about Australia. From the opening desert shot to Onus standing in front of a map of Australia in the first introductory sequence, the animal extras (emu, kangaroo, koala, turtle, and so on), the diagetic sound and the locations – Lake Tyers in the far east of Victoria, a sheep station near Balranald, the Dandenong Ranges just outside of Melbourne and Wilsons Promontory – *Alcheringa* is rooted in Australia. It is important to remember that the audience for this series had a very different experience of national audio-visual culture than that of a contemporary audience. In the first instance, they had a relatively limited exposure to images of Australia on television. After all, this is before the Leyland Brothers and *Bush Tucker Man*. Theirs was an audiovisual culture dominated by cinema and the newsreel, by images in magazines and books, by advertisements and newspapers. So, while *Alcheringa* does not use locations that we now take as iconically national – Uluru or the Bungle Bungle Range (Purnululu), for example – almost all of what we see on screen is immediately identifiable as Australian. So, in one important sense, 'our primitives' are, in this televisual rendering, occupying 'our' country. Our primitives live in tribal lands, use trade routes across the country, have a remarkable body of knowledge about animals, plants and other natural resources, and their spiritual belief systems are intimately attached to place.

But there is a strange paradox in the indigenous occupation of 'Australia' in *Alcheringa*, because the country is both occupied and empty. In the archive of film-making about indigenous people, there is, in general, a strong preference for filming large groups. We can see this convention in the archetypal anthropological wide shot of ceremonial performances.[16] In all these cases, the frame of the camera and, by extension, the location itself, is full of people. *Alcheringa* is closer to that other more melancholic imaging tradition in which Aborigines form a minor or even absent element within a landscape. The paintings of Eugène von Guérard or Albert Namatjira are strong examples of work that resonates with the broader cultural conception of Australia as an empty continent.[17] So, while we are told by the narrator that a 'tribe' occupies the story-space of the series, in most episodes, the actual televisual space is only occupied by a four-person family group. This was certainly a result of a very limited budget.[18] But the relative emptiness of the mise en scène certainly connects the world of *Alcheringa* to the cultural imaginary of *terra nullius*.

So, *Alcheringa* invests heavily in primitivism 'with its aura of unchangeability, voicelessness, mystery, and difference from the West'.[19] While these first two characterisations, 'unchangeability' and 'voicelessness', can, and probably should, be thought of as negative attributions, I am not so sure about 'mystery' and 'difference', especially if we consider the ways in which the series was consumed. *Alcheringa* was for me and many other viewers first and foremost an educational television series structured around teaching and learning.[20] I mean this in a double sense, referring both to the series as storytelling, and about the discovery of objects of fascination. The narratives and the voice-overs remind the viewer repeatedly that the various activities on screen are a means of teaching the children (particularly the son) the skills needed to survive and prosper. This is especially the case in the episodes 'The boomerang' (episode 1), 'Making a stone axe' and 'Bark canoe' (episode 4), in which we are told:

> For this young boy, living in close harmony with nature and learning to utilise the many materials she provides had been an important experience. Just how well he its details will determine his future success as a hunter and provider for his family.

All three of the books that accompanied the series also strongly emphasise pedagogy. For example, the preface to *The Stone-axe Maker* reads:

> A long, long time ago, many Aborigines lived here in our land of Australia. In those days the hills, the valleys, and the deserts – in fact, all the land belonged to them. The boys and girls were taught by their fathers and mothers all they should

know – how to track animals, how to find food in the bush, and how to make the things they needed, such as spears, boomerangs, and stone axes. This is the story of such a family living in a desert area.[21]

These aspects of the series are heavily accentuated (again in both the television and book series) by the loving attention to shot details in the scenes and processes of making the boomerang, the stone axe and other tools. The use of close-ups, in particular, works to produce *Alcheringa* not only as a didactic educational experience but also as an experience of fascination. And that's how I remember watching the series and reading the books. The historian Stephen Atkinson has written evocatively about his relationship with *Whiplash* in which the television series seems to have energised his fascination with 'things Aboriginal'.[22] Similarly, *Alcheringa* helped me make sense of a stone axe and a boomerang that my father brought to Melbourne from the Northern Territory in the early 1970s; it was an incitement to curiosity.

It seems to me now that Frank Few might also have been curious about indigenous people, and wanted to incite that curiosity in others. Like me, he had come from the United States to Australia; Few after serving in the Pacific during the Second World War and me as a child. Perhaps for Frank Few that transition provoked questions about indigenous Australia and the presence of the disavowed past of his adopted country. But unlike me, Frank Few was a Native American. Perhaps that personal history, about which I know little else, led him to make television that was inquisitive about the world of Aborigines as Stone Age primitives. Such curiosity is neither good nor bad, and nor is it necessarily racist. There is nothing objectionable about either producing or marvelling at a filmic reconstruction of making a boomerang, or being enthralled by images of living in a world in which one had to hunt and harvest food every day. But it is objectionable in *Alcheringa* because it is curiosity without any reflective impulse. It has no capacity to imagine how that curiosity comes about, how questions of difference become important, how indigenous people have been fixed in time to serve particular non-indigenous needs. It is also curiosity in the absence of any consciousness of the historical experiences of indigenous people, experiences fundamentally entwined with non-indigenous people.

A COLONISED PEOPLE

One of the crucial characteristics of indigenous people rendered as Stone Age primitives is that they are *always* Stone Age primitives: they are outside of history, fixed in another time to both modernity and the present. In one sense, we see this in a very pure form in *Alcheringa* as a series that recreates life in an unspecified but clearly very distant past. Bill Onus, the series host, emphasises this when he introduces episodes with expressions such as 'Let's watch the past ...' and 'Come back with me ...' That past, as I have already noted, is characterised as 'a timeless land' and 'an unchanging world'. And, importantly, it was and is (interchangeably) a world, a way of life and a people 'now dying'. Yet, both the viewers of the series and we ourselves know that the series depended on indigenous moderns as actors and narrators, as well as an array of modern technologies, and that *Alcheringa* was, in part, the product of a colonial history. The very framing of the series is performed, and some of the words are spoken, by an indigenous man, who identifies himself as Aboriginal in a number of ways. To put it differently: a series about some Stone Age primitives (a people now dying) is introduced to the viewer by a genial and articulate man who is very much alive and very much indigenous. I want to explore these contradictions – of 'a people' both alive and dying – as an example of a particularly Australian colonial conundrum of living in (at least) two places and (at least) two times, and to consider how such a conundrum is worked through in *Alcheringa*.

The notion of Stone Age primitives was first given voice in

Europe to name people who, for Europeans, had once been in *their* place but who were no longer. It referred to people of 'the first, earliest age, period or stage'.[23] In Europe, primitives were dead people and necessarily absent people, precisely because they preceded history and the triumph of civilisation. They were, like the fossilised bones of long-dead creatures, signs in the archaeological strata. Their time was not the time of Europe. Yet, this did not mean that living primitive people were an impossibility for the European imagination. Indeed, according to the *OED*, at the end of the 18th century when 'primitive' was used to refer to 'inhabitants of prehistoric times' (in Europe), it was also used to refer to 'natives' in non-European lands. It did, however, mean that – both before and after the adoption of evolutionary models of human biological development derived from Charles Darwin – reports about, images of and even the bodies of living primitives could only come to Europe from elsewhere, and thus from other times. Because Europe is possessed of historicist thought, the primitive is necessarily anachronistic.

The term 'anachronism' plays an important role in the key contribution on historicist thought by historian Dipesh Chakrabarty, *Provincializing Europe*. Chakrabarty begins from a simple proposition: 'That Europe works as a silent referent in historical knowledge'.[24] He means this in the practical sense that the histories of non-Europeans are understood as backward, underdeveloped, incomplete and lacking in relation to Europe; 'the "first in Europe and then elsewhere" structure of time'.[25] In this sense, the primitive is indissolubly linked to the modern, objectified as a vestige of another time or place:

> Historical evidence (the archive) is produced by our capacity
> to see something that is contemporaneous with us – ranging
> from practices, humans, institutions, and stone-inscriptions
> to documents – as relics of another time or place. The person
> gifted with historical consciousness sees these objects as
> things that once belonged to their historical context and now

exist in the observer's time as a 'bit' of that past. A particular past thus becomes objectified in the observer's time.[26]

But the 'gift' comes with a cost when, instead of seeing different ways of being human that coexist in the present, historical consciousness produces a hierarchy.

For Chakrabarty, philosophy itself is infused with the historicism that Walter Benjamin called the secular, empty and homogenous time of history, such that:

> Reason becomes elitist whenever we allow unreason and
> superstition to stand in for backwardness, that is to say, when
> reason colludes with the logic of historicist thought. For then
> we see our 'superstitious' contemporaries as examples of
> an 'earlier type,' as human embodiments of the principle of
> anachronism. In the awakening of this sense of anachronism
> lies the beginning of modern historical consciousness.[27]

Chakrabarty's project is to think historical difference. To 'provincialize Europe in historical thought' is not to do away with European thought, but rather:

> to struggle to hold in a state of permanent tension a dialogue
> between two contradictory points of view. On the one side
> is the indispensable and universal narrative of capital ...
> On the other side is thought about diverse ways of being
> human.[28]

He stages a dialogue around a mobile triangulation of Europe (as a hyper-real category), the modernised colonial subject and/or state (modern Indians and India) and the peasant ('a shorthand for all the seemingly nonmodern, rural, nonsecular relationships and life practices that constantly leave their imprint on the lives of even the elites in India and on their institutions of government').[29] While we cannot map that particular triangulation directly onto the Australian colonial experience, we can join him in the spirit of thinking historical difference in specifically Australian ways.

European Australians were split in different ways. In the first place, they lived in a place that was both not Europe – Australia as a continent that predated colonisation – and a place that was European – Australia as a colony and then a nation-state that came into existence through European discovery and colonisation. It was also a place of multiple temporalities: archaically prehistoric (indigenous), incompletely modern and underdeveloped (first as a European outpost and then as an emerging nation), and as completely modern and fully historical (as Europe transplanted or an autonomous complete nation). Traditional Australian historiography has focused almost exclusively on the question of Australia's development from primitive colony to civilised nation; that is, on the universal narrative of Australia becoming fully modern. It is no surprise that such historiography ignores the simple fact that being fully in the time and space of Australia could only be conceived in relation to the place and time of indigenous people in Australia.

We have already touched on some of the generic 'solutions' to the contradictions between archaic Aboriginal being and pure white modernity: the fantasy that the continent was unoccupied; the genocidal desire, acted on at small and larger scales, to remove indigenous people from the country; the belief in the present as a transitional moment before their inevitable 'departure'; the myriad practices to effect the eradication of Aborigines as a distinct people; and of course, forgetting. But real as these ideas and practices are, they were at the same time imaginary 'solutions' to the actual intercultural experience of colonisation. Being in Australia meant that indigenous and non-indigenous peoples coexisted; they watched each other, listened to each other; they interacted through the complexities of conquest and governance, of punishment and dialogue, of theft and trade, of employment and sex, and much more. Here I want to explore how *Alcheringa* negotiated what we might call the actuality of such colonial complexities, actual intercultural relationships so often obscured by forgetfulness, and refusals to see or hear.

When Bill Onus appears on screen after the opening sequence, he reminds me today of my paternal grandfather. The two men were almost the same age. My grandfather's parents were children of Irish immigrants. Bill grew up on Cummeragunja. Both had snowy-white hair, and seemed possessed of patrician seriousness and stubborn dignity. In front of a camera (Onus) or at church (my grandpa), both wore similar respectable and honest three-piece suits. These are the very first words that Bill Onus utters in *Alcheringa*:

> Yes. My people, the Australian Aborigines, knew of
> Alcheringa, which means from the very beginning of time.
> Their ways were the ways of their forefathers. These ways
> were good. They need not be changed. Let's look back
> through the mists of time and see some of the ways of my
> people before the future overwhelmed them and the white
> man's time began.

At one level, the first three words, 'Yes. My people', entirely undo the ways in which *Alcheringa* locates Aborigines as both Stone Age primitives and prehistoric to the historical time of Australia. Onus's historical consciousness, far from objectifying 'his people' as a bit of the past, claims Aborigines, in cultural studies scholar Stephen Muecke's wonderful phrase, as both ancient and modern.[30] In other words, the kind of settlement implied in much of *Alcheringa* – that with the coming of history to the continent of Australia, an archaic people were naturally displaced and became a dying remnant – is unsettled, as its re-enactment is staged by a man who is both articulate and very much alive in the present and claims primitives as 'my people'. How can we make sense of these seemingly contradictory aspects of the television series?

According to John Murray, the decision to feature Onus as the 'host' was not made until after shooting the series was completed. He says, 'There was a lot of talk about it. But we felt that it was necessary. It gave the series a continuity and structure.

Bill Onus making boomerangs, c. 1950s. (With the permission of the
Australian Institute of Aboriginal and Torres Strait Islander Studies)

Without that, the episodes were very disparate. [Onus] sort of held it together.'[31] Betty Few, who, while not credited, co-wrote the series with her husband Frank, says that Onus was involved prior to this in at least two ways: Frank had already discussed aspects of the series with Bill, and Bill had assisted in recruiting the two children who appear in the series.[32] In these ways he was working as, what we would call and credit today, a consultant or adviser. Betty Few, however, also insists that Onus was not involved in writing the script, which she and Frank produced after extensive library-based research. John Murray, on the other hand, says of Onus that 'He had a knowledge of Aboriginal culture and Frank and Betty tapped that.'[33]

Even so, there are some stark differences between the texts of the omniscient narration within the episodes (which as I have already indicated purport to be expert, anthropologically inflected commentary) and Onus's framing narrations. Whether or not Onus wrote these pieces, they are a distinct element in the film text. Onus speaks in the first person and repetitively produces a living connection between himself and the subjects of the films not only through his filmic presence, but also by saying 'my people'. He also uses the Wurundjeri language (the language of his people) to name artefacts and spiritual beliefs. Through his powerful on-screen presence, Onus thus establishes strong continuity between precolonial indigenous people and himself. And he claims for himself the status of being a modern Aborigine. He speaks of the film being about 'primitive Aborigines' in a way that is analogous to the contemporary expressions 'classical' or 'traditional' Aboriginal culture. The way he handles and talks about a boomerang, axe and spear makes a point of both his knowledge of these objects and their artefactual status. These things 'belong' to Onus and his time, but they also belong in another time when he says in episode 5, 'Come back with me and see how the Aborigine used this spear.'

In a sense, this coexistence of 'ancient and modern' is of a piece with Onus's life. He grew up in a famous Aboriginal reserve community and, while a teenager, worked as a drover and shearer. He was a wharf tally clerk and a justice of the peace. After the Second World War, he was instrumental in reviving the Australian Aborigines League, while also organising with Douglas Nicholls such theatrical performances as *Corroboree* (1949) and *An Aboriginal Moomba: Out of the dark* (1951). He was a champion boomerang thrower who gave exhibitions around Melbourne, and in 1952 he established Aboriginal Enterprises, which was a:

> tourist outlet for Aboriginal art in Belgrave (Victoria). Funding for this venture came from compensation Onus received for injuries sustained in a traffic accident, which left him an invalid for a year. Unable to return to his former employment as a wharf tally clerk, Onus sought an alternative means of income. Aboriginal Enterprises offered a wide variety of merchandise: bark paintings from Arnhem Land and locally made artefacts, furniture, textiles, and pottery decorated with motifs from traditional Aboriginal art. With additional branches in Narbethong (Vic.) and Port Augusta (SA), Bill Onus provided employment and training and fostered a strong sense of cultural pride among a new generation of urban Aborigines.[34]

We could consider Bill Onus's life as archetypal of generations of 20th-century Kooris in south-east Australia. He was deeply connected to his Yorta Yorta traditions through a community refashioned by colonial settlement and government policies of segregation and concentration. His experience of life and labour was both rural and urban. Archival records and living tradition attest to his energies in cultural, political and entrepreneurial ventures. His son, who died in 1996, was not only a very significant artist but also an institutional bridge between the aesthetic, cultural and political worlds of his father and a new century.

So, rather than think of Onus in *Alcheringa* as an unfortunate ventriloquist's dummy, we might imagine him as speaking to both an indigenous and a non-indigenous audience about precisely the historical context for this life: the experience of colonisation. At the conclusion of the first episode, Onus stands in front of a map of Australia and says:

> At the coming of the first European, it is estimated that there were about a quarter of a million Aborigines in Australia. This number was broken down to about 525 tribes or sub-tribes. They occupied every corner of the continent from the burning deserts of the centre to the jungle-covered coastal areas.
>
> The tribal area of my forbears, the Wurundjeri, extended along this part of the Murray River, a place of plentiful water and game.
>
> From the primitive man's viewpoint, an excellent place to live.
>
> Unfortunately for the Aboriginal, the new settlers from Europe also found the area most suitable for colonisation. In the skirmishes that followed, the primitive Wurundjeri lost, and as a tribe ceased to exist.

In this little scene, Onus puts colonisation on the historiographical map of Australia. He remembers indigenous occupation of the country in ways that were already integral to Koori land rights claims of the 1960s, and would reverberate ten years later in national demands for the recognition of land rights. He remembers the place of his people, 'the tribal area of my forbears', not as disappearing but as continuous with a colonised place, 'along this part of the Murray River'. And he remembers the impact of invasion for the Wurundjeri, a defeat that was only partial, qualified by the phrase 'as a tribe' and attested to by his presence, which announces in everything but the words themselves that, 'As a people we have survived.'

Another way in which we can recognise, and remember, the actual presence of colonialism in *Alcheringa* is suggested by John Murray's recollection about producing the series. Murray remembers:

We had to cast the jolly thing and that was diabolical. Frank
and I travelled all over Victoria and southern New South
Wales to the mission stations and anywhere Aborigines were
living, on the banks of the Murray or whatever river it was,
in humpies. We finally, after a long search which was not
successful, found the female lead [Doris Simpson] working
as a domestic two streets up from Ripponlea Studios [the
ABC studio in suburban Melbourne] and we found Arthur
working on the assembly line at General Motors [Holden, at
Fishermans Bend in Melbourne].[35]

I like this story because of the contrast between the presupposition
made by Murray and Few – that they would discover Aboriginal
actors by searching country Victoria for 'Aborigines in humpies' –
and their actual experience of recruiting from a Melbourne suburb
and a transnational company's factory floor. But it is not a story to
be told at Murray's expense; in fact, it reminds us that, more often
than not, film-making (and much other cultural production) about
Aborigines relies on actual interactions and exchanges between
indigenous and non-indigenous people, asymmetrical though those
relationships may be.

The exchanges that produced *Alcheringa* extended to the first
shooting location, Lake Tyers, perhaps the most significant site
of continuing indigenous and non-indigenous interactions in the
south-east corner of the continent, and an important memory
place.[36] The connection of *Alcheringa* to Lake Tyers came during
a turbulent period. The 1957 Board of Inquiry into the Aborigines Act of 1928 'had recommended the dispersal of the 186 Aborigines still living at Lake Tyers'.[37] According to historian Anna
Haebich:

Moves to close Lake Tyers in the early 1960s drew strong
protests and the Board was forced to adopt a compromise
where it pushed residents to leave while agreeing to maintain
the land as a permanent Aboriginal reserve. Families who left

Lake Tyers experienced considerable difficulty in adjusting to their new way of life, often with tragic consequences, as one woman recalled in evidence to the National Inquiry into the Separation of Aboriginal and Torres Strait Islander Children from their Families.[38]

Albert Mullett, a respected elder and spokesperson for the Gunai/Kurnai people, grew up on a fringe camp at Lake Tyers. He remembers:

> There was only full-blood Aboriginal people to live on Lake Tyers. So all part-Aboriginal people, we lived across the lake. And we were sort of then the, I suppose you would say, fringe dwellers then. Living outside of the mission because the government policies didn't want part-Aboriginal people. In their devious ways, saying: 'We cannot afford to keep these people. They've got to assimilate into wider society and they've got to survive by the best way they can.'[39]

John Murray came into this situation with the actors and crew of *Alcheringa*, and remembers being shocked by the man who ran what was then the Lake Tyers Aboriginal Station: 'He was a real brute, a real bastard of a man and we were shocked by the attitude he had to the Aborigines, you know, absolute contempt.'[40] He went on:

> What happened was our lead was arrested on the location at Lake Tyers. I had these tents, and I had Arthur's tent next to mine, so that you know if he wanted anything ... he wouldn't feel too isolated. And I put the door of the tent round on the other side to give him some privacy ...
>
> And suddenly one day, we're filming on the bank of the Lake, and the police arrived and they just arrested him on the spot for carnal knowledge ... It seems that a young girl who was underage, had been going into Arthur's tent. I

Production shot from Alcheringa. *Arthur Johnson.*
Photo: John Pearson. (With the permission of the ABC)

couldn't see at night. And he [Arthur] seemed to think that she wasn't underage at all and I really believe him.

... But the police wouldn't take no for an answer and they just took him. You know, we were left stranded there and we had to find another lead ...

Arthur was put in jail in Lake's Entrance and I went in to take him some clothes and food and so on and it was as bad as anything you could imagine of South Africa. You know, the attitude of the police was just complete loathing and contempt.

It was a great shock to me, I had no conception of the Aboriginal problem until then ... that in Australia that we would treat and have attitudes like we did was a real shock.[41]

Arthur took no further part in the production of *Alcheringa*, but John Murray had one further moment of contact in relation to his imprisonment:

At one stage, ... much later, I got a call from a woman who was ... looking after Arthur after he was charged ... She wanted me to appear as a witness for him ... I was about to go off on the Balranald leg [of the *Alcheringa* shoot] and I also felt well I'm an employee of the ABC and so, I don't think that's my role ... I hadn't seen anything anyway and I had no knowledge of him other than when we hired him and it was in the first week or the second week, and I felt no, it's wiser under all the circumstances that I didn't go. But I'm very sorry that I didn't go. I should have gone and done something.

Because it may have made a difference to his prison sentence. So I was very sorry that I hadn't taken that step.

In fact it's one of the saddest things of my life.[42]

The Gippsland Times reported:

Michael Arthur Johnson (24) an aboriginal, laborer, Gibbs St, Collingwood pleaded guilty to three counts of carnal knowledge at Lake Tyers between January 23 and 25 this year.

Sentencing him, Mr Justice Adam said Johnson's bad record merited a heavy sentence but he was prepared to make an allowance because he was a victim of circumstances.[43]

WARLPIRI ON TELEVISION

I came to the television program *Alcheringa* initially as a way of talking back to white amnesia in Australia. I wanted to recall how images and stories about Aborigines were part of the ordinary array of primary school training in the 1960s. Like singing the national anthem at Monday assembly, learning to respond to a roll call and playing football, Aboriginality was part of my everyday life as a child of perhaps eight or nine years of age. Growing up in Melbourne in the 1960s, I cannot possibly claim, as others have done of earlier periods, that I was taught nothing, knew nothing, had never seen images of nor heard about Aborigines before some moment of coming to consciousness. That my personal memories are different is, in and of itself, insignificant. They are useful here only because they directed me to a text, *Alcheringa*, that played a role in the memory culture of school-aged children in the 1960s. In this television series, Aboriginal people were visible to me. In *Alcheringa* we can see that indigenous people were present at the very beginnings of television in Australia. In seeing these short films in suburban Melbourne, I met and learned about Aboriginal people. These memories have provoked me to revisit *Alcheringa* in order to think about the actual presence of indigenous people on television in the 1960s, and to consider how such a program might be remembered today.

It may also be that *Alcheringa* persists as more than mere memory; that somehow it might be related to Warlpiri television. Like most 'inventions', the Warlpiri invention of television didn't take place in a vacuum but relied on a whole range of pre-existing technical facilities and conventions, a significant textual archive and a world of cultural knowledges and practices. The short film *Bush Mechanics* (1998) and the television series *Bush Mechanics: The series* (2001) were both made by the Warlpiri Media Association at Yuendumu and were co-directed by and featured Francis Jupurrula Kelly.[44] These two films are in one sense stories about the creative and crazy stuff that a bunch of Warlpiri guys do with cars in the bush. The films are also part of a longer tradition of cultural explorations about the uses of cars in and by indigenous communities.[45] But for my purposes here what's interesting about both the film *Bush Mechanics* and *Bush Mechanics: The series* is that they revisit and remember some of the very conventions of film-making about Aborigines that structured *Alcheringa*, and in doing so they reinvent history.

Bush Mechanics uses, parodies and replies to a whole raft of conventions about imaging indigenous people.[46] Let me mention only two obvious examples. The graphical title 'Bush' (as it appears on screen, DVD/video covers and the website) is assembled from bits and pieces of cars – pistons, shock absorbers, brake shoes – and appears to mimic the ways in which the title in *Alcheringa* is assembled from boomerangs. And there's another kind of reply to *Alcheringa* (and other similar anthropologically inflected films about Aborigines) in the opening scene when Kelly performs as if he were a primitive under the anthropological gaze, except he's not only the actor but also the co-director, and rather than performing an anthropological script, he's remembering a story of his countryman, Jack Jakamarra Ross. This is a thoroughly 'two ways' cultural product: its relations and conditions of production making it a historical not a 'prehistorical' text.

Bush Mechanics begins with Francis Kelly playing the Mayal (one of the two characters that he plays, the other being Bush Mechanic) sitting and eating by a campfire. He says to himself, in Warlpiri that's translated in subtitles, 'Mmm birds singing. It's getting late. I better look for some more meat.' He gets up, grabs spears and a woomera, and walks into the red sand and spinifex country where he finds kangaroo tracks. As the camera follows Kelly tracking the kangaroo, Kelly's voice is replaced by that of Jack Ross, who begins a story:

> We left our old camp and were hunting as we walked towards Wayirdi. It was near there that we came across the strange track.
>
> 'What's this thing?' we asked each other.
>
> We looked east to be sure there were no more strange things. Then we looked south but saw nothing. I thought this thing must be some sort of a monster.

As we listen to this narration, we watch Kelly finding and following a car tyre track. Then we cut to Ross completing the story. A distinguished old man wearing a magnificent cowboy hat and red-checked shirt tells of 'the first car'. The rest of *Bush Mechanics* follows the Jupurrurla gang through a series of mechanical misadventures with their car on a bush trip. These adventures are intercut with various indigenous people reminiscing about cars, and with Kelly (now in blue overalls) and Ross as bush mechanics, demonstrating to the viewer various *nyurulypa*, 'good tricks', such as making a clutch plate from mulga wood, repairing a flat tyre with spinifex grass, and using Omo soap powder and water to make replacement brake fluid.

Bush Mechanics: The series also begins with Kelly out in the bush, this time looking for a goanna and chatting away to himself in Warlpiri. We cut momentarily to Jack Ross, who takes up the story, establishing the sense that Kelly is re-enacting Ross's first encounter with a motor car – the same story that, on the *Bush Mechanics* website, Ross says was told to him by his grandmother. Kelly comes across two white fellas at a camp site. In a little comedy spoof, Kelly asks of the men, 'What's that covering your skins?' He takes a cup of tea from them, tastes the hot drink and then tips the 'black water' out (but keeps the mug). He takes a tin of meat that the men offer and then, as he heads off, is startled by the sight of their truck and asks:

'What this big monster?
  It must be sleeping. Might be a big lizard. I better go before
it wakes up.

We cut back to Jack, who says, 'I was frightened of that truck. So I ran into the bush for good. True.'

Like the 'original', *Bush Mechanics: The series*, which consists of five 30-minute episodes, follows a group of indigenous men on car adventures. But in the series the adventures are more elaborate: they drive to their first gig, bring a cousin back from jail in Alice Springs, chase car thieves from a rival football team and drive to Broome to bring back pearl shells for a rainmaker. And like the 'original' too, the wrecks of old cars provide sites for older indigenous men to tell stories about cars. But in the series there is a more fully developed attempt to use car wrecks and car stories as sites of memory that provide a way of telling the history of colonisation. Again, there is an echo from *Alcheringa* here: it's as if the map in front of which Bill Onus talked about the colonisation of his people is replaced by a landscape dotted with car wrecks which can be used to map first encounters, the arrival of pastoralists and confrontations with police, the Coniston massacres and the establishment of stations. In *Bush Mechanics*, these 'histories' litter the landscape and provide an excuse to restage the past in the present.

But there is one final feature of *Bush Mechanics* that's suggestive for thinking about the patterns of remembering and forgetting Aborigines that this chapter has explored. In the short film and the television series, Kelly plays both Bush Mechanic and a Warlpiri man from the old days who appears in moments of historical recreation, principally of encounters between indigenous and non-indigenous people. In one sense, these are not two characters but a single character who takes different forms at different times, moving between old days and new days. As Kelly puts it on the *Bush Mechanics* website, the trickster character both emphasises cultural continuity and, equally, offers a deep challenge to historicist ways of thinking:

> In old days they had a skill, today they still have a skill
> but they're mixing two skill together to use the tricks on
> motorcars like when radiator leaks, they break battery and
> use the lead from battery or put pepper to stop the leak ...
> Those sort of things.
>
> And we've been thinking about making bush mechanics – the
> old ways and the new ways of using the skill ... Learning both
> the old ways and new ways to make things run better for their
> future and make other people follow on.
>
> ... Old Jack Jakamarra used to tell us; in old days they used
> to use their skill and he's using new skill to work better.[47]

Kelly's character performs this role by appearing and disappearing in various times and places. The ability to make things appear and disappear, like the capacity to transform one thing into another, is a kind of magic. It's not necessarily something positive or negative; indeed it might be both at the same time, and its outcomes may well be unexpectedly creative or destructive. In a sense, Kelly appears in the present (as a bearer of both new and old skills) when he is needed, such as when a car breaks down and his people need to remember some skills for the present. In other words, he is there all the time, even when we don't actually see him. Perhaps, like Kelly, the history of Aboriginality in this country is there all the time, but it appears and disappears for complex reasons, some practical and some magical. Remembering as a form of appearance and disappearance might be a way of thinking that avoids the crude positivism of presence and absence. It might be a way of non-indigenous Australians avoiding the arrogance of consciousness, the bad faith of asking 'Why weren't we told', the fleeting outrage of discovering injustice and the quick-drying tears of indignation. Remembering a different kind of history-in-the-present can, I believe, help us fashion a more ethical future.

Although Warlpiri television is considerably richer and more culturally complex than *Alcheringa*, beyond sport, news and current affairs, today images of indigenous people on television in Australia are rare. By contrast, over the last three decades, Aboriginal art has become a ubiquitous part of public culture. The next chapter is concerned with some of that art and particularly with how the value ascribed to authentic Aboriginal art has enabled a forgetting of the artistic entanglements between indigenous and non-indigenous art that stretch back to before Papunya.

3 OLD AND NEW ABORIGINAL ART

When we were growing up, my generation knew nothing and cared less about Aboriginal culture. Indeed, those two words – Aboriginal and culture – seemed a contradiction in terms, a classic oxymoron. The view from the Melbourne suburbs? Aborigines were a dying people and a dead issue. This seemed confirmed by the fact that none of us had actually met an Aborigine. Most of us hadn't even seen one, although my father, wearing his army chaplain's uniform, did point to a couple as we crossed Melbourne's Princes Bridge in a tram during World War II. They were playing gum leaves, begging for coins.

If Aborigines were mentioned at school, it was with plangent piety, in a sorrow devoid of guilt. 'Abos' were a primitive people, stone-age leftovers who'd run out of time. Out of time and space. (In short, exactly the view expressed by Western Mining's Hugh Morgan as his response to Mabo.) As for their culture, that was confused with mulga wood ashtrays, crude motifs on tea towels and plastic boomerangs in tawdry souvenir shops.

Phillip Adams[1]

For Mungo MacCallum, attempting to remember his experience of Aboriginality in the 1950s meant explaining denial. By the 1960s and 1970s, the sheer political and cultural visibility of indigenous people made the denial of indigenous existence unsustainable. Instead of whether an experience of Aboriginality was repressed, accounts of this period tend to be more concerned with the adequacy of remembering. So in this quote, Phillip Adams, another prominent cultural commentator born in the first half of the 20th century, recalls indigenous culture as consisting of 'mulga wood ashtrays, crude motifs on tea towels and plastic boomerangs in tawdry souvenir shops' to evoke a time and a world of bad images of and about Aborigines. Unlike Aborigines being thought of as anachronistic, this characterisation condemns Europeanality as anachronistic. Adams's polemic stages a reversal: once his generation thought 'Aboriginal culture' was an oxymoron; today, anyone who does not properly and respectfully acknowledge indigenous culture would themself be a moron. The first sentence of his recollection could be rewritten thus: 'Now that we've grown up, my generation knows something, and cares, about Aboriginal culture.' In fact, this paraphrases the dominant liberal conception of the journey made by decent Australians in the postwar period. It brings together two crucial elements that vouchsafe a non-indigenous calibration of progress in, and hope for, the status of indigenous people in the nation-state: knowledge and compassion. This conception imagines that where once there was ignorance, now there is understanding, and where once there was abuse, neglect or indifference, now there is sympathy. Such is progress.

If there is one, single piece of evidence likely to be called upon to support this liberal sense of progress, it is Aboriginal art. Today, galleries and auction houses don't display shields (as ethnographic artefacts) or plastic boomerangs (as tourist keepsakes), but certified high art produced by master artists. In the early 21st century, Aboriginal art is the most widespread and perhaps significant manifestation of indigenous culture in the public sphere. Its presence is ubiquitous, from ordinary advertisements to blockbuster shows at the National Gallery of Australia. In important respects, indigenous art has become the most visible international sign of Australian-ness. Aboriginal art is widely collected by public institutions, businesses and private individuals in a market worth well over $100 million per annum.[2] The secondary art market now routinely sells scores of works for five-figure sums and, increasingly, a number of six-figure sums every year. Commercial, public and corporate galleries; curators, prizes and periodic exhibitions; auction houses and collectors, forgers, critics, advisers, publications, government support, artists' organisations and many other elements are all part of an elaborate art system that now sustains Aboriginal art.

There is now a conventional history of the emergence of Aboriginal high art. It consists of a series of landmark moments stretching from the 1960s. At the very beginning of this period, the Yirrkala Church Panels (1962–63) and the Yirrkala Bark Petition (1963) were produced. Ten years later marked, what for now I'll call, the 'invention' of modern Aboriginal art at Papunya. Another decade on, large canvases by Papunya artists – 'vast compendiums of Western Desert culture, mapping out the artists' custodial responsibilities over vast areas' – were included in Australian Perspecta 1981 at the Art Gallery of New South Wales, a moment which art historian Vivien Johnson has described as marking 'the beginning of the end of the long denial of Aboriginal art by the Australian art establishment'.[3] In 1988, the exhibition *Dreamings: The art of Aboriginal Australia* was shown in New York and then toured Chicago, Los Angeles, Melbourne and Adelaide. And in the new millennium, *Papunya Tula: Genesis and genius* was shown at the Art Gallery of New South Wales, while paintings by Emily Kame Kngwarreye, Clifford Possum Tjapaltjarri and Rover Thomas Joolama became among the most sought-after Australian contemporary art both nationally and internationally.

In this chapter, I want to tell a different story. In addition to regarding this work as simply 'extraordinary and exhilarating'[4], I want to think about the emergence of Aboriginal art as producing forgetfulness in the domains of Aboriginality. I'll argue that the history of the creation of an Aboriginal high art between 1961 and 2000 is shadowed or perhaps haunted by other histories and other memories of Aboriginal art in relation to white Australia. This 'other world' of image-making and Aboriginality produced a seemingly endless supply of Aboriginal kitsch and Jacky Jacky statues. It was a world of Qantas menu cards replete with 'Hunting motifs from Australian Aboriginal Art' and the 'Honey-bee totem Christmas card' designed by Estonian-born Gert Sellheim; of 'Kangaroo Hunt' textiles by Douglas Annand and Frances Burke; of Byram Mansell murals, Lloyd Piper playing cards and Rita Chin mugs; of the theft of a David Malangi design for the Australian one-dollar note (introduced in 1966); and much else besides. These objects, designs and artworks share one thing: they are in some respects *derived from* versions of indigenous art practices. But rather than creative practice in the domain of 'authentic Aboriginal art', this is 'Aboriginal art' produced by non-indigenous people. Such works are about popular image-making: closer to 'Mulga wood ashtrays, crude motifs on tea towels and plastic boomerangs in tawdry souvenir shops' than unique works of art in galleries, more reproduction than authentic, more light and offensive than serious and genuine, more of mundane everyday culture than of extraordinary genius. The contemporary celebration of authentic Aboriginal art has, in the main, consigned this world of Aboriginal kitsch to the dustbin of history as image-making practices to be forgotten because it was made by the wrong people and based on the theft of indigenous tradition. But this new 'respect' for indigenous art also forgets a long history of artistic entanglements between indigenous and non-indigenous Australians.

I want to make this argument by reconsidering the recent consolidation of Papunya Tula as 'perhaps the greatest single cultural achievement of Australia's post-settlement history'.[5] One of the effects of this cultural achievement has been that 'new' and 'authentic' Aboriginal art has come not only to dominate the terrain of contemporary Aboriginal art but also to obscure how, in the not-too-distant past, Aboriginal art was possessed in very different ways by non-indigenous Australians. As well as marking the beginning of a movement, Papunya might also be the beginning of the end for Aboriginal kitsch. My starting point for this contrast is Roman Black's 1964 book *Old and New Australian Aboriginal Art*, in which 'new Australian Aboriginal art' refers to the work of non-indigenous artists, designers and potters using indigenous art as a resource and inspiration for their artistic practice. This work opens up the terrain of Aboriginalia or Aboriginal kitsch as an ambivalent culture space of Aboriginality. What's remarkable about the inheritance of Aboriginalia today is that, while it's forgotten and disavowed by respectful white collectors and critics, it's being reworked by artists such as Destiny Deacon and Ross Moore. Their work provides me with a conclusion to this chapter.

BARDON AND BOARDS: REMEMBERING PAPUNYA

> By some strange paradox, as the Aborigine becomes less a primitive man and his way of life recedes into the past, his culture becomes more and more a part of the Australian heritage.
>
> Dennis Dugan[6]

Today, the word 'Papunya' works metonymically to both describe a dominant conception of Aboriginal art and tell a particular story about how it came into existence. Howard Morphy neatly describes the shape of the now conventional account:

> In 1971 Geoffrey Bardon was teaching art and craft at Papunya school. He was interested in ways of including traditional art in the school curriculum and he encouraged some of the community's elders to paint murals on the school walls. The first designs were painted by Long Jack Phillipus

Tjakamarra and Billy Stockman Tjapaltjarri who were employed as school groundsmen. The project captured the interest of other members of the community and soon more elders became involved. Once the murals had been completed, the artists wanted to continue to paint; they therefore asked Bardon to provide them with painting boards and pigments. Some of the paintings were sold to cover the cost of materials, and it was not long before they began to be exhibited and marketed throughout Australia.[7]

Paradoxically for a project that begins with paintings on a wall, 'Papunya' very quickly became a travelling culture. The artists themselves travelled, not nomadically but to outstations such as Yayari in search of better health and autonomy, in what Fred Myers called a process of 'Pintupi separatism'.[8] As the outstation movement gained momentum in the 1980s, 'Papunya' travelled with the Pintupi to Kintore and then Kiwirrkurra. Amid significant changes to the policy regimes applied to indigenous people, the key innovations of Papunya – story painting, a market orientation, artist- or community-controlled co-operatives and classically rooted aesthetics – took new forms at Yuendumu and Napperby, Utopia, Haasts Bluff (Ikuntji), Ernabella, Hermannsburg (Ntaria), Lajamanu and Balgo, and beyond. And the paintings travelled too in circuits that created a new market segment: to homes, to galleries in Alice Springs and southern capitals, to public galleries within and beyond Australia, and to the secondary market. The status and value ascribed to the work was also on the move. Fred Myers argues that 'This "Aboriginal art" acquired status as "fine art" with a much-publicised show in 1988 at the Asia Society Gallery in New York, entitled "Dreamings: The Art of Aboriginal Australia"'.[9] Others would date the acquisition of fine art status to 1972, when the Museum and Art Gallery of the Northern Territory purchased 105 early Papunya works, or to 1975, when the Aboriginal Arts Board curated *Art of the Western Desert* at the Australian National University, or to the 1981 Australian Perspecta, which included works by Clifford Possum Tjapaltjarri, Tim Leura Tjapaltjarri and Charlie Tjapangati. But whatever date is pinpointed, it's undeniable that by the late 1980s, as 'Papunya' went global, within Australia it defined a new mode through which indigenous people were recognised by White Australia. And so, with each new style and each new star came headlines such as 'Six months after picking up a brush, Sally, 83, a top seller'. These were repeated across the country: indigenous people in relatively remote communities kept picking up brushes, often through government-sponsored programs, and produced startlingly new and deeply authentic transportable art for sale to non-indigenous buyers, public and private institutions.[10]

This sketch of 'Papunya', and of its 'repetition' across the country, is not historically accurate. Those who were involved as painters or advisers, and those with a serious stake in Aboriginal art as critics, historians, anthropologists or curators, also know that 'Papunya' as a metonym is a selective condensation of varied stories and actual historical experiences, a figure that stands in for the contingent and particular reality of historical processes. The centrality of 'Papunya' is, in a sense, registered by the two most common (and entirely accurate) contemporary scholarly and curatorial gestures in relation to Aboriginal art: the historical gesture – (modern) Aboriginal art predates Papunya – and the field gesture – there's more to Aboriginal art than just the 'style' of Papunya. Here my claim is simply that 'Papunya' has become a culturally powerful way of thinking about Aboriginal art, what Geoffrey Bardon himself described as 'the public face of Australia for the world'.[11]

I want to consider some of the consequences of the cultural significance of Papunya by examining two recent and important publications: *Papunya Tula: Genesis and genius*, the catalogue produced to accompany a majestic exhibition at the Art Gallery of New South Wales in 2000, and Geoffrey Bardon's posthumously published record of his work at Papunya in 1971 and 1972, the massive and beautifully produced *Papunya: A place made after the story: The beginnings of the Western Desert Painting Movement* (hereafter *Papunya: A place made after the story*). These are only two recent examples of a huge body of scholarly, curatorial and popular works that have solidified 'Papunya' as culturally iconic, foundational and unique. Geoffrey Bardon himself began to document the movement as it was being created and reported on it as early as 1972.[12] A BBC documentary of the mid-1970s, *Desert Dreamers*, was followed by Bardon's books *Aboriginal Art of the Western Desert* (1979) and *Papunya Tula* (1991, with second and third editions in 1999 and 2002).[13] There have also been other television programs and documentary films, many exhibitions and exhibition catalogues, as well a small library of academic and popular books concerned with aspects of Papunya.[14] Even so, I want to explore how, taken together, a major exhibition and its catalogue, and a lavish testimonial book (a record of witnessing Papunya), seem to pose a common question: what kinds of forgetting are involved in the recognition and remembering of Aboriginal art as inaugurated by Papunya?[15]

In their essay 'Genesis and genius: The art of Papunya Tula artists', the editors of *Papunya Tula*, Hetti Perkins and Hannah Fink, cite a very moving story told by Bardon which we can take to be the genesis of the painting movement:

> I recall most vividly a group of Aboriginal men, some of
> whom I had not met before, knocking at the door of my flat
> one cold night, and silently filing in. They sat in their clothes
> all crushed and seemingly used up and it was then that I first
> saw Kaapa Tjampitjinpa, as himself. He secretively handed a
> piece of paper to Old Mick Tjakamarra and kept whispering
> and making signs to Mick to hand the paper to me. There
> were gestures and coughing and clearing of throats, and at
> last the paper was handed to me. I unfolded it and this fellow,
> as yet unnamed and unintroduced, pointed at it from where
> he stood and said, 'Design'. I nodded, and looked at it. It was
> a rough composite drawing of the mural they planned to paint
> on the school wall – a series of lines and what seemed like

arabesques, but all very simple and basic ... This outline was the first conceptualisation of the great honey ant mural, the first public affirmation of Aboriginal culture at Papunya.[16]

It's a painful and beautiful story. Into a cold and miserable place controlled by the 'drunken, foul-mouthed and violent men who ... were the settlement's administrators' comes a sign of life brought by other men who, like their clothing, seem crushed and used up by the violence and horror of the penal settlement that was their home.[17] In a re-enactment of so many cross-cultural exchanges, gestures and performances, a rudimentary shared vocabulary and an inscription signals the beginning of something new, the mural as the 'climactic public affirmation of Aboriginal identity at Papunya'.[18]

This very careful formulation is, I think, perfectly balanced. Even before he arrived, Bardon certainly knew that there was plenty of indigenous culture at Papunya; indeed, this fact was what had drawn him to take up the teaching position.[19] But his implicit argument is that before the painting of the mural, Aboriginality was simply abject:

> The people of the Welfare Branch said to me so often that I beheld a living museum, and an overarching thought among the teachers and administrators was that not only Aboriginal culture but the Aborigines themselves were set in a death-mould and that nothing in this world would save them.[20]

Bardon's response to such thinking is made clear in the chapter 'The children come first'. He was clearly a generous, thoughtful and gifted teacher who challenged himself to find pedagogic strategies that would work for his students. And like all good teachers, he began by learning, by watching children 'drawing tracks and signs in the red sand'.[21] In doing this, he acknowledged the children's enthusiasm for incising stories of 'travelling tracks that told of dingoes, kangaroos, emus and camels' and he acquired a name,

'Mr Patterns'.[22] With the help of his teaching assistant, Obed Rag-gett, Bardon began to bring the red sand into the school building, allowing the children to draw and paint on the floor, urging them to produce what he thought of as Aboriginal patterns, which, later that year, were reproduced in the *Papunya School News*.[23] So the children were first not only in the sense of his professional commitment to them as a teacher but also in the sense that together, Raggett, Bardon and his students produced the classroom as a space for Aboriginality in which indigenous culture could be affirmed. The same communicative possibilities come into being as a tiny sketch of the mural is passed from hand to hand in Bardon's flat amid 'whispering and ... signs ... gestures and coughing and clearing of throats'. What comes together in both instances is, on the one hand, indigenous knowledge and cultural practice, and, on the other, Bardon expressing his interest in this knowledge and practice by making available resources and spaces at his disposal: the classroom, art materials and walls of the school. As historian Paul Carter writes, 'Bardon was asserting, as anthropologist TGH Strehlow had before him, the possibility of a genuinely Australian culture emerging from a creative meeting of indigenous and non-indigenous poetic systems.'[24] The 'public affirmation of Aboriginal culture at Papunya' occurs when new, intercultural spaces are created. These are shared communicative spaces that are neither black nor white; as simple as drawings in a school newsletter and a design on a government building.

Papunya: A place made after the story is an extraordinary book that is unashamedly and justifiably focused on documenting Bardon's experiences as part of a remarkable cultural moment. Yet, while it is a magnificent document, as a study of memory, it is perplexing. Bardon introduces memory as a key concern in the book's dedication:

This book is dedicated to those twenty-five or more towering artists of my experience in the Western Desert, and to all their marvellous kith and kin; but also it is a justification, amply and I hope, unforgettably seen, of what in the darkness of time sometimes can be mislaid and lost, because it was not understood for what it was.[25]

More than anything, this seems to refer, on the one hand, to the fact that the white authorities at Papunya did not understand what Bardon and the men had created and, on the other hand, to the real danger that Bardon himself may have mislaid or lost his memories of Papunya as a result of the terrible treatment – a time of darkness – that he experienced at Chelmsford, a psychiatric hospital, after his breakdown at Papunya. In a sense, the book is his response to the prospect of forgetting. But there is simultaneously a concern with indigenous memory. Indeed, Bardon's first paragraph in *Papunya: A place made after the story* makes this clear: 'The Western Desert Painting Movement of my experience was always about recollection and cultural memory, a bringing-to-consciousness of those people who lived in the Western Desert of our Northern Territory.' Paul Carter, too, writes of the movement: 'The systematic dismembering of identity somehow flipped over, inaugurating its antithesis, an extraordinary act of collective remembering.'[26] But what this confidence obscures is how fragile were the achievements of the painting movement in 1972 and 1973. The Honey Ant mural on the school walls was painted over by order of the settlement's authorities and both ill health and lack of institutional support made it impossible for Bardon to stay. During this time, Bardon writes that 'the painters worked, seemingly, in recollection of me'.[27] This is one way of making sense of the strange subtitle, 'a place made after the story'. In important respects, this book is about remembering with an eye to the future, trying to reconstruct the foundations of a 'painting movement', which, although it was to become strong, began with a whole series of delicate moments.

It seems entirely right to think about the invention of Aboriginal art at Papunya as a massive remembering, a pouring forth of that which had been repressed from this strange and new hybrid zone seemingly controlled by whitefellas. But, the weight given to memory in this account comes at the cost of forgetting. We can identify this in some of the things we don't see in the records of Papunya. The exhibition *Papunya Tula: Genesis and genius* consisted of more than 150 paintings; the first, a 1971 untitled, double-sided painting on composite board attributed to Tutuma Tjapangati, and the last four huge canvasses – the Kiwirrkura Women's Painting, the Kintore Women's Painting, the Kintore Men's Painting and the Kiwirrkura Men's Painting – all painted in 1999 and auctioned to raise funds to purchase kidney dialysis machines. Nothing in the exhibition predates Papunya and there's a strong emphasis on the aesthetic development of the work of individual painters and of communities over time. Similarly, in *Papunya: A place made after the story*, we see almost no images of art produced before Bardon's arrival, nor read any account of art being produced by Western Desert people before 1971. Instead, we begin with the boards, those luminous works described in this way by Paul Carter: 'over a thousand paintings whose sudden appearance *ex nihilo* might well suggest a comparison with the events of Genesis in the Old Testament'.[28] And this too is how the market imagines early Papunya Tula. The boards – a finite corpus perfectly suited to the speculative logic of the secondary market – are regarded as both reaching deeply into time immemorial (they are profoundly authentic) and seemingly without artistic antecedents (they are pure innovation).

While this evaluation is influenced by Bardon's accounts of the establishment of the 'painting movement' at Papunya, I don't believe that he actually thought that the paintings appeared *ex nihilo*. He knew that the men who worked with him were not amnesic, mere blank slates nor outside of history.[29] He knew that many of them had long produced art both for market and non-market purposes, including various kinds of woodcarvings, watercolours and artefacts. He knew that the extraordinary work that he and the painters accomplished at Papunya in 1971–72 was impossible to even imagine without there already being both a desire to paint and the existing epistemological, aesthetic, familial, cosmological and iconic resources of the indigenous communities at Papunya. Yet, despite this, and despite the widespread knowledge of a long tradition of indigenous art-making (in a Western sense), there is a great deal in *Papunya: A place made after the story* that contributes to the sense that contemporary Aboriginal art was invented at Papunya.

The way in which Clifford Possum Tjapaltjarri comes into view for the reader of *Papunya: A place made after the story* as he enters Bardon's world is a strong case in point: 'His visits to Papunya from February 1972 interested him in continuing with his brilliant wood carving and entering into tribal painting within the Anmatjira Aranda [Anmatyerre] tradition.'[30] Clifford Possum, circa 1972, seems a very different man in Vivien Johnson's account, which accompanied a major retrospective of the artist: 'When Clifford Possum began to paint for Geoffrey Bardon in early 1972, he was not taking his first tentative steps as an artist ... he had probably carved or painted almost every day of his life for the past twenty years.'[31] Johnson makes a careful and detailed argument that prior to Bardon's arrival at Papunya in 1971, Clifford Possum and his countrymen Kaapa Mbitjana Tjampitjinpa and Tim Leura Tjapaltjarri were already practising artists (in a recognisable Western sense). They were already experimenting with 'turning traditional art into a commercial form – paintings on flat surfaces'.[32] Already one of these paintings, Kaapa's 1971 *Galgardi*, had won the Caltex Art Award in August 1971. This work, writes Johnson, 'was the product of an artistic practice based in Western Desert traditions which existed independently of and prior to the events comprising the now familiar tale of the origins of painting at Papunya'.[33] Even more important than the work they were producing was that these men shared 'the idea of themselves as artists and craftsmen'. Johnson argues persuasively that this idea and their artistic practices can be linked to the contact that these Anmatyerre men had, through their work as stockmen, with the Arrente school of watercolourists.[34]

The differences in emphasis between Bardon and Johnson are, in part, relatively arcane issues of detail in art historical scholarship. But the point has a wider significance for my argument here. In addition to recalling Bardon's forgetfulness in relation to the Anmatyerre artists (while at the same time not wanting to downplay the significance of what was begun by Bardon and the painting men), Johnson makes a crucial link to the zone of Aboriginality that is the chief focus of my concerns. She also writes of Clifford Possum and his countrymen: 'Their aspiration to become professional artists like Albert Namatjira was critical to the emergence of Papunya painting.'[35] The substantial links between the Anmatyerre men and the second-generation Hermannsburg painters, whose 'daring counter-appropriation of the traditions of European landscape painting to their own expressive ends' fed into Papunya where the same strategy took different forms.[36] Thus, for Johnson, the 'origins' of what became Papunya are rooted not only in the relatively autonomous Anmatyerre culture, but also in Anmatyerre familiarity with producing carvings and paintings for commercial sale in Central Australia. In other words, a different account of Papunya might emphasise less the appearance of the boards *ex nihilo* and more their connection to painted boomerangs and pokerwork on mulga plaques. And this link takes us not to the emergence of an Aboriginal high art at Papunya but to the circulation of Aboriginal things and images in the non-indigenous community in the late 1960s. Bardon himself thought initially that pottery fired in an already-existing kiln might be worth a go: 'My idea was for the black people to learn ceramics, so as to link traditional design and pattern from their painting to a craft pottery for there had been real success with the school lessons and firing of the kiln.'[37] Had they done this, the people of Papunya would have been turning out ceramics for a market already flooded with so-called 'Abo art' made by white Australians.

FORGETTING AßO ART

In thousands of Australian shop windows one can see
examples of pottery, wooden boxes and trays, table-mats,
textiles, and various knick-knacks and souvenirs decorated
with aboriginal designs. To a visitor from abroad this is
like a breath of fresh air: here at last is something that is
different, that is typical of the country, that is good. When
I made inquiries I discovered that the production of these
articles forms quite a large industry … thousands of pieces of
pottery decorated with aboriginal motifs are made annually
by white Australian potters … passengers of Qantas Empire
Airways use table-mats decorated with aboriginal designs …
contemporary interior decorators use textiles hand-
painted with aboriginal patterns. Besides these products
of craftsmen, there are paintings and murals inspired by
aboriginal art that are little known in Australia, and, alas,
quite uncommon in England.

Roman Black[38]

In this passage, Roman Black describes a world of 'new Aboriginal art' that he came across as a visitor to Australia in 1963. From
the vantage point of the early 21st century, this world is hard to
imagine, despite echoes in contemporary textile production. That's
not the case with the other half of Roman Black's concerns, 'old
Aboriginal art'. 'Old' refers to what today is often described simply as indigenous art and material culture: rock engravings, rock
and bark paintings, ground sculptures and sacred objects, carved
trees, incised boomerangs, shields, pearl shell, boab nuts, spears,
basket work and carved figures, grave posts, and so on – indeed
Black's book provides an inclusive inventory of the repertoire of
artistic work produced by indigenous people.[39] In *Old and New
Australian Aboriginal Art*, Roman Black celebrates the creativity of 'old Aboriginal art': 'The aboriginal's cultural life – his art,

his music, and his dancing – is particularly rich ... the aboriginal is a true artist: he paints for the joy of it and not for the pleasure of possessing.'[40] Perhaps the only moment of discomfort for a contemporary reader – apart from the fairly typical patronising and condescending tone common to 'friends of the Aboriginal' in the 1960s – arises in recognising that, while Roman Black's 'old' Aboriginal art was in some small measure 'still living art', he was primarily referencing historical artefacts accessible in museum collections. But the real shock of this book comes with what Roman Black means by 'new Australian Aboriginal art'. This refers to a disparate body of indigenous-derived images and objects made by non-indigenous artists – painting and design, pottery and textiles; not only the commodities produced for tourist or popular markets such as mulga wood ashtrays, tea towels and garden figures. Black also includes to high prestige examples of design (such as cover art for literary journals), costume designs for ballet productions and significant public murals. Taken together, new Australian Aboriginal art had a significant presence in public culture.

I want to revisit this world of Abo art in order to consider some of the shapes and patterns of cultural exchange that are legible in this almost forgotten domain of art. I'm using the term 'Abo art' to describe this work for a number of reasons. It's a term that is contemporary to the production of this work. I want the term to carry all its racist force rather than, in polite fashion, avoid it as unfortunate. For the purposes of this discussion, I don't want to make any distinction between tourist souvenirs (as Aboriginalia or Aboriginal kitsch) and Aboriginal-inspired fine art: oil paintings, graphic design and expensive fabrics. It's all Abo art. The term 'Abo art' is also preferable to Roman Black's notion of 'new Australian Aboriginal Art'. For Black, the idea that indigenous people could produce new art was an oxymoron. He was familiar with and reproduced works by contemporary indigenous artists painting on bark at Oenpelli, Groote Eylandt and Yirrkala, but for him, they were simply reproducing old Aboriginal art. The contemporary work of Namatjira and his

Playing cards designed by Lloyd Piper and featured in Roman Black, Old and New Australian Aboriginal Art. *(With the permission of HarperCollins)*

heirs was regarded as 'not primitive enough'.[41] The only reason to not use the term 'Abo art' is that it might offend some indigenous readers of this book. Nevertheless, I feel it's appropriate to use this offensive term because it's about offensive images and things which are worth thinking about. I stress that my use of the term highlights the appropriation of indigenous culture by non-indigenous cultural producers. Richard Bell's 'Bells theorem: Aboriginal art – it's a white thing' certainly applies fully to Abo art; it's only about indigenous art to the extent that it's reusing, copying and applying some aspects in indigenous image-making in a different domain.[42]

The world of 'new Aboriginal art' that Roman Black encountered when he dropped in on the Australian art world was already old in 1963. Nicholas Thomas, in a much broader argument encompassing the entire sweep of post-1788 art practice in Australia and New Zealand, connects Abo art to questions of image-making and cultural belonging: if white Australians were becoming native, how were these new natives to exist in relation to older natives?[43] Thomas draws our attention to a number of processes. As 'the first Australian became almost invisible in the cities and more densely settled areas', indigenous people were excluded almost entirely from high art, in part because 'undignified, acculturated and dispossessed indigenous people about town did not constitute appropriate subject-matter'.[44] Yet, at the same time, nationally specific motifs became centrally important to an emerging Australian nation-state in search of distinctiveness. Wattle and eucalypt, emu and kangaroo, boomerang and spear became widely deployed in national iconography. For Thomas, the 'disappearance' of indigenous Australians from high art was one of many 'shifting accommodations' that led him to examine the 'chequered history of the use of indigenous references in design and decoration in Australia and New Zealand, and explore the curious slippage that enabled indigenous figures and motifs to have both native and national connotations'.[45]

From the 1920s, there were successive attempts to interest non-indigenous artists in Aboriginal art as a source of inspiration. Baldwin Spencer urged craft workers to 'visit the museum and "copy some of the designs of the Australian aborigines"'.[46] A few years later, Margaret Preston began her promotion of indigenous design as the basis for an Australian art, while in 1938, anthropologist Frederick McCarthy published *Australian Aboriginal Decorative Art*, which, through a number of editions, sold over 100 000 copies.[47] McCarthy was also centrally involved in the Australian Museum exhibition *Australian Aboriginal Art and Its Applications* held at galleries in the Sydney department store David Jones.[48] By 1955, the Martin Boyd Pottery in Sydney employed 50 people to decorate ceramics with Aboriginal designs.[49] Two aspects of Thomas's argument are relevant to these, and many other, examples in the domain of Abo art. First he suggests that:

> In settler societies, cultural colonization proceeds most energetically not by the 'theft' of motifs or art styles that are reproduced in creole culture, but through forging national narratives that situate indigenous people firmly in the past, or in the process of waning, while settlers are identified with what is new and flourishing and promising. In this way, the potential paradox arising from the use of natives to affirm the native status of settlers is mediated by a narrative of succession: future is to past as settler is to savages.[50]

Roman Black's *Old and New Aboriginal Art* provides a very clear example of this 'narrative of succession'. While Black is deeply interested in some aspects of 'old Aboriginal art', this art (with some minor exceptions) is found only in museums, the work of unnamed and now dead artists. Abo art is art without Aborigines in the sense of it being produced by non-indigenous people, but also it is radically forgetful of both Aboriginal history and contemporary indigenous presence. Abo art literally replaces 'old Aboriginal art' as settlers are imagined to have replaced indigenous peoples. Second, Thomas writes that in this process of succession, 'Settler nationalists clearly understood the relation between indigenous reference and emergent national culture as one of incorporation rather than exchange.'[51] In other words, Aboriginal art was a resource for settler artists, an untapped 'vocabulary of forms', as described by the art critic Robert Hughes in 1960.[52] But crucially for Thomas, this mining of Aboriginal art in an effort to 'localise settler culture' was not just another form of dispossession but rather another, and ultimately unstable, moment in colonialism as a 'conflict which is never definitely resolved'.[53]

Writing within an art-historical framework, Thomas's thesis is that Abo art gradually becomes dominated by what art historian Judith O'Callaghan calls the 'amateurism and commercialism of the souvenir trade'.[54] It became kitsch. In the 1940s and 1950s, Abo art was associated with forms of modernist high design in theatre, literary culture, architecture and elsewhere.[55] But by the 1960s, Roman Black was swimming against the tide. Architect Robin Boyd's bitter ditty better expressed the value accorded to Abo art:

I'm picturin' a little vision
On a sunburnt subdivision
Brick veneer in every fashion hue
Wall to wall on every floor
And abo drawings on the door –
A two-tone Holden Special, and You.[56]

Thomas works his way through this in a brilliant account of Margaret Preston as the only 'new Aboriginal artist' whose work 'rose above the level of kitsch'.[57] Whilst Preston advocated the indigenisation of white Australian culture through the incorporation of Aboriginal art, her art actually achieved something very different: in quoting indigenous motifs, it *pointed towards* Aboriginal art. Her work makes 'the fact of difference explicit, and this is surely to lay bare the contrivance of synthesis ... Preston presented combination rather than fusion, a possibility rather than an accomplishment, a problem rather than a solution.'[58]

> Just as the 1941 Australian Museum exhibition inadvertently
> revealed the aesthetic strength of indigenous forms that were
> introduced only to display their potential 'applications',
> Preston's work deflected viewers' attention, drawing them
> not toward her grand notion of a national culture, but
> 'irresistibly' toward the neglected indigenous art traditions
> themselves. Those traditions pointed in turn toward the
> indigenous presence, spotlighting a stubborn and enduring
> obstacle to the idea of settler nationhood.[59]

Thomas's key point is that Abo art was self-subverting in that it
kept alive the instability at the heart of settler nationalist culture:
what places and positions are available for indigenous citizens in
the nation-state? His argument looks forward (in all senses) to the
emergence of a new Aboriginal art produced by indigenous people
and (gradually) validated within the art world from the 1980s.

If Thomas is attentive to how Abo art called forth Papunya
into the world of the gallery, Carolyn Lovitt is concerned with
how that art found a place in domestic homes. Lovitt focuses on
the period between 1934 and 1966. Following anthropologist AP
Elkin, she argues that 'In the early 1930s, Australia was coming to
grips with a period of recent violence that had drawn the attention
of local and international media. Race-relations became a matter of household debate.'[60] It was also a time when there was a
growing presence of Aboriginal people and things in public culture
through popular novels, travel writing and children's books. For
Lovitt, there were multiple underpinnings to the domain of Abo
art. Like Thomas, she wants to emphasise how it provided distinc-
tively national motifs for those artists and consumers interested in
marking an aesthetic break from European influences. She's also
attentive to the ways in which the 'Aboriginal style' had 'tremen-
dously commercial viability' and thus was particularly applicable
to the mass production of ceramics and fabrics. But to this list,

From Roman Black, Old and New Australian Aboriginal Art.
(With the permission of HarperCollins)

Lovitt wants to add a third aspiration of Abo art: a 'humanitarian ambition to override the racism of the Australian public and government policy'. This involved a paradoxical stress on 'common humanity' as the source of such artworks.[61]

Lovitt's account is not, however, an abstract study of how ideas (such as those of Franz Boas, Elkin and McCarthy) produced a new and more humanitarian understanding of indigenous peoples. Her interest is in the larger argument that 'Space for Aboriginal culture was first negotiated through the "domain of the decorative".'[62]

In this frame, the 1941 David Jones exhibition to which I referred earlier becomes important because, in creating a living room containing both items of indigenous material culture and Abo art, it 'demonstrated the compatibility of Aboriginal art with modern everyday living ... [as] a direct challenge to those who argued that Aboriginal culture had no place in modern Australia'.[63] Lovitt is not suggesting, as Elkin did, that 'the incorporation of Aboriginal art into everyday Australian life ... would usher in an acceptance of Aboriginal people'.[64] Instead, she wants to revalue the domestic, the feminine and the commercial against the condescension of modernist heroes and critics who railed against ornament. She wants to think about the home not simply as an aesthetic domain but as a space of 'social pedagogy and control'.[65] It's here that we can connect Lovitt's argument with Anna Haebich's account of one important example of Abo art from the 1950s:

> Australian governments of the time [1950s] were adopting
> symbols from 'primitive' Aboriginal cultures to represent
> the new modern Australian nation of the postwar period.
> Designers were incorporating the hybrid commodities based
> on Aboriginal and modernist forms to create the latest look in
> fashionable interiors. Stylised shapes of boomerangs, together
> with human and animal figures, motifs and designs from rock
> art and bark painting, floated across the surfaces of textiles,
> ceramics and the host of ephemeral objects that adorned
> corporate and domestic spaces around the nation. A cruel
> irony was that non-Aboriginal artists and designers were
> the principal creators of these hybrid works and they were
> inspired by anthropologists' reproductions and interpretations
> of Aboriginal art. Aboriginal artists and custodians were left
> out of the loop.[66]

In her brief but punchy essay, Haebich discusses the ballet *Corroboree*, commissioned for the 1954 visit of Queen Elizabeth II and Prince Philip, as an archetypal high culture example of Abo art. The ballet was created by American dancer and choreographer Beth Dean and her husband Victor Carell. It featured music by John Antill and costumes and sets by William Constable. Dean and Carell were inspired to come to Australia by a lecture and film screening presented by the anthropologist Charles Mountford during a US tour. They recalled him conjuring 'leaping, virile young men, their dark glistening bodies ochre-daubed and decorated in fantastic designs of feather down'.[67] Like many promoters and producers of Abo art, Dean and Carell thought of *Corroboree* as a work that would encourage respect for Aboriginal culture. Haebich argues the contrary. She sees the ballet as a hybrid transgression for two reasons: first because the production breached Aboriginal cultural protocols, and secondly because, 'The all-white performance reinforced the impression that Aboriginal culture was indeed dying and that assimilation was the only way forward.'[68]

As in the case of the overwhelming majority of Abo art, 'Aboriginal custodians were not financially compensated for the commercial use of their cultural property, which was often misinterpreted and misused.'[69] However, the question of breaching protocols in relation to historical cultural practices is a difficult one. Dean had certainly made a field trip to the Northern Territory to conduct research. Haebich writes that Dean 'wove a narrative of dance based on the public ceremonies of initiation which she had been invited to observe in Central Australia'.[70] Although it's very unlikely that Dean observed indigenous cultural protocols in the ways in which we would deem appropriate in the 21st century, can we ask that of her? The uses made by Dean of indigenous performance is really something that could only be adequately addressed by those indigenous people who had and have cultural rights in relation to those performances. Without such authority, how are we to judge Dean's choreography as formally different from the creative hybridity of the contemporary dance company Bangarra? In the final analysis, it's the fact that in *Corroboree* 'Dean danced the lead role of the male initiate' that enables Haebich to assert that 'Today a production that so clearly breached indigenous cultural protocols would have no hope of being presented in any Australian theatre'.[71] That's almost certainly true but of little use in making sense of a 50-year old ballet. Besides which, our contemporary cultural ethics would stamp a very long list of both indigenous and non-indigenous cultural productions in the past as 'Not To Be Performed'. But performed they were.

The issue of the relationship between Abo art and government policies in pursuit of assimilation is a more accessible one to me, as a non-indigenous writer, because it concerns the domain of Aboriginality. Haebich is very persuasive on this point. The original sketches for *Corroboree* envisaged that 'an Aboriginal elder ... from Central Australia ... would sit on stage prior to the performance and then move discreetly off stage as the curtains opened to reveal the opening scene of the ballet.'[72] The sense in which an indigenous presence disappears (discreetly) and is succeeded by vital and mobile white performers in dark woollen body suits clearly makes indigenous people literally absent. This mirrors the 'disappearance' of indigenous people which was occurring as Abo art incorporated Aboriginal things and knowledge into a non-indigenous cultural world. For Haebich, the coincidence of Abo art and the high-water mark of assimilation policy is no accident. Abo art was a 'hybrid transgression' of modernism that stole from indigenous people. Assimilation was a policy which deployed 'race' in order to discipline and eradicate indigenous people. Lovitt is also concerned with how many of the uses of Abo art can be read as metaphors for assimilation, understood as a new kind of subordination of indigenous people to the (white) nation-state. But unlike Haebich, Lovitt maintains 'that the version of Australia that artists signalled by the use of Aboriginal art was also loaded with imaginative possibilities of what Australia might look like as it negotiated a new relationship with Black Australia'.[73] For Lovitt, 'By 1950, Aboriginal art was fully accepted in the "sitting room" while its place in State art galleries was still uncertain.' In a sense, 50 years of Abo art prepared both the art world and the home for the 'coming' of Aboriginal art in the 1980s. Abo art was unstable, in-between, ambiguous stuff in the domain of Aboriginality.[74] And it took Geoffrey Bardon to Papunya. Before it became his mission to drive whitefella influence from the repertoire of his painting men, it was an aspiration not unlike that of Margaret Preston that lured him to the desert:

> I had an abiding interest in the Western Desert graphic
> designs yet also I had a purpose for my own art, since with a
> small grant of $150 from the Interim Film Council, I wished
> to make an animated film. A graphic art style was something
> that I very much wished to develop and it was this idea that
> had brought me, in part, to Papunya and the concept of
> authentic Aboriginal art, and what it said and might portend
> and show.[75]

Already interested in Aboriginal bark paintings from Arnhem Land and no doubt familiar with Abo art, Bardon expected that the local art production would furnish him with suggestive designs which might be incorporated into a graphical language that would stamp his animated film as distinctly Australian. An artist interested in film, he expected the relative isolation of Papunya to provide him with the leisure to fulfil an ambition – the creation of a 'recognisably Australian style of animation'.[76]

KITSCH AND KOORI

> First I labour for an idea, one that usually ends up being sad
> or pathetic, and then during the agony process of getting the
> image done, somehow things take a turn towards the ironic.
> Humour cuts deep. I like to think that there's a laugh and a
> tear in each picture.
>
> Destiny Deacon[77]

Today, the objects and aesthetics celebrated by Roman Black have been either largely forgotten or surface as examples of 'Aboriginal kitsch'. *Barry Humphries' Treasury of Australian Kitsch* achieves both ends.[78] Amid the gleeful mockery of 'utilitarian art' – kookaburra name plates, ceramic marsupials, big pineapples, bottles, bananas and cows, roo-skin postcards, silver yabby pendants and mosquito cufflinks – only two items of Aboriginal kitsch appear. The first is captioned 'A range of popular garden ornaments. Marsupial optional.' It consists of three garden figures assembled as a family group: an Aboriginal man with spear poised, an Aboriginal woman holding a coolamon and an Aboriginal child cradling a koala. The second is an image of a boomerang-handled beer mug featuring an Aboriginal face. The caption reads: 'The traditional "Toby" jug is here unequivocally translated into local idiom. Thinking Australians would think twice before quenching their thirst from any other vessel.' Such a paltry selection suggests that even a satirist as iconoclastic as Humphries becomes nervous when confronted by these objects. The presumption that contemporary Aboriginal art's significance resides in the authenticity of its producers makes it difficult to imagine Abo art as anything other than inherently fake, delusional or bizarre, the product of cultural insensitivity at best or, at worst, simply theft or unjust cultural appropriation. And, as Thomas, Lovitt, Haebich and others have argued, this unease is reinforced by the fact that kitsch was Abo art's fate; 'Aboriginal style décor eventually lost the power to challenge the observer, passively reinforcing stereotypes instead.'[79]

Overwhelmingly, it's indigenous artists who have been the energetic and creative memory-workers in the archives of Aboriginality. I think of photographic work like that of Leah King-Smith's haunting ghost pictures and Fiona Foley's *Survival II* (1988), *Giviid Woman and Mrs Fraser* (1992) and *Badtja-la Woman* (1994). I think of film work by Tracey Moffatt and Michael Riley, and of Gordon Bennett's paintings, some of them dealing directly and explicitly with the inheritance of Abo art in general and Preston in particular. But the queen of this kitsch is

Destiny Deacon, White Australia's Aboriginal Artefacts, *1995. Installation view,* Welcome to Never-Never *at Gallery Gabrielle Pizzi, Melbourne. (Courtesy of the artist and Roslyn Oxley9 Gallery, Sydney)*

Destiny Deacon. Her art certainly begins from the ruins of colonialism, but the most distinctive aspect of the work is Deacon's capacity to hold her nerve, to be fearless in the face of kitsch and embrace it with compassion. Even so, my purpose is not to add to the significant critical commentary on indigenous artists in relation to the history of image-making about indigenous people. Instead, I want to consider how a non-indigenous artist, Ross Moore, has approached Abo art. I've not chosen Moore because his work is any 'better' or more interesting than the work of Bennett and Deacon. Rather, I think his art provides us with a lonely example of a non-indigenous contribution to what needs to be (at least) a two-sided dialogue.

Dear Primitive was exhibited in a former Masonic Hall in Melbourne in 1994. On approach, it looked a little like one of those 'thousands of Australian shop windows' that took Roman Black's fancy in 1963. High up on the walls of the entry to the main gallery were hung a number of very roughly painted banners featuring crude Aboriginal figures. In this antechamber, the visitor could hear the second component of the exhibition, a soundtrack swelling from inside. All the time songs were in the air: 'Tie me kangaroo down, Sport' (Rolf Harris), 'Carra birra wirra canna' (Rolf, again), 'Bush tracker' (Eric Jupp) and 'My boomerang won't come back' (Charlie Drake). Written in 1957 then briefly a number one hit when it was first released in 1960, 'Tie me kangaroo down, Sport' begins with a wobble board laying down a rhythm. The sound of that odd but simple instrument somehow evokes a meld of didgeridoo and bullroarer, and is able to produce an aural space that seems to expand slowly but insistently. Then comes Harris's distinctive British-Australian voice pitched somewhere between

Ross Moore, Floor tiles. Installation view, Dear Primitive, *Temple, Melbourne, 1994. (With the kind permission of the artist)*

the simulated authenticity of Leonard Teale and the satiric mockery of Aunty Jack. The first verse (as I remember it) is squeezed out in talkin' Strine:

> There's an old Australian stockman ...
> Lying ...
> Dying ...
> An' 'e gets himself up on one elbow
> An' turns to 'is mates who're gathered round him
> An' 'e says ...

Today, 'Tie me kangaroo down, Sport' might be remembered as a funeral dirge that marked a passing. In postwar, Anglo-Celtic Australia, the archetypal man-of-the-bush was a phantom born to be mourned, a figure who only came into existence as an absence – an imaginary means of refusing indigenous existence, women's presence, homosocial and urban culture, national dependency, ethnic pluralism and global interdependence. Harris's rendition of the dying stockman was an occasion for last rites more than anything else, a ceremony in which business was tidied up, sins were forgiven and the remnants of a body were preserved as a tanned hide. The old bloke's koala was to be returned to the bush, Blue was to play his didgeridoo through the final moments and, most important for my purposes, Lou was to let the stockman's Abos go loose.

To hear that line (now usually erased from the song) was shocking. That Moore certainly intended the soundtrack and many of the obviously racist images in the show to be shocking is clear in his carefully developed argument in the catalogue essay. He suggests that non-indigenous people should take responsibility for having been so obsessed with making images of the 'OTHER'; he muses on memories of his family's reactions to Aboriginal people while he was growing up in Broken Hill; he discusses the links between the cultures of racism and homophobia, and condemns the continuing erasure of history that occurs when racist images are forgotten, cast off or cleaned up. For Moore, it's important that the

words of 'Tie me kangaroo down, Sport' and the racism of white image-making are experienced as shocking. It's a way of refusing the comfort of disavowal.

The counterpoints to these aspects of *Dear Primitive* came in the second and third exhibition spaces. The second room was constructed so as to conjure the aura of the museum and contained a number of plastic shields on display plinths. Here institutional forms were familiar; these were false artefacts on display – clearly products of white imagination – and I was being asked to gaze at my (cultural) self in a mirror of mis-recognition. The final room contained a floor-piece made of more than 100 white tiles each printed with an identical image of three 'dancing Aborigines' and a cute little plane overhead. It was stunning, so regu-

Ross Moore. Installation view, Dear Primitive, *Temple, Melbourne, 1994. (With the kind permission of the artist)*

lar, so clean, so modern, efficient and reproducible in form, so Australian – those 'performing Blacks' that have been indispensable to Europeanality.

Dear Primitive was an aural and visual sampling of non-indigenous culture in the curio shop, the museum and the craft rendering of Abo art. It took inspiration from everyday culture of the 1950s and 1960s which had trained people for modes of life faithful to the fictions of progress and civilisation. The exhibition was a brave, cannibalistic gesture in the shifting communicative space of Aboriginality. It seemed to me concerned with the voracious non-indigenous desires to know, speak, map, measure, classify, question, photograph, demarcate and film. Unlike a line being drawn under Australia's colonial entanglements, Ross Moore's *Dear Primitive* produced lines of connection rather than conclusions, lines of rearticulation and lines of intensities, pain-filled moments in the search for places to live. That's perhaps why the songs keep coming back to him, because they're still there, because the new songs haven't yet been sung.[80]

JACKY JACKY

Abo art was produced at a time when the lives of the vast majority of indigenous people in Australia were controlled and dominated by state agencies, and when, as a result of colonial and postcolonial oppression, they were socially marginal and economically impoverished. Indeed, Abo art can connect us to the real effects of postcolonial regimes of power, a connection made shockingly clear by health scholar Ian Anderson in his essay 'Post-colonial Dreaming at the end of the whitefellas millennium':

> Most Australians are familiar with the figure of the Jacky.
> He is found in suburban garden kitsch, a three-foot black
> plaster miniature with a red lap-lap and spear, or perhaps
> inside the house as a cutesie receptacle for cigarette butts:

the tea-towel image of Aboriginality. It is the Jacky who features in blokey bar discourse – as butt of racist jokes. This derogatory representation of Aboriginality is a pitiful figure of the bewildered 'traditional' Aborigine who has wandered into modernity, yet at the same time also maintains notions of a pristine and authentic Aboriginality.

Jacky Jacky is a drunk. He is disadvantaged and trapped in a cultural void. Jacky is not an industrious or smart operator in a capitalist economy. He is a living fossil – a 'primitive' among 'moderns'.

… Arthur Moffatt was a Koori from country Victoria … On the day that he died, Mr Moffatt travelled by train between two local country towns. Prior to the journey, he had been seen drinking with some friends, yet was not reported to have displayed any signs of intoxication. However, by the time that he reached his destination, he was agitated, sweaty and confused. Removed from the train, he was left semi-conscious on the station platform. Here a station guard called the police, who despite removing him to police custody also called for an ambulance. The ambulance officers assessed that Mr Moffatt was drunk, and took no further action. Later that evening Arthur Moffatt died in a police cell, alone and unattended.

The Royal Commission [into Aboriginal Deaths in Custody] inquiry into the death of Arthur Moffatt concluded that he had most probably died because of a hypoglycaemic coma, a complication of his diabetes. Some symptoms of hypoglycaemia can reasonably be confused with drunken … The police and ambulance officers who assessed Mr Moffatt were apparently so confident in their own diagnosis of drunkenness that they failed to secure a medical assessment of his condition. This most probably cost Mr Moffatt his life.

We can only speculate about the extent to which notions of 'Jacky as a drunk' were influential in shaping the actions of those in authority on this occasion. At best, these colonial stereotypes probably reinforced a series of errors in professional judgement.[81]

Ian Anderson is not arguing that negative stereotypes killed Arthur Moffatt in 1987. He is, however, arguing that culture can and does produce effects beyond mere representation and abstract ideas, and that 'Aboriginal art has the potential to provide non-Aboriginal people with new or enhanced insights into Aboriginal people and their cultural history.'[82] Hetti Perkins, the senior curator of Aboriginal and Torres Strait Islander Art at the Art Gallery of New South Wales, adds an explicitly political element to her appraisal:

> The emergence of a distinctive and strong indigenous voice
> through the visual arts over the preceding decades has been
> a catalyst for a re-evaluation of Australia's history and its
> potential to emerge into the twentieth-first century as a nation
> reconciled with its past.[83]

While such hopes can be associated with indigenous art, it's equally clear that indigenous art works in the fluid and polysemous world of Aboriginality which connects indigenous and non-indigenous people in many ways. Well-heeled ex-patriots are keen paddle-wavers in London and New York auctions. In Australia, a colour-field Freddie Timms canvas might be attractive because it matches a peach wall in a mansion, a small painting on bark might be a keepsake of a holiday in the north or a work by Phyllis Thomas might be a memento of working in an indigenous community in the Kimberley. In this chapter, I've made two small contributions to thinking about such a complex field. I've argued that the rise of contemporary indigenous art is inseparable from Abo art. Secondly, I've suggested that despite this, and with few exceptions, Abo art has been forgotten, disavowed and repressed. It may be that the cultural and political ambitions for indigenous art may depend, in part, on non-indigenous people recalling what they have inherited from Jacky Jacky and Abo art. The next chapter is concerned with precisely these questions of 'inheritance' as they were debated and contested in the 1980s and 1990s. From the bicentennial year, 1988, Aboriginality fuelled a heritage crisis focused on the historical legitimacy of the nation.

4 THE SPECTRE OF HERITAGE

We cannot dismiss the Australian state's recognition of culture, heritage and, in limited way, history, as merely a shallow cloaking of a deeper rejection of alterity.

Gillian Cowlishaw[1]

In 2007, the Australian federal government introduced a citizenship test for individuals wishing to become Australian citizens. The computer-based multiple-choice test aims to assess whether prospective citizens have 'a basic knowledge of the English language' and to measure 'knowledge of Australia and the responsibilities and privileges of citizenship.'[2] Heritage is mentioned only six times in the 46-page booklet produced to assist those preparing to become citizens: referring to 'Australia's history and heritage', 'a British political heritage', 'cultural heritage' (as something which should not confer disadvantage), 'Anglo-Celtic heritage', 'World Heritage' and 'Judeo-Christian heritage'.[3] The term 'memory' is absent and 'remembering' occurs only four times referring, in fairly anodyne ways, to Governor Lachlan Macquarie, those who 'served and died in war' (twice) and the goldfields. Despite the relative absence of these terms and their lack of emphasis, I think that remembering and heritage are central to this new process of 'becoming an Australian citizen'.

The capacity to remember is demanded by this test. Prospective citizens need to remember answers to questions such as 'In what year did the European settlement of Australia start?' and 'Which one of these Australians is famous for playing cricket?' More important, the test connects remembering to that which grounds the Australian nation: its heritage. In this sense, 'heritage' invokes something more than mere history. It is both property passed between generations and 'inherited customs, beliefs, and institutions held in common by a nation or community ... [and] natural and "built" landscapes, buildings and environments held in trust for future generations'.[4] This meaning encompasses heritage as both grounding the nation – emerging ideally in historian Perry Anderson's evocative phrase from deep roots in an 'immemorial past' – and the ways in which heritage is evoked in media, political and commemorative spaces.[5] My use of heritage includes, but is not reducible to, 'preserved things' or 'the things we want to keep', as the Hope inquiry into the Australian National Estate defined the term.[6] Yet it also suggests an older ethical and evaluative meaning along the lines of historian Ernest Scott's praise of 'the splendour of our heritage and the greatness of our possibilities' and echoes the not-yet-archaic racial-nationalism expressed in Henry Parkes's celebration of heritage in the form of a 'crimson thread of kinship'.[7]

In this chapter, I move from the ways in which 'forgetting Aborigines' has occurred in television and art to consider how Aboriginal people and things have been at the centre of a mundane heritage crisis or, at the very least, a moment of significant instability in the taken-for-grantedness of heritage since the 1980s. Most cultural institutions articulate inherited customs and beliefs through a sense of heritage, which, in turn, certifies their authenticity and legitimacy. Parliamentary convention, halls of fame and honour boards, much judicial ritual, the use of uniforms and anniversary commemorations of all sorts are strong examples of such practices. In a more specific sense, codified notions of heritage as things held in trust explicitly organise the work of many cultural institutions. Museums, the Australia Heritage Commission, sites registered on the National Estate, libraries, archives, some aspects of education, academic research, urban planning and large parts of tourism all partake in 'the heritage industry'.[8] Because heritage is one of the key modes in which 'the past' is put to use in cultural institutions, it can be regarded as a crucial element of the institutional and citizenly collective common sense that underpins public culture.[9]

The historian Elizabeth Jelin provides a way of connecting social memory to these notions of heritage. Jelin's book *State Repression and the Labors of Memory* is concerned with the relationship between memory and historical justice in Latin America. Like a number of scholars, she is critical of how some accounts of contemporary memory tend to regard memory as predominantly belonging to individuals and consisting of 'words'. Instead, Jelin wants to renovate an older tradition of thinking of remembering as always 'embedded in networks of social relationships, groups, institutions and cultures'.[10] Rather than thinking of memory as belonging to collectives, Jelin historicises the processes through which memories gain authority and particularly 'the institutions which legitimise them'.[11] In this light, a focus on heritage can direct us to institutions and utterances in and through which historical understandings and habits of memory are deployed in relation to governance. Not just any conjuring of 'the past' or evocation of history falls within the territory of heritage, but specifically the deployment of history in imagining and defining citizenship and governance. At the risk of drowning in generalities, here I want to consider heritage even more broadly as a constitutive and organising rhetoric across the field of cultural institutions and practices. In this chapter, heritage refers to the mobilisation of historical understanding and social memory in *institutional and citizenly* forms.

If there is a crisis legible in the government booklet *Becoming an Australian Citizen*, it is in the puzzling placement of indigenous people as the coda to part 2 of the book, 'Our land, our nation'.[12] After running through demography, geography, government symbols and rituals, national holidays, 'A story of Australia' – which features Captain James Cook, convicts, explorers, diggers and the Anzac legend, economy and politics, sport (and pride of place to the Don), nationalism and Nobel laureates – at last we come to the 'First Australians'. The booklet tells the reader that:

> Aboriginal and Torres Strait Islander People have been living in Australia for between 40 000–60 000 years. Australian Indigenous culture is the oldest surviving culture in the world ... [but there is 'a great dilemma facing Australian society'] many of the Aboriginal people in ... remote locations do not live well ... Australia faces an ongoing challenge to ensure that the Aboriginal people fully share in the life and prosperity of the nation.[13]

This captures perfectly the spectre of Aboriginality haunting Australian heritage. After the 1967 referendum, indigenous people were both progressively admitted to the rights of citizenship and governed in new and distinctive ways. Through various movements and achievements around land rights and forms of self-determination in the 1970s, indigenous people established what Tim Rowse has called the 'indigenous sector'.[14] During the same period, indigenous people and things were installed as belonging to the nation, perhaps most powerfully in the commissioning of Michael Jagamara Nelson's mosaic for the forecourt of the new Parliament House opened in 1988. Yet two decades later, indigenous people are not fully of the nation.

My argument is that forgetting aborigines is part of this 'great dilemma'. Three reference points organise and orient my remarks here. First, I consider the legacy of the 1988 Australian bicentennial celebrations. I draw attention to the pluralist and inclusive versions of national heritage that predominated. These tropes were

built on a tradition of cultural criticism that confidently uncov-
ered and disavowed pre-existing 'myths' of Australian heritage,
but was vague as to the images, narratives and evocations that
could replace these discredited legends in civic culture. So 1988
as a 'race portrait' seems, from this distance, not only anxiously
white but genuinely insecure and thin. Second, I turn to consider
the consequences of the indigenous boycott of the bicentenary. I
argue here that post-1988 indigenous people and their supporters
have built a new and powerful place for Aboriginality and heritage
in public culture. These transformations of Aboriginality and heritage are elaborated in relation to the Royal Commission into Aboriginal Deaths in Custody and the *Bringing Them Home* report
and include the decisions of the High Court in the Mabo and Wik
cases. My argument is that remembering Aborigines, like native
title itself, is authorised by significant governmental institutions
in new, contested and unfinished ways. Third, I turn to some of
the political disputations around heritage in the so-called 'Battle
for History' and the rise of the One Nation Party as further evidence of a mundane heritage crisis. One Nation (like the opposition to Mabo, Wik and reconciliation from within the federal
government) was shaped by paranoid heritage myths and relied
heavily on a singular and exclusionary notion of national heritage. The success of this political assemblage derived, in part, from
the absence of credible political alternatives affectively rooted in
national heritage. But the phenomenon of One Nation was built on
the unsustainability of the pluralist heritage proffered in 1988. In
this sense the formation of One Nation was, like John Howard's
sense of 'future directions', a protest against remembering Aborigines in part because of the extent to which this was regarded as
necessarily degrading of Australian heritage.

Having outlined some of the dimensions of a heritage crisis, I
conclude by offering some suggestions about how heritage in the
vernacular might be one way of thinking about a postpluralist heritage. Vernacular heritage is a loose way of describing historical
meaning shared by relatively small groups of people; it might be

locally specific in terms of idiom and themes or it might be familiar principally to those who share a common language or set of experiences. It is certainly particular and lived rather than general and abstract. My suggestion is that thinking about heritage in the vernacular may offer productive possibilities for cultural institutions. This is important because heritage will remain a key point of insecurity and longing as globalisation, market challenges to public culture, new information and media economies reshape the institutions of culture. Heritage matters today not because there is too much of it, nor because an earlier model needs to be reconditioned, nor because it's impossible, but because the desires stoking its production address an urgent problem: how specifically local and national historical traditions can provide sustaining resources in the face of globalised media and commodity flows.[15] Rather than a repetitive oscillation between remembering and forgetting Aboriginality in relation to national heritage, vernacular memory might provide one resource for trafficking between past and present.

1988: A STRATEGY OF REFUSAL

> Even people's confidence in their nation's past came under
> attack as the professional purveyors of guilt attacked
> Australia's heritage and people were told they should
> apologise for pride in their culture, traditions, institutions
> and history.
>
> John Howard[16]

In 1988 Australian heritage reached a conclusion of sorts and became something new. The exhaustion of certain notions of heritage was, in part, the result of shifts in the meaning and significance of heritage under pluralist and democratic pressures. Although there is a long history of heritage in Australia, the coincidence of new kinds of history-making and cultural dynamism in the 1960s and 1970s was far from arbitrary.[17] The new nationalism of the short-lived Whitlam government deployed heritage in the service of reform. Not only did Whitlam's government promulgate preservationism in the shape of the Australian Heritage Commission but, more broadly, it conceived of heritage as a means of articulating a 'useable past'. This national past held all the magical and tragic powers of myth and was supplemented by a faith that cultural nationalism would contribute to building a better future. This configuration of heritage drew on and elaborated the single most important innovation of 20th-century historical scholarship: an expansion of history's purview to include those who had previously been regarded as ephemeral historical subjects – convicts, the working classes, women, migrants, (so-called) minority identities and Aborigines. In the postwar period, new demotic and nationalist historiography blossomed as the heritage culture of the 1960s and 1970s began to rediscover and reinvent the signs and sounds of a nation – in preservation, collections policies and stamps; in popular ceremonies, anthems and civic rituals; in film, song and story. Democratised history gave to heritage a relentless positivity at the end of last century; its representations should be communal, they should include everyone's story, this one, the next one, and then some. By the 1980s, this cultural work had modernised and revivified Australian heritage as constitutive of a new bedrock for the Australian nation.

The bicentennial celebrations of 1988 made apparent some of the tensions and limits in this inclusive and pluralist configuration of Australian heritage.[18] Its vision of heritage was a grand hug-in of spatial togetherness in the form of symbolic journeys, collective spectacles and hi-tech panoramas. Whether in analyses of the Australian Bicentennial Authority, the NSW *First State 88* exhibition, stamps, *Images of Australia*, ephemeral material, *Australia Live* or the bicentennial exhibition, analysts have concurred as to the centrality of 'cultural diversity and racial reconciliation'.[19] David Goodman and Peter Cochrane called this strategy 'tactical pluralism', referring to the Australian Bicentennial Authority's attempt to include 'all the groups clamouring for recognition within the scope of the celebrations'.[20] This unanimity of analytical opinion did not, however, guarantee any common set of judgments as to the significance of these bicentennial phenomena. One conservative writer complained that Australia appeared as a 'land of incoherent diversity', while other commentators bemoaned the lack of a critical edge or wondered why 'many began to feel that in their empty, undiscriminating openness, there were few possibilities of liberation'.[21] Still others despaired that 1988 represented a 'pallid official amnesia'[22] or pondered the ramifications of such happy postmodernism representing Australia as a 'space wide open' for tourism and foreign capital.[23] It is possible to identify three features that may help us to make sense of 1988 as both disappointing and ineffectual: first, the absence of 'strong nationalism'; second, the exhaustion of a particular (nationalist) mode of cultural criticism; and third, not so much the pallidness of 1988 but the fact that it was downright white. I'll briefly discuss each of these propositions.

If the heritage products of 1988 lacked a strong nationalism, this is explicable in terms of forces both intrinsic and extrinsic to the field of heritage. The impact, reach and pace of the (ongoing) internationalisation of economic and cultural life in Australia since 1983 has been profound. This has certainly produced new moments for nationalist outpouring such as Bob Hawke's rapture at the 'national triumph' of winning the America's Cup. While there is no single model that can make sense of how 'national' achievements will be figured in the globalised fields of sport, culture, capital and military intervention, the balance between articulating the nation as the first among many and understanding the nation as an occasionally significant moment in multiple global fields, has shifted decisively to the latter. For many people, the disappointment of a franchised nation was made symbolic in January 1988 by the Coca-Cola icon adorning the spinnaker of one of the First Fleet re-enactment vessels that

*Sue Passmore (Australia Post Design Studio), Australian Bicentennial
X, The First Fleet Arrival–Australia Day, 1988. (With the permission of
Australian Postal Corporation)*

sailed into Sydney Harbour – a new Australia sailing under a new
flag. Powerful though that sign might have been, more broadly
there were serious narrative difficulties in founding nationalism
in a replay of (somebody else's) imperial adventures and precious
little nationalist meat in the establishment of a small penal colony, the beginning that grounded the celebration.

These very real problems were exacerbated by the seeming ina-
bility of 1988 to generate affective images and narratives of the
national. The problem was not in the volume of mediatised and
popular articulations of history and heritage. Nor was the problem one of excluding critical or argumentative engagements with
history. On the contrary, the bicentenary 'fostered a wide interest in "history" in every sense of that term ... [It] pluralised, or
rather multiplied, historical consciousness in Australian cultural
life'.[24] But this inclusiveness was shadowed during the bicentenary
by a particular model of cultural criticism. Meaghan Morris has
suggestively identified some problems of coupling banal pluralism
with ritual unmasking in her discussion of Russell Braddon's 1988

series *Images of Australia* broadcast on ABC television. This series was structured as a quest for national identity that took the form of 'a journey through disillusion'.[25] The series revisited relatively clichéd stories and stereotypes of Australian history, proceeded to debunk and, regretfully, disavow these mythic foundations until the critique of heritage left nothing but the future as the space of (prospective) inheritance. Morris notes that in this 'critical quest':

> Criticism's job is to banish the phantom by demonstrating
> its lack of reality. Thus Braddon's first program revealed that
> most Australians are not and never have been hardy bush
> pioneers, that we aren't all white or male, and that Ned Kelly
> was a criminal ...
>
> The logical conclusion of the adventure is not the capturing
> of an identity but the projection of a big picture – a vision
> of a *future* Australia in which 'true' identity may at last be
> seized. Braddon's picture had familiar features: a pluri-racial,
> double-gendered, multi-cultural society with Japanese as
> a second language, the three R's re-imposed in schools, a
> healthy debate about republicanism, and hi-tech economic
> outlook ... The quest for identity is a metaphor of a polemic
> about the present.[26]

This model of cultural criticism has a long history, but for our purposes we can identify a reference point closer to home: Australia, in the title of historian Richard White's influential book, has been 'invented'.[27] In *Inventing Australia*, White pursued the proposition that 'Australia' is a way of thinking that was made – geographically, politically, culturally – rather than essential. His thesis is widely misunderstood. One critic of the book took White to be a vacuous nihilist.[28] Elsewhere, White suffered the fate of those, such as Robin Boyd and Donald Horne before him, who are deft with titles: first, his insights were truncated and then they were wielded with the delicacy of a sledgehammer to break shackles holding Australia back from a multicultural, republican and postcolonial future. In such attacks, the nation and the outdated essences of heritage on which it relies are unmasked, denaturalised and denied their mythic power. In general, this mode of criticism has few of the virtues of empirical historical scholarship; it's actually possible to write about settlers who thought of themselves as bush pioneers. Such criticism has an extremely poor sense of historiography and popular historical imagination to the extent that it's uninterested in when, by whom, how and to what effects history was seen as territory that was both male and white. It has no grasp of the affective dimension of history: why might I feel that Ned Kelly was much more than a criminal? Nor does it possess a self-reflexive sense of what is at stake in cultural criticism: why engage in gestural demystification and with what results? Conjoined with the bicentenary, this kind of demythologising cultural criticism produced some very peculiar results.[29] With the demotically inspired multiplication and inclusion of historical identities (or perhaps more accurately, back-projected identity politics), 'the past' became both a space for nostalgia and a source of frustrating lack, hence the resort to the future. The 'invented-ness' of the national past meant, in this framework, that heritage could not offer any ground from which to speak.

And, to make matters worse for those enamoured with 1988, the indigenous boycott completely transformed the bicentenary. The boycott was radically unlike earlier indigenous protests around national historic commemorations such as the 1938 celebrations or those in 1970 marking 200 years since Cook visited the continent.[30] There were significant protests in 1988 and, while the boycott was not universal, the protests and the boycott were, perhaps surprisingly, not a request to be included or a call to add another meaning to 1988. Instead they claimed that the celebrations were a 'big lie' because 'White Australia has a Black History' going back 40 000 not 200 years, and that this fact fundamentally undermined the authority of the bicentenary to represent Australia. The boycott figured indigenous people as other to and outside the nation-state. Thus the absence of Aboriginality produced by the boycott made the unresolved aspects of colonialism central and present. Art historian Terry Smith has described this as keeping 'nationality open, like a promise and a running sore'.[31] We might also regard it as an act like that of the delegates to the 1997 Reconciliation Convention who turned their backs on the Prime Minister. In this sense, we can think of the boycott as a 'labour of the negative', a strategy of refusal that generated new conditions of possibility.[32] It was, and remains, an extraordinarily productive cultural and political intervention, which contributed significantly to Aboriginality and heritage becoming newly foundational for cultural institutions in Australia. Of course, if this has occurred, it could not have happened without the long history of indigenous organising and the post-1988 work of indigenous people and their supporters in a myriad of organisations and forms. Even so, I do want to suggest that the decade of the 1990s saw Aboriginality and heritage assume animating and transformative roles in unexpected places, which were enabled by the forceful demonstration during the bicentenary that white heritage could not carry the burden of the past in the present. In this sense, John Howard was right to observe that 'Even people's confidence in their nation's past came under attack as the [critics] attacked Australia's heritage.' For Howard and many others, heritage was something to be reclaimed from the cultural critics who found it damaged and wanting, and from an indigenous boycott that found it broken and irreparable. They wanted to renovate and reinstall an older unitary heritage marginalised by the pluralism of 1988 – a proud race portrait both antiquated and radically minoritarian in its rigorous exclusions. The model of cultural criticism that informed much of 1988, on the other hand, could find no viable heritage model and hence projected a race portrait of happy multicultural families on fast forward. Both were haunted by the spectre of Aboriginality. After 1988, the cultural authority of a singular Australian heritage waned.

FROM THE DEAD TO THE STOLEN

> To the Aborigines who are proud of their heritage it is
> indeed a day of mourning; we mourn the death of the many
> thousands of Aborigines who were brutally murdered; we
> mourn the loss of our land and the rape of our women by the
> white invaders.
>
> An Aboriginal Petition to the King, 1937[33]

The 1991 Royal Commission into Aboriginal Deaths in Custody was charged with inquiring into the deaths in custody of 99 Aboriginal and Torres Strait Islander men and women between 1 January 1980 and 31 April 1989. Its final report runs to 11 volumes and contains sweeping recommendations encompassing police and custodian practices, health, drug use, education, post-mortem practices, self-determination, reconciliation and much else besides. Yet on page 7 of the National Report Overview is a section headed 'The importance of history', in which Commissioner Elliot Johnston draws the readers' attention to the 'legacies of the history of two centuries of European domination of Aboriginal people' and goes on:

> I include in this report a chapter on that history. I make no
> apology for doing so. I do so not because the chapter adds
> to what is known but because what is known is known to

historians and Aboriginal people; it is little known to non-Aboriginal people and it is a principal thesis of this report that it must become more known.[34]

This is clearly a contribution to remembering in the domain of Aboriginality. He's suggesting that significant questions of public policy bearing on a range of governmental institutions cannot be comprehended without non-indigenous people 'knowing' a history. This is the first in a series of examples of institutional practices of memory in the period 1991–97 that reconfigured the relationships between Aboriginality and national heritage.

It's significant that the commissioners felt 'history' to be central to their report in the sense of it being a story to which the audience had a duty to listen.[35] But the passion with which the royal commission argued its historical case is also strikingly similar to the judgments of Justices Deane and Gaudron delivered in the Mabo case a year later:

> We have used language and expressed conclusions which
> some may think to be unusually emotive for a judgment in
> a court ... [T]he reason which has led us to describe, and
> express conclusions about, the dispossession of the Australian
> Aborigines in unrestrained language is that the full facts of
> the dispossession are of critical importance to the assessment
> of the legitimacy of the propositions that the continent was
> unoccupied for legal purposes and that the unqualified legal
> and beneficial ownership of all the lands of the continent were
> vested in the Crown.[36]

These comments reinforce the 'importance of history', and add a second element that is new in relation to the status of Aboriginality and heritage within public culture. It is not just that 'a distortion in the history of Australia' has to be corrected.[37] A *new* history is required, a new history that not only tells different stories about indigenous people but also tells different stories about non-indigenous people. In Mabo, this is implicit in the question of whether 'the continent was unoccupied for legal purposes'. In the Royal Commission into Aboriginal Deaths in Custody report, the problem is posed more explicitly:

> There is the other side of the coin, the effects of history upon the non-Aboriginal people ... [F]or a complex of reasons the non-Aboriginal population has, in the mass, been nurtured on active and passive ideas of racial superiority in relation to Aboriginal people ... which sits well with the policies of domination and control that have been applied.[38]

In other words, it is not just a question of 'adding' a black component to Australian history but of indigenous history transforming the category of Australian history itself.

For Aboriginality to assume a new and distinctive role in public culture required a shift from history to heritage. Telling a new historical story is one thing and a significant gain at the level of representation. But putting a new historical understanding into effect, making it play a role in governance, shifts the matter to the terrain of what I'm calling heritage. It was almost there in the royal commission, but the emphasis was not so much on the past in the present as on the 'legacy of history [explaining] the over-representation of Aboriginal people in custody'.[39] It was almost there too in the Mabo judgment, in which the High Court found that, although the Crown gained radical title over the territory, it:

> did not become the beneficial owner of the land, which remained in the possession of the indigenous people [and] that the Crown extinguished native title in a piecemeal fashion over many years as the wave of settlement washed over the continent, but native title survived on the Murray Islands.[40]

The emphasis on the piecemeal extinguishment of native title effectively meant that native title survived on the Murray Islands as a historical anachronism or perhaps because of the incompleteness of colonisation. This logic enabled a judge in a subsequent native title claim to assert that 'the tide of history' had washed away the rights to land of the Yorta Yorta people in south-eastern Australia – that is, to valorise only one side of history in the present.[41] The decisive steps necessary to install Aboriginality and heritage at the centre of public culture came in the Wik case and *Bringing Them Home*.

In the Wik judgment, brought down in December 1996, the High Court extended the Mabo ruling by holding that native title rights could coexist (subject to certain important restrictions) with rights held under a pastoral lease. The court found that the inheritance of two different kinds of legal rights – native title rights and rights in relation to land under Crown law, each with different historical legitimation – continued to co-exist in the here and now. Finally, *Bringing Them Home*, the Human Rights and Equal Opportunity Commission report into the history and consequences of removing indigenous children from their families, made fully explicit a new governmental sense of heritage.[42] Even as they wrote the report, Commissioners Ronald Wilson and Patrick Dodson were, I think, responding to pre-emptive attacks already in circulation. The conservative magazine *Quadrant* was prominent in these efforts which continued in 2000 with John Herron, the Minister for Aboriginal Affairs, denying the existence of a stolen generation. Subsequently, these attacks have attempted to both undermine the historical veracity of the report and/or place the events, policies and responsibilities around the stolen generations firmly in a past radically disconnected from the present. This second disposition underpinned Prime Minister Howard's refusal to offer an apology. Somehow, Wilson and Dodson seem to have already heard these protestations when they wrote:

The actions of the past resonate in the present and will continue to do so in the future ... In no sense has the Inquiry been 'raking over the past' for its own sake. The truth is that the past is very much with us today, in the continuing devastation of the lives of Indigenous Australians. That devastation cannot be addressed unless the whole community listens with an open heart and mind to the stories of what has happened in the past and, having listened and understood, commits itself to reconciliation.[43]

Bringing Them Home has been the subject of many popular, journalistic and academic analyses. For my purposes, John Frow's account of the report as concerned with 'a politics of stolen time' is particularly powerful and relevant.[44] Frow is attentive to the consequences of citing first person testimony: 'The Report of the National Inquiry listens to witnesses and reports their words in two ways: by repeating them directly, and by turning them into the

Chris Cook, The Taking of the Children, *Great Australian Clock, Queen Victoria Building, Sydney, 2003. (Photograph by Brian Jenkins)*

material of a larger and more comprehensive narrative.' It's in this way that the report bears witness to the consequences of policies designed to ensure that children 'were to be prevented from acquiring the habits and customs of the Aborigines'. One of the terrible consequences of these policies traced by the report is the absence of memory produced by the removal of children from families and communities. In many cases, witnesses do not have memories of family, law, country or language, not because these have been forgotten, but because the time during which these experiences would have been acquired was stolen. Stolen time cannot be returned.[45] Frow argues that in giving public voice to witnesses, in tracing the scars, and in enumerating policies and practices, the report enables remembering to open up a space of listening in the present and, perhaps, to reshape a contemporary conversation about pain, ethics and justice.

The performance of remembering in *Bringing Them Home* produces a new and distinctive configuration of heritage and Aboriginality that was immediately taken up in Corroboree 2000, the conference and march across Sydney Harbour Bridge that was the culmination of ten years' work by the Council for Aboriginal Reconciliation. After the 'silence' was broken, after the 'other side of the frontier' was acknowledged, after indigenous history and memory was validated, after the doubleness of colonialism's impact on black and white was recognised, Aboriginality became a material, institutional and potent component of history in the present. A transformed notion of heritage decisively grounded not only reconciliation but also many attempts to fashion just relationships between indigenous and non-indigenous peoples. The inheritance of colonisation, for both indigenous and non-indigenous people, was refigured. An 'old' Australian heritage became untenable and a 'new' ambiguous and unsettling inheritance was placed at the centre of governance, potentially affecting notions of territory and cultural identity, political representation and authority at the most basic levels.

To write in this way is to imagine that somehow these issues have been fully worked through in public culture, when in fact institutional questions of reparation, reconciliation and a treaty remain unresolved and cultural questions of belonging, ethics and difference are persistently ossified. In fact, the years after 1996 have been described by one scholar as being marked by a 'frenzy of forgetting'.[46] As political historian Judith Brett notes, the attempt by John Howard's government to incorporate these transformations involved a recognition that the treatment of indigenous people represented a 'blemished chapter in our history'. Yet, Brett writes, 'In choosing "Blemish" it seems to me Howard reveals the repressed thoughts the word is designed to deny – the role that skin colours played and continue to play in Australia's history.'[47] There is no denying, however, that Aboriginality and memory have a new valency: 'For Howard, the terrible thing about the blemish is that it *is* on the record, it is his archival inheritance, and no amount of rhetorical quibbling or conservative historical revisioning can change this.'[48]

The philosopher Paul Patton has noted that Mabo (and by extension, I'd suggest the decision in Wik, the royal commission on deaths in custody and *Bringing Them Home*) 'draws attention to the differences of cultural historical situation which separates indigenous and non-indigenous citizens'.[49] These cultural historical differences reside, for Patton, Aileen Moreton-Robinson and Henry Reynolds, in a recognition of sovereignty that is unfinished: while 'Aboriginal law is not fully recognised as a body of law grounded in the sovereign authority of indigenous peoples the issue of sovereignty will remain with us for some time to come'.[50] A similar, although far from welcoming, assessment was made by historian Geoffrey Blainey, who objected to the decision in Mabo because it posed a threat to 'the sovereignty and unity of the Australian people'.[51] Blainey is both right and wrong in his assessment. He is right because this constellation of reports and judgments actually destabilises two of the central underpinnings of the nation: the 'historicity of a territory and the territorialisation of a history'.[52] However, it does not necessarily follow, as Richard Mulgan asserts, 'That the undermining of non-Aboriginal legitimacy is a potent obstacle to reconciliation'.[53] In fact, only some versions of 'non-Aboriginal legitimacy' are undermined by the cultural transformations I've discussed here. Equally, the new status of Aboriginality and heritage actually creates the conditions of possibility for thinking and constructing different kinds of nationhood based on different models of sovereignty and collectivity. The beginnings of such processes are already evident in regional land-management agreements, in AFL football, in some ventures in Aboriginal tourism, in music and elsewhere. But these are not cultural and political configurations waiting to be discovered, they are 'reconstructive practices towards nationhood'.[54] Before turning to these questions in the final section of this chapter, I want to examine some of the impediments to beginning this process visible in another 'race portrait' – a new assertion of whiteness.

ONE NATION

> One regime values permanence and accumulation, the
> other transience and turnover. One fears invasion, the
> other metaphorically solicits it. Threatened by the 'foreign',
> the 'primitive' and by 'ghosts', imperialist discourse tends
> towards closure: it paranoically defends the borders it
> creates. A touristic space must be liberal, and open: the
> foreign and the primitive are commodified and promoted,
> ghosts are special-effects: the only 'barrier' officially
> admitted is strictly economic.
>
> Meaghan Morris[55]

After the boycott of 1988, indigenous organisations and their supporters continued the long march of 'pragmatic and dogmatic gradualism' through governmental, judicial and cultural institutions.[56] By contrast, and in response to the heritage conundrums posed by the bicentenary, a very different ideological and rhetorical battle took place in the sphere of national politics. In February 1992 (the year in which the Mabo judgment was delivered), the then Prime Minister, Paul Keating, was alleged to have 'handled' or touched the Queen in a manner that breached archaic protocols in relation to the body of the monarch. His actions provoked a minor outcry in the United Kingdom. In response, John Hewson, leader of the Opposition, attempted to use this incident to mark Keating's disrespect for Australia's cultural and political heritage and to articulate this disdain with support for an Australian republic. The Prime Minister struck back: 'The Opposition, Keating claimed, were relics of the past, "xenophobes" who remained British to their bootstraps despite that nation's decision not to help Australia defend itself against the Japanese advance in 1942.'[57] This was not the first time Keating had mobilised historical rhetoric during his tenure as Prime Minister, and his heritage speech at Redfern is regarded by some as the greatest historical speech given by an Australian prime minister. For an array of reasons including his personal predilections, the importance of social memory in the political culture of the NSW Right and the skills and inclinations of his staff (particularly those of Don Watson, one of his speech writers), Keating had 'a readiness uncommon in recent prime ministers to take note of recent trends in historiography and to use them in the service of promoting a particular myth of nationalism'.[58] More broadly, he had remarkable talents in mobilising history in the service of his 'big picture' politics.

Keating was more than happy to engage in a 'battle of history' (as it's been called) in heritage disputation about Robert Menzies and Gough Whitlam, White Australia, Kokoda and Singapore, republics and monarchies, Asia, immigration, modernity and so on. But by the end of his period as prime minister, Keating had lost this battle, not in relation to these specific issues, but on the key heritage terrain identified by Howard in the expression 'black armband' history and elaborated by One Nation in terms of Aboriginal privilege. The enormous differences between Keating and Howard in style and political persona often obscured the fact that they both depended significantly on occupying particular heritage positions. As Meaghan Morris argues:

Howard's triumph ... was to provide a historical framework that made this new, future-oriented and violently divisive rhetoric seem to be a way of *returning* to a more secure and socially cohesive past ... when so many rural and working-class people were economically ravaged *and* feeling culturally despised ... his aura of drabness and littleness gave Howard a formidable power to be *historically* 'shifty'.[59]

At least as early as 1988, in shaping the *Future Directions* document, Howard was laying claim to his 'antiquarian' version of heritage. But it was not until he articulated his objections to a 'black armband' view of history that Howard proudly hung his own race portrait:

This black armband view of our past reflects the belief that most Australian history since 1788 has been little more than a disgraceful story of imperialism, exploitation, racism, sexism and other forms of discrimination.

I take a different view. I believe that the balance sheet of our history is one of heroic achievement and that we have achieved much more as a nation of which we can be proud than of which we should be ashamed.[60]

This is a classic example of the divisive logic at the heart of Howard's *historically* shifty vision of both politics and heritage, each either heroic or disgraceful, certainly not both, and other things besides.

The continuities between this kind of heritage rhetoric and that adopted by the freight train that was One Nation during 1996–98 have been widely discussed.[61] Here I want to examine the efforts of one cultural critic to think historically about the use of heritage within formal politics. Just before the 1998 Queensland election, Janet McCalman, a celebrated Melbourne historian, wrote about One Nation on the op-ed page of *The Age* under the title 'Two Nations arise to threaten a peaceful land'.[62]

McCalman's account begins with a description of the last day of teaching a course in Australian history at the University of Melbourne. The 'moment of truth' in the classroom comes when an American student, after enumerating some of the lessons grasped during the semester, says, 'But you have a good country here. It's safe and peaceful. It's a very good place to live. You are very lucky.' McCalman concurs with the judgment and then writes, 'This makes the rise of One Nation ... all the more heartbreaking ... One Nation ... wants to create two nations, one of insiders and another of outsiders. *And yet this is to fly in the face of our history* [my emphasis].'[63] While it might not be defensible, this is a clear and definite position. The new party is historically aberrant. One Nation is either not *in* Australian history (perhaps it travelled from the United States on one of the neoconservative rafts that have provided flotsam for some right-wing Australian beach scavengers since the 1970s) or One Nation is not *of* Australian history and hence is unsustainable in Australian historical conditions.

A fortnight later, in another column piece, this time analysing the results of the Queensland election, McCalman wrote about the work of two scholars who had conducted detailed qualitative studies of the electoral base of One Nation.[64] This work found that 'the poor', 'the dispossessed', 'the unemployed', 'the working poor' and 'the truly forgotten people' were not Hanson supporters. On the contrary, One Nation drew its support from, in McCalman's words, 'the classic Australian whingers – aggrieved souls who imagine they are forgotten because they have not done quite as well as they had hoped'. Yet, after taking considerable succour from the fact that nearly three-quarters of Queensland voters did not vote One Nation, she writes, 'In One Nation's heartland of the Atherton Tablelands and in the sugar-growing country that was built on indentured labour, their racism has deep historical roots.'[65]

Herein lies a problem. For McCalman, One Nation is a historical aberration, yet One Nation's supporters live in regions where

The Bulletin, *22 October 1996. (With the kind permission of acpsyndication.com)*

racism is deeply historical. This is a contradictory, yet illuminating, position. McCalman's 'safe and peaceful' present (much like Howard's 'relaxed and comfortable' Australia) cannot admit a heritage that is rooted in colonial racism (along with many other 'traditions' more palatable to contemporary cultural critics). This contrasts sharply with the way Justice Brennan grounded his judgment in Mabo – 'the dispossession of Aboriginal people underwrote the development of the nation' – and which, as I've suggested, goes some way towards developing a different idiom for heritage.[66] Paradoxically, McCalman's pluralist and inclusive heritage (very reminiscent of the bicentennary) simply cannot admit One Nation as a product of actual historical processes. So the only heritage mechanism available for understanding One Nation is as an anachronism, a cultural formation belonging to another time. This was precisely the strategy employed by the *Bulletin* with a cover image of Hanson tucking into a plate of pie and chips with a beer on standby. It's also the same tactic used when *Sixty Minutes* sought to position Hanson as a throwback to the 1950s. Even more damning for urban political elites is the fact that One Nation was a home-grown anachronism belonging to those places (such as the Atherton Tablelands or certain whingeing suburbs) that ought not have any role or status in defining Australia or Australian heritage in or to a globalised world. In other words, both One Nation and McCalman (along with many other critics) share a common understanding of the role of heritage – to unite and underpin a singular nation polity. For One Nation, the problem is with 'minority' attempts to threaten this unity of past and place by foreigners, Aboriginal people and metropolitan citizens of the globe. For many critics, One Nation was a 'minority' attempt by ideologues, whingers and outdated yokels to undermine the 'good country' which history has delivered. Thus we flip back and forth in simple inversions. Might it be possible to think of a model of heritage that does not rely on a solid unitary or, its flip side, the disreputable minority?

VERNACULAR HERITAGE

> The accents, idioms and imageries that characterized
> them were foreign to the lexicon of a post-Enlightenment
> Reason that provided historiography and nationalism with
> much of their distinctive vocabulary. They defied generic
> incorporation into historical discourse, and were put into
> words by genealogists, balladeers, story-tellers and wise old
> people – that is, by the custodians of communal memory
> – rather than by historians.
>
> Ranajit Guha[67]

Sometimes explicitly and sometimes implicitly, questions around Aboriginality and cultural memory have been insistently dissonant in relation to the heritage discourses of 1988, a series of governmental inquiries and judicial rulings, and the One Nation phenomenon. In listening to these reverberations, I've suggested that they can alert us to some of the tensions that have bedevilled the idea of national heritage. The year 1988 marked a terminus for demotic articulations of national heritage. On the one hand, the admission of everybody's stories left older notions of heritage substantially (if nostalgically) intact while, at the same time, producing such diverse and incoherent heritage gestures that their meaning and significance seemed ineffective. On the other hand, by taking indigenous citizens out of the nation-state, the indigenous boycott of 1988 exposed the absolute limits of its pluralism; Aboriginal heritage simply would not be one more positive addition to an affirming story of Australian civilisation. The centrality of Aboriginality in relation to history and memory in the 1991 Royal Commission, Mabo, Wik and *Bringing Them Home* effectively made it clear that, institutionally, Australian heritage has depended on the exclusion of Aboriginality. These government or official initiatives explore how exclusions might be remedied in the ruins of national heritage. Both One Nation and some of its critics have taken a different route, preferring to stake out true heritage as guaranteed by history's gifts to those seated at the table: the rest are mere servants, beggars or interlopers. Together, these heritage discourses seem to open up the question of Aboriginality and a postpluralist heritage. Is it possible to think about the deployment of history in relation to citizenship and governance in ways that might avoid some of the limitations exemplified in these crises of heritage? I want to suggest that thinking about heritage in the vernacular offers some real utility.

For a long time, it has been recognised that a central problem of history as a general category has been its claim to universality. Rather than history being an aggregation of particular routes from events in the past to events in the present, universal history has been understood as a grid on which any of those events might be traced.[68] So, for example, histories of nations, while specific in their timing, pace and leading players, are usually thought of as histories of development and achievement or of destiny not yet accomplished. For this reason, actual micro-histories tend to suffer one of two fates at the hand of history-in-general. Either they are incorporated into the grid of a larger historical narrative – Ballarat appears significant as a gold-mining town because it contributed to Australian history – or they are absences, mere traces, like so many other ghost towns which failed to contribute to the larger story. This does not mean that the micro-histories disappear, only that most have no place in grand historical narratives. When it comes to heritage – that is, the use of historical understanding in citizenly and governmental registers – these processes are usually even more exclusionary, because heritage, and particularly national heritage, is necessarily more formal and often codified. A national register of historic houses, for instance, contains only those houses that possess heritage as assessed in terms of architectural taxonomy or large-scale historical significance. The idea of such a register including all houses possessing heritage significance – your heritage significance and mine and the next person's – makes no sense because the role of democratic heritage is to exemplify by selection those objects and narratives which can represent a general collective historical understanding. Nevertheless, we also know that specific or micro-heritages – often in the form of remembering – are enduring and significant forms of social memory. It's these kinds of understandings that I want to identify as vernacular. Vernacular history can describe ways of making the past present that are marginal to or silenced by the authority of 'official' heritage; vernacularity might reside in language or idiom, in shared but particular historical experience, such as that of displacement or suppressed cultural identities and rituals.

Ranajit Guha has provided a stimulating discussion of vernacular histories in the context of postcolonial India.[69] He argues that vernacularity exists (and existed) in 'accents, idioms and imaginaries' foreign to the lexicon of post-enlightenment reason. In this sense, they are 'unspeakable' in the language and rationality of colonisation. This does not mean, however, that vernacular pasts disappear with the advent of colonisation, only that once they are articulated in the province of history they must 'speak' the grammar of power. In his particular argument, they must find a place in a terrain mapped by nationalist historiography. Guha argues that vernacular histories have taken two forms in India, each of which preserves the force of the Latin root of vernacular: *verna* meaning 'home-born slave'. There is the discourse of the happy slave – Indian history as the story of England's work in which the slave parrots his master from within the place that colonising history has reserved for his story. There is also the idiomatic story of the slave who, though employing her master's language, is *not* speaking in her master's voice. This second story is not an authentic, precolonial or nativist voice, but it is historical to the extent that it preserves traces of the violence that enables the story to be told in the language of domination. So, the transposition, translations, silences and violence that enable speech in the master's language still resonate with the memory of slavery. How does an understanding of vernacular heritage as a 'third term' between formal history and 'unspeakable' micro-histories help illuminate the notion of vernacular heritage in

Australia? First, it is important to recognise that the term is not evaluative; that is, vernacular histories are not necessarily good or bad, accurate or inaccurate. Second, while vernacular histories are not authentically subaltern, they do not answer Spivak's question 'Can the subaltern speak?' Even so, vernacular histories preserve elements of experience that have been marginalised or excluded from general historical discourse. Third, vernacular histories exist in tension to official history; they are not reducible to elements of a historical narrative, but seem to have a capacity to disrupt or reorganise historical understanding. Fourth, vernacular histories are memory performances. Finally, the primary site of vernacular histories in Australia is surely Aboriginality.

We can explore some of the consequences of thinking about Aboriginality, memory and vernacular history by turning to a recent book by historian Robert Kenny. *The Lamb Enters the Dreaming: Nathanael Pepper and the ruptured world* is a study of the life of Nathanael Pepper, a Wotjobaluk man who, in 1860, became a convert to Christianity at the Morovian mission at Ebenezer in the Wimmera in western Victoria. That Kenny's thoughtful and persuasive account is directly concerned with vernacular rather than history-in-general can be seen in this epigraph from Richard Rorty:

> What might the cultural history and sociopolitical of the West look like if we tried to narrate both without mention of major turnings? What would they look like if they were written as histories of a very large number of small campaigns, rather than as the history of a few great moments? What would our past look like if we decided ... that history is an endless network of changing relationships, without any great climatic ruptures or peripeties and that terms like 'traditional society', 'modern society' and 'postmodern society' are more trouble than they are worth?[70]

In what follows, Kenny wants to make sense of Pepper's life in both its particularity and through a transnational historiography connecting colonisation and the Wotjobaluk. He wants to remind us that the 'pioneers' were not the respectable men who appear in late 19th-century photographs but 'young men – barely adults with braces of pistols in their belts and rifles in their saddles' and that missionaries were not all of a piece.[71] More important for my purposes, Kenny wants to produce a sense of what kinds of understanding and transformation – rather than simply misunderstanding and domination – were produced between Wotjobaluk and Europeans in the first decades of contact. He provides a number of vivid examples of the *Bun-yip* and of the *Myndie* as creative indigenous responses to European colonisation, and of Wotjobaluk men not only keen to acquire European axes and steel but the technology of writing too: 'the young Wotjobaluk sat around the fire with their spelling books'.[72] Kenny's account of Pepper's faith is at the core of the book. He wants to restore spiritual, cultural and political authority to Pepper rather than regard him as an indoctrinated victim of an imperialist religion. This involves thinking about conversion as a complex transaction between Christian and Wotjobaluk beliefs, one in which the blood of sacrifice and the lamb entering the Dreaming played key roles. We can think of Pepper's understanding of colonialism as a vernacular history because it's a story of suffering in which becoming Christian and being Wotjobaluk are not posed as binary alternatives. In fact, when Pepper first preaches the word of the Lord, in his mother tongue, to his people soon after his conversion, he leads them not into a church or a European settlement but into the bush.[73]

My use of this example of vernacular history may seem less esoteric if I return to the questions of Aboriginality and heritage that have already been discussed in this chapter. The royal commission, the judicial proceedings I've discussed and *Bringing Them Home* were all governmental instances in which indigenous and non-indigenous people produced spaces in which otherness (including vernacular histories) and difference were recognised. The practical import of this recognition necessitated translation, which, as

Patton reminds us, the philosopher Jacques Derrida describes as 'an always possible but always imperfect compromise between two idioms'.[74] In other words, commissions and courts had to recognise and acknowledge the particularity and partiality of their idiom in order to listen to another idiom being translated for them, a dialogue which was then, paradoxically 'returned' in another form.[75] So Aboriginality and heritage actually includes and extends Noel Pearson's understanding of native title itself 'as a concept which belongs to the space between two bodies of law and by means of which one recognises the other under certain conditions: Native title is therefore a space between two systems, where there is recognition'.[76] Metaphorically, these encounters produce new cultural spaces that I've described as spaces of Aboriginality and heritage – reports, rulings, commentary, organisations and agreements – which exist between indigenous and non-indigenous people but belong exclusively to neither. It is in this sense that this new space of Aboriginality and heritage is vernacular.

Conversely, 1988 and One Nation can be seen as examples of heritage discourse that failed to take up the virtues of vernacular heritage. The bicentennial celebrations of 1988 depended on an irredeemably white and narrowly national history, yet simultaneously critiqued and mourned such heritage and indulged in gestural pluralism by celebrating heritage as an inclusive patchwork. In contrast, we might think of another bicentennial example. On 25 January 1988, after marching through Sydney, indigenous people and their supporters gathered at Kurnell to perform vernacular ceremonies at a place where Cook had come ashore. This articulation of vernacular heritage as a shared commitment to reconciliation in place has since been elaborated across the country as indigenous and non-indigenous people have come together to hold meetings, share stories, produce inscriptions and make commitments to a future they share under the rubric of reconciliation.[77] Some of the building blocks that made One Nation came from the kind of marginalised heritage given voice in Les Murray's poetry, heard when loggers take on conservationists and proclaimed in the primitive socialism of the National Party. One Nation transformed this 'raw' material. Hanson was adept at fuelling a sense of ordinary people as besieged and damaged (as many people's lives had literally been damaged by a decade of economic reforms). As a political party, One Nation generalised these reactions in the form of a program that called for national defence against a host of enemies. In doing this, One Nation was producing a paranoid, xenophobic and exclusionist politics of blame, playing suffering off against suffering. It relied on a capacity to forget indigenous dispossession in favour of demonising indigenous people as the undeserving recipients of special treatment.

For Runajit Guha, vernacular histories are always marked by slavery, whether in traces of subordination and/or shadows of pain. To think of Aboriginality as a space of memory and the vernacular is to imagine the forgetting of dispossession as the spectre haunting Australian heritage. This might encourage a more circumspect approach to speaking of national heritage as singular and unified. No doubt there are some moments when it is important to invoke national heritage; for example, to prohibit the export of cultural property. But generally, rather than thinking in terms of heritage and civilisation, race or nation, rather than stitching many plural historical experiences into one national heritage quilt, perhaps we could be content with a more disaggregated sense of heritage. To think of Aboriginality as vernacular history means to understand the embeddedness of the past in the present as various and shifting. It may also be an effective antidote to the paranoid and defensive hollowness of 'the story of our people ... for all our people ... broadly constituting a scale of heroic and unique achievement against the odds'.[78]

In the next chapter, I turn from a general consideration of heritage and the vernacular to a specific account of the memory work of the museum. These venerable institutions have become some of the most dynamic institutional sites working through the practical postcolonial question of what comes after a heritage crisis.

5 OBJECTS AND THE MUSEUM

And it seemed to me then that the lines and sweeps and swatches of colour in his paintings and gouaches speak not just of charming dreamtime figures and their ceremonial landscapes, but of all that remembered love and pride and anger burning in the artist's heart, burning now, like a hidden, unquenched bushfire, across all the Gija realm and beyond the frontier.

Nicholas Rothwell[1]

If the terrain of heritage in Australia has been significantly reshaped over the last two decades by memory-work relating to Aboriginality, then museums have been central to these trans-formations. Or perhaps public memory has just caught up with museum historical consciousness? Surely, the one cultural insti-tution immune from the charge of 'forgetting Aborigines' would have to be the collecting machine that is the museum. From the earliest contact between indigenous people and the British (if not before), the collection of indigenous objects was a crucial form of (uneven) cultural exchange. With colonial settlement came more collecting of indigenous things and bodies; then later amateur and professional collecting filled the new Australian museums with stones and spears, skulls and songs, secrets and shields. Australian museums became quintessentially modern 'sites of memory' where the 'records' of indigenous and non-indigenous interaction were preserved and ordered. It is now well known and widely deplored that, historically, indigenous bodies have been displayed as exemplifying the story of human biological evolution, and indigenous artefacts and art have been arranged for view so as to demonstrate hierarchies of civilisation.

Over the past three decades, relationships between museums and indigenous peoples have been debated and contested and renegotiated in significant ways. We can see this particularly in relation to the ownership of cultural property, the procedures through which museums work with indigenous people and things, and the techniques used in the display of indigenous cultures. Indigenous desires for the repatriation of collections have been and remain a powerful motivation.[2] Some museums have responded to these pressures by reconsidering their policies and procedures in relation to indigenous peoples, sometimes developing innovative and distinctive processes to deal with such difficult issues. Other responses have focused more on creating new ways of representing indigenous people, and of indigenous people representing themselves, in specific exhibitions.[3] On the face of it, museums would seem to be the outstanding examples of memorial institutions. Museums could be thought of as working through the complex issues which result from collections and institutional practices deriving from a colonial world that now exist in a postcolonial world where indigenous people have recognised rights as citizens and cultural custodians. They seem to have made the transition from being memory machines for colonialism and race to being memory machines for a postcolonial future.[4] In other words, museums, as sites of memory, seem to be doing what they should be doing, remembering for us.

There's much to be said in support of the view that, in general, Australian museums are genuinely creative cultural institutions. They often produce challenging exhibitions concerned with Aboriginal people and things, and with the historical and contemporary intercultural zones between indigenous and non-indigenous people in Australia. Yet this kind of broad proposition tends to regard museums as primarily explicable in ideological terms: museums are appraised either as ideologically progressive or ideologically reactionary. Ideological critique has certainly been the dominant mode in which museums have been thought about in the 'new museology' and this kind of analysis has been undoubtedly productive.[5] However, after a couple of decades of such analysis, the distance between ideological critique and how most museums actually work seems more disabling than enabling. In particular, thinking about museums as principally ideological has tended to reduce these complex organisations to texts that can then be read as producing more or less adequate accounts of social relationships. A diverse range of scholarship now emerging seeks to account for museums not as texts but as cultural institutions or, what sociologist Tony Bennett calls 'cultural assemblages'. Bennett argues that if we consider museums as assemblages of 'texts, rules, bodies, objects, architecture etc', we provide a stronger basis on which to think about how objects work in the museum. He draws our attention to how, in the museum, objects acquire certain qualities, how various kinds of knowledge produce new kinds of relationships between objects, and how people are placed and moved around in distinctive ways.[6] In this chapter, I follow in his footsteps by analysing a particular kind of museum object, Aboriginal breastplates, and the place produced for indigenous people in the design of two new museums in Australia, the National Museum of Australia and the Melbourne Museum. But before I do that, I want to supplement Bennett's perspective on the museum by considering another theorist of the museum, the Gija artist Rusty Peters.

Gamerre – What's this Museum? by Rusty Peters appears, at first glance, to be representing a hard contrast between indigenous and non-indigenous culture. The left-side element of the trip-tych, the gamerre side, is strongly black and formally similar to many of Peters's 'dreaming' paintings.[7] The two right-side elements seem, like the white borders that surround the six small inserts, to ask the question 'What's this museum?' As Victoria Lynn writes, 'These smaller images are presented against a white background as if they are paintings hanging in a museum.'[8] And the gallery notes on the painting reinforce this impression:

> This work is a result of the artist's time spent crossing the
> gulf between two worlds, the world of his own country
> and that of his parents and grandparents, and the world of
> Europeans, including visits to cities and museums. He has
> often told Tony Oliver: 'We don't have museums. We have
> rock paintings and the country itself.'[9]

To see the painting in these ways is to think about it as a text representing two cultural worlds. So the image stands in for the dichotomous relationships between white and black worlds: the whole and integrated world of black country and cosmology; the fragmented and alienated world of white institutions and knowledge. Through particular aesthetic strategies, the painting makes a white world amenable to critique. But what if, for both Rusty Peters and some viewers, this painting is not a representation? What if this painting is making present the actual things that Peters has painted? What if this work, like those of the Central Desert artists discussed by anthropologist Jennifer Biddle, 'do not have to represent the past because they enact it … literally bring to life country, Ancestors, people … by literally enlivening us, the spectator'?[10]

If we look again at the image and at some of Peters's words, *Gamerre – What's This Museum?* seems less like a contrast between two radically different worlds and more like a comparison or a transaction between different worlds. Peters says explicitly that both the left element of the triptych and the lower right element are gamerre: 'the earth where we all live'. Then in response

Rusty Peters, Gamerre – What's this Museum? *2005. Photograph by Paul Green. (With the permission of Jirrawun Arts)*

to a question from Frances Kofod, 'For all humans? Or just your family?', Peters says, 'For everybody in this place white, black, everybody, no matter what colour.' Also, the significant objects in the painting – spears, stone axe, boomerangs and so on – clearly have a place in both the world of gamerre (as rock paintings) and in the world of the museum (as canvas paintings):

> When they put them painting in the museum, not for sale. All the tourists go in inside and have a look, and not for sale they only see the painting there. Well that's the way this rock painting, we have a look that country, rock painting in that hill. Well that painting there remind man, this one there forever. You can't pull that thing, just like a museum they got them painting. Like a gamerre that place. The rock painting round the gamerre he there forever for everybody. We can't pull em out painting from rock.[11]

Both the domains of gamerre and the museum value and enable preservation, respect and learning. In this light, *Gamerre – What's*

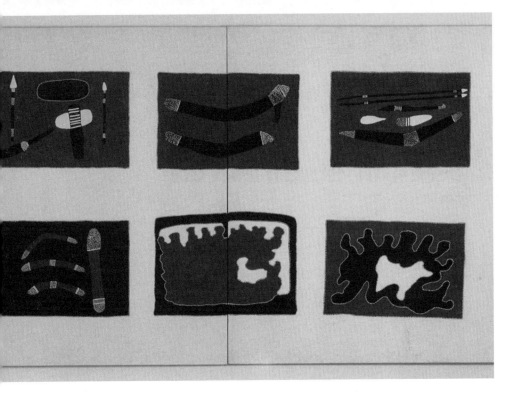

This Museum? speaks 'not just of charming dreamtime figures and their ceremonial landscapes' but as an explicit challenge to a non-indigenous spectator based not on an ideological reading of white people and their museums but on Peters's analysis of museum practice. His analysis might be restated in the following way. You put important things in the museum in a respectful and proper fashion; those things are not for sale but are there for everybody to learn from mimetically. The problem is that you don't treat country in the same way. Things, like rock paintings, in gamerre are not for sale, they are there forever and for everybody. Gamerre needs to be treated with the respect that you reserve for objects in the museum because that is, in part, how we sustain life, by reproducing appropriate relations between bodies, objects and knowledge in the world. To put it another way, both Tony Bennett and Rusty Peters seem concerned with the civic role of museums: how the organisation of things in the world and the museum acquire certain qualities and capacities, how expertise and things exist in mutually constitutive relationships,

and how different kinds of 'objecthood' enable different kinds of
work on the self. They both seem concerned with the museum as a
site in which memory and Aboriginality are actually at work.

BREASTPLATES: GETTING IT IN THE NECK?

DENTI
KING OF TORQUAY
PRESENTED BY
W. GERATY
FOR HIS HONESTY
1889

The first use of breastplates in Australia was recorded in 1815.
In that year, Lachlan Macquarie, Governor of New South Wales,
gave to Boongaree a regimental uniform and a plate engraved:

Boongaree Chief of the Broken Bay Tribe 1815

Both uniform and breastplate, it seems, were soon thrown away.[12]
This minor setback did not deter Macquarie, who, in the following year, presented a number of plates at the first of what would be
annual 'friendly gatherings' at Parramatta held until 1835. Those
Macquarie wished to confer with 'chieftainship' were presented
with engraved brass plates. The design of the plates derives from
gorgets, military decorations worn by British regiments in the 18th
century, which in turn derived from armour used to protect the
throat, a piece of metal that stopped the wearer from getting it
in the neck. Distributed until the 1930s, primarily along the east
coast but probably in all Australian colonies except Tasmania,
the plates and their inscriptions evoke numerous colonial narratives. They are about ownership of country and dispossession;
about political accommodation, strategic co-operation and mis-
recognition. They marked alterity and attempts to make indig-

enous people familiar by conferring titles such as 'chief' 'king', 'queen' and 'prince'. And they recognised service, friendship and heroism.[13]

Breastplates connect me emotionally to Australian colonialism as imagined in Nick Cave's gothic nightmare *The Proposition*, a depraved and intolerably miserable world of everyday brutality, fratricide and hate.[14] Breastplates evoke colonial domination of indigenous people. As historian Tania Cleary writes in the substantial survey put together as a catalogue to the exhibition *Poignant Regalia*, 'Collectively the inscriptions on the breastplates tell the story of European domination and subjugation through years of indiscriminate slaughter and martial law imposed on Aborigines.'[15] I want to return to these shameful objects here in order to consider if my emotional association of breastplates with a (past) moment of colonial conquest is supported by historical evidence. As it turns out, breastplates are better thought of as cross-cultural objects wrought out of the ambivalences of colonial encounters.[16] But that's less than half the story. As well as belonging to colonial history, breastplates are constitutive of contemporary historical imagination. They been collected by individuals and institutions, and are displayed in contemporary museums such as in the Australian Gallery of the Melbourne Museum. So, I am also concerned with the processes involved in postcolonial remembrance of breastplates. These objects are connected not only to a relatively distant colonial past, about which we might or might not want to pass judgments, but also with the collecting and memorial processes that constitute our present. Breastplates are products of memorial cultures that belong not only to dead generations but also burden the living. To get to these issues, we have to deal with the characterisation of breastplates as two-sided.[17] On the one hand, 'breastplates show ... attempts on the part of the Aborigines to somehow come to terms with the needs of the Europeans'.[18] On the other hand, they were a means by which non-indigenous people conferred 'titles' on indigenous people. Let's begin with those two sides.

'ABORIGINAL BREASTPLATES': WHOSE PLATES ARE THESE, ANYWAY?

BUDD BILLY II

KING

OF JAVIS BAY

In 2007, a brass breastplate was to be auctioned in Melbourne. It was engraved with the words:

> Presented to [blank] by the Exploration Committee of
> Victoria for the Humanity Shown to the Explorers Burke,
> Wills & King 1861

The plate was reported to have been found some six years earlier near Innamincka in remote South Australia by brothers Eric and Klaus Ganzert, 'two knockabout blokes who run a tiling business and take three weeks off every winter to go bushwalking together in the outback'.[19] This was no ordinary breastplate. It was linked to Robert O'Hara Burke and William John Wills (and John King), the most famous 'explorers' of Australia who died around the end of June 1861 on the return leg of a journey attempting to cross the continent from Melbourne in the south to the Gulf of Carpentaria in the north. When it learned of the forthcoming auction, the South Australian Government, through Aboriginal Affairs and Reconciliation Minister Jay Weatherill, evoked powers under the Aboriginal Heritage Act to declare the breastplate 'an Aboriginal object of significance' and so halt the sale.[20] The auction house, Bonhams and Goodman, disputed the claim that the breastplate was an Aboriginal object, but the minister referred the matter to the Government Investigation Unit because he determined that, under the Act it was, prima facie, an 'Aboriginal object'. He went on to claim: 'This breastplate is a significant piece of our shared Australian history. It is one of the earliest symbols of reconciliation between Aboriginal and non-

Aboriginal Australians. As such it has enormous historical value to both Aboriginal and non-Aboriginal people.'[21]

Here Weatherill is sliding too comfortably between his twin ministerial portfolios. Because breastplates are regularly sold by auction houses without government intervention, he probably made his determination in part because of the connection to Burke and Wills. And this connection certainly inspired Bonhams and Goodman to quote an estimate of up to $500 000, perhaps ten times the price likely to paid for a comparable non–Burke and Wills breastplate. This impression is reinforced by the fact that Weatherill's decision was made by ministerial fiat in the absence of any evidence of indigenous ownership. Most existing breastplates were given to specific, and often named, indigenous people, so in this sense they are objects that have belonged to indigenous people. It's not clear, however, whether the breastplate found by the brothers Ganzert was ever given to an indigenous person or persons, despite that being the intention of the Exploration Committee. For gifts to be owned they have to be accepted or avowed in the terms offered by the exchange. An ungrateful recipient can become unworthy of a gift and conversely a gift given without worthy intentions can be rejected as worthless.[22] Immediately, then, we confront the question: in what ways did indigenous people understand and make use of these gifts?

Take the photograph of Bilin Bilin wearing a plate inscribed 'Jackey Jackey – King of the Logan and Pimpama'. The plate, the chain and the conventions of photography produce a Yugambeh elder as a shackled criminal on display. His nakedness and the breastplate make him appear as a lone authentic indigene. Implicit in this solitude is the image's melancholia animated by the notion of Aborigines as a 'vanishing people'. He is both a primitive in tableau and one of 'the usual suspects'. The image seems to both document captivity and evoke those 'frontier photographs' of indigenous prisoners in the desert bound together with heavy chains attached to manacles around their necks.[23] In a very moving article, 'Bilin Bilin: King or eagle?', Ysole (Yuke) Best,

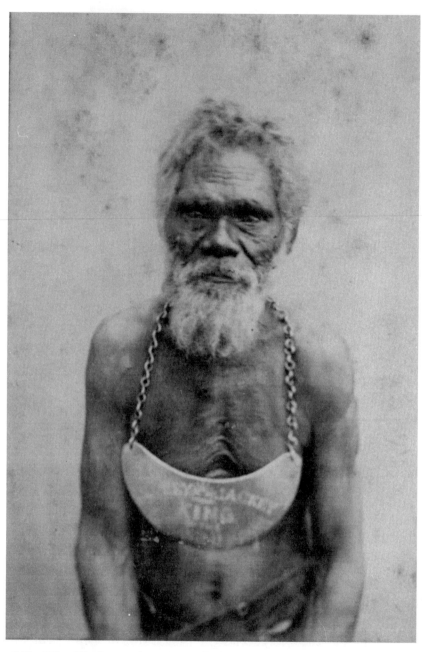

Bilin Bilin. The breastplate is inscribed, 'Jackey Jackey/King of the Logan and Pimpama'. (With the kind permission of Yugambeh Museum, Language and Heritage Centre and the State Library of Queensland)

great-great granddaughter of Bilin Bilin, writes about the photograph of her ancestor wearing the plate:

> Look into the eyes of *Bilin Bilin*, yes, they tell a story of the burden he was forced to bear when these intruders failed to respect his family and land. The metal plate and chains are symbols of his burden.[24]

These words make a lie of the white fantasies emanating from the image. Another photograph of Bilin Bilin at the Deebin Creek Industrial Mission also suggests he had considerable success in ensuring the survival of many of his people, but at what cost? In the second photograph, too, he is wearing the plate, stage right but somehow central, and surrounded by people who are respectably dressed, industrious in an industrial mission and most definitely surviving. Perhaps the breastplate here is, like the European suits and clothing, a burden to be borne as a sign of accommodation. Or perhaps, as Phil Gordon suggests, the 'recipients may have been looked down upon because they were seen to be assisting the white man's never ending quest for land and control over the land and Aboriginal people'.[25]

In the absence of substantial documentation of indigenous interpretations of the plates contemporaneous with their gifting, these questions about Bilin Bilin are hard to answer with any certainty. More broadly, we can't be sure about how indigenous people understood and used breastplates as semiotic objects deployed in the often violent, sometimes mutually baffling and unequal worlds of colonial exchange. Certainly, the plates were understood as part of the power play of signs and exchange; they were both target and shield. Maybe the plates were simply uncomfortable or impractical. Certainly, one recipient is reported to have found her plate too heavy and she was rarely seen wearing it. There may also have been moments of shared recognition and mutual regard in their receipt. But do we have to decide if the plates identified canny tacticians or collaborators – as if such labels could tell us a great deal?

Deebin Creek Mission, c. 1896–97. Bilin Bilin is seated in the front row, right-hand side. (With the kind permission of Yugambeh Museum, Language and Heritage Centre and the State Library of Queensland)

The few existing records of indigenous responses or reactions to breastplates are the product of white interpretations. In late 19th-century Queensland, the German 'ethnographer among cannibals' Carl Lumholtz thought that, 'Every native is anxious to become "king", for the brass plate, which is considered a great ornament, also secures the bearer many a meal.'[26] In 1835, a Reverend Handt wrote that when invited to join him at his fire, three indigenous men who possessed plates refused, saying they were gentlemen. Cleary interprets the account thus: 'The import of their reply was that it was a gentleman's privilege to give not take orders'.[27] This conclusion seems confused on at least two fronts. First, the relationship between an invitation to join someone at a fire and taking 'orders' is not clear. Of course, 'invitations' and 'status' can be deeply imbricated, but we get little sense of how these complicated relationships were understood in this instance. Second, and this is a mistake widely shared among those non-indigenous people writing about the plates, there is a clear assumption that the white *intent* inscribed on the plates is transparently adopted by those who possessed them. In this case, the intention is (assumed to be) that the wearers were being granted the status of European gentlemen and that their recipients adopted this European status as their own.

Cleary relates another instance, from 1849, in which a similar, if even more transparent, understanding of the meaning of the plates is demonstrated:

> the Commandant at Brisbane had given a breastplate inscribed 'Moppy, King of the Upper Brisbane Tribe' to an influential Aborigine: 'The rest of the tribe could not, of course, read the inscription on the plate; but being shrewd enough to discover that it had meaning, they requested the supposed Boraltchou [a runaway convict assimilated into the tribe] to explain to them what it meant. And when told that it signified that Moppy was their master, and that they were all his servants, they got into a prodigious talking at his supposed usurpation of kingly authority over themselves, as

free and independent natives of Australia, and insisted that
Moppy should carry back the plate to the Commandant,
under pain of death'.[28]

This story may have served some purpose for its narrator – to
show the egalitarian impulses of indigenous people – or it may
well tell us more about Boraltchou's role in his adopted community. Certainly, the story alerts us to the ways in which non-
indigenous people understood the political role of breastplates.
But, I think it's a white fantasy to imagine that breastplates func-
tioned as a command for indigenous people. Just because the plate
names Moppy as 'King of the Tribe', it doesn't make Moppy the
'King of the Tribe'. Moppy might well have used the plate to pro-
mote his authority, or thought the plate to be demeaning or unat-
tractive. Perhaps it was traded or used for other purposes beyond
the white semiotic intent engraved on its surface. Whatever the
case, breastplates were unlikely to achieve the effect they named;
white magic was simply not that strong.

For indigenous people contemplating these plates today there
are further complicating factors beyond the instability of the
objects themselves, particularly the questions of how they were
collected, their current ownership and the emotional resonances of
the plates. The provenance of many existing plates is vague. There
is, however, enough ambiguity in the accounts of finding breastplates to indicate that some may have been found as a result of
deliberate and 'accidental' grave robbing. Plates are described as
being 'unearthed at the old Aboriginal Reserve'[29], discovered on a
property that included 'their burial ground' and exposed after big
floods 'unearthed his remains and swept them away leaving the
heavier metal plate'.[30] Notes about one plate suggested that 'Aborigines generally buried their dead in an upright position ... They
did not dig very deep graves so their heads would not be very deeply buried. If Mulwaree Tommy's plate was hung around his neck in
death, this is perhaps how it came to be ploughed up'.[31] For some
collectors, bodily remains were just as collectable as breastplates[32],

and ominously too, if only in terms of impressions, many of the plates now in the collection of the National Museum of Australia were previously held by the Institute of Anatomy. These associations are, inevitably and understandably, painful for indigenous people and recall the implications of museums and their collections in such practices. Ysola Best is keenly aware of these possibilities:

> Bilin Bilin died c1901 and it has been alleged that he was buried seated in an upright position, in a high rocky shelter overlooking the Albert River in the nesting place of eagles. Has he been left in peace or has the sanctity of his burial place been invaded by scavengers seeking to gather human remains for scientific studies and brass plates for museum collections?[33]

So, for some indigenous people at least, although the plates might act as mnemonic objects that can invoke an ancestor or provide a more general link with the past, breastplates are overdetermined by their origin; they are objects of colonialism's world deployed for colonialism's (worst) ends.

Phil Gordon, writing 'an Aboriginal point of view', offers a more heterogeneous perspective. He evokes the strongly conflicting emotions experienced in the face of the plates and their images: 'anger, hate and sorrow [and] pride ... because they also symbolise not only past inequalities but the fact that Aboriginal people have survived and continue as a people against huge odds today'.[34] When I first read this sentence, I was puzzled as to how Gordon could feel pride in staring at these ambivalent objects. The anger and the hate make sense to me, not only in terms of the past but also through the ways in which breastplates articulate with other 'brandings' such as the 20th-century Queensland mission 'dog-tickets'. A sense of sadness, too, seemed appropriate. Sorrow is, I believe, an emotion that can be shared when confronting some of the losses inaugurated by colonialism – despite indigenous resilience, the absence of all those peoples, all that knowledge and all those languages is a deeply sorry inheritance. But why pride? For Gordon, breastplates can be regarded with, or inspire, pride because they are signs of colonialism's failure. Because breastplates are not 'monuments' to a successful genocide, Gordon's celebration is a simple but profound one: 'Aboriginal people have survived and continue as a people against huge odds today.' To understand how breastplates can mark that extraordinary achievement, we have to dwell on their meanings for non-indigenous people.

'DEGRADED SYMBOLS OF COLONIALISM' [35]

BERRY TO BROUGHTON
FOR DIGGING A CANAL
SINGLEHANDEDLY
A FEAT NO WHITE MAN COULD EMULATE

So far, in drawing together widely disparate records of historical and contemporary indigenous understandings of breastplates, I've said little that's original.[36] But, in order to consider the uses of breastplates by non-indigenous people, this context is vital because it was in relation to Aboriginality that these 'two-sided' objects were deployed. Indigenous uses of and memory-work around breastplates recall that these objects are memorials in the sense of being actually part of colonial dispossession. Much more than 'symbols of reconciliation', these objects promise to put us in touch with historical events and, at the same time, make clear the absence of those events. In other words, non-indigenous people might approach them anxiously, with a kind of foreboding about being brought close to and actually remembering the world that enabled their production.

And this impulse is right. Take this example of vicious satire in relation to royal titles from *The Australian*, 27 May 1844:

Distinguished Foreigners. Among the distinguished visitors at the levee at Government House on the Queens Birthday, by some unlucky oversight (for which we humbly apologise to their sable Majesties) the names of King Bungaree and Queen Gooseberry, who were in attendance in full regal costume, were omitted. Her majesty was attired in a new pink robe of very curious workmanship, and a Dunstable straw bonnet, wearing the order of her tribe in the form of a crescent, suspended by a brass chain from her ebon neck, and a natural rose, in honor of her Royal Sister Victoria, on her forehead. The King – bless his sable Majesty! – appeared in a rusty cast-off suit, enveloped in a new blanket, which hung in graceful folds about his royal person, rendered irresistibly monarchical by a short pipe being thrust, transversely, through the cartilage of his royal nose.[37]

The 'joke' for this white writer, and no doubt for many of his readers, is simply mockery of the uncivilised, which is then doubled by the absurdity of a primitive claiming sovereign status. Its witticism is like a torturer's amusement at the damage they've been able to inflict. But the contempt of the humour is also directed at those whites so stupid as to believe that the granting of the status of royalty could be anything other than a bad joke. In other words, the arrogance and hatred in these lines is about how plates were read and understood by those fools, both black and white, who believed in them as anything other than buffoonery.[38] This aspect of the production of plates is missed if we think of them as being about the conferring of 'fantasy titles'. By focusing on white fantasy, we forget the actual use of the objects in colonial worlds. Breastplates were certainly in no sense adequate or mutually recognised signs of exchanges between equals. But what gestures, words and artefacts of cross-cultural interactions are? Hostility and accommodation, mutual support, mis-recognition and murder, captivity and exchange, disdain and wonder, and much else besides, were all part of the actual historical processes that constituted the possessing of country and the dispossession of indigenous peoples. If breastplates are not simply bad colonial signs, then the problem becomes one of articulating the specific historical use of breastplates in colonial performances. If we accept that there were (many) whites, such as the writer in *The Australian*, who saw no use in breastplates, then we need to ask what kinds of purposes the plates served for some non-indigenous peoples?

In the first place, the breastplates were a state initiative. The earliest Australian breastplates were, you will recall, conferred by the representative of royalty in the colony. They were, as Cleary writes, 'a token of recognition from one "chief" to another'[39]. Macquarie's rule, more than that of any other colonial governor, exemplifies the contradictions of autocracy, 'liberalism', violence, dispossession, incorporation and acceptance with which indigenous people had to deal. While he was holding his picnics for Aborigines, Macquarie had issued proclamations that outlawed armed Aboriginal people or unarmed groups of six or more from coming within a mile of any town, village or farm occupied by British subjects. Aboriginal men in breach of this proclamation could be shot by landowners or convict servants – in which case, Macquarie instructed that their bodies be hung 'on the highest trees and in the clearest parts of the forest'.[40] Those men who abided by the proclamation were offered a '"passport" or certificate, bearing his signature, that would permit them to move across their land and protect them from being injured or molested'.[41] In this context, breastplates were an attempt at domination of a different order from systematic shooting. Macquarie regarded Aborigines as his (that is, the Crown's) subjects. Unfortunately for him, they were subjects who had yet to knowingly consent to that status. So, Macquarie's seemingly ambiguous actions – shoot some Aborigines and 'reward' others – makes sense as a repertoire designed to establish the conditions of governance. The plates were a technology in that repertoire.

Even before Macquarie returned to the northern hemisphere, his monopoly over the distribution of plates became a matter of some concern for other colonists. With Macquarie's replacement by Thomas Brisbane, however, the distribution of settler-bestowed breastplates throughout New South Wales proliferated significantly between 1830 and 1850 as the acreage under white control expanded relatively unchecked by colonial governance. This led to the use of lead and other metals, to stylistic variation and major changes in the kinds of inscription on the plates. Cleary interprets this 'privatisation' of the distribution of breastplates as leading to their debasement as they became a 'medal' bestowed independently of the Crown's representative and for any number of reasons. This is certainly evident in inscriptions such as 'Mr Verge's King Charlie' and 'Mr Verge's King Michie' granted in the Macleay River district. In these cases, sovereign recognition has been replaced by the nomenclature of slavery. But I'm also struck by two more productive aspects of this privatisation. First, it makes transparent the fact that the colonisation of the continent (and hence our contemporary sense of how non-indigenous Australians might remember and respond ethically to the consequences of those processes) depended on both state initiatives and those of relatively autonomous settlers. Even in the first half-century or so of colonisation, the complex process of 'contact' – the literal dispossession of indigenous people, episodes of negotiation, intimidation, accommodation, subordination and so on – was performed at least as much by individuals as by state functionaries. Second, and this is particularly noticeable in the variety of breastplate inscriptions, the non-government distribution of breastplates highlights some of the more intimate and personal aspects of colonial relationships. Compare, for example, the impersonal act of Macquarie conferring the generic title of 'King' with a much later inscription:

Paddy/For Saving Life

Would it be too much to imagine some shared respect in the use of the honorific in this inscription?

Mr Briney of Pialliway

Isn't there a sense of mutual gratitude or even common warmth in the following inscription?

Presented to Baraban by Sheperd Laidley
In remembrance of 9th Decr 1867

This plate features an engraved scene of a drowning child being rescued. My point is a simple one: breastplates vary. In their forms and inscriptions and in written accounts of their use, they served a number of non-indigenous goals. Breastplates are neither exclusively indigenous nor non-indigenous, but transactional objects produced in various modes of (unequal) colonial exchange from instrumental control to intimacy. The postcolonial remembrance of breastplates, however, is a different matter.

REMEMBERING GENOCIDE

JENNY
QUEEN OF BROULEE
SOUTH COAST
NSW

Remember the double nature of Macquarie's first breastplates: they were insignia given to people who could be shot, and they were tokens of recognition – target and shield. This doubleness was repeated more than a century and a half later when, in the early 1980s, a breastplate sold at auction in Sydney for $6500. A report of the sale noted: 'Farmers in the Narrandera district used to nail them to trees for pot-shot practice. Keen bidders at a recent Sydney auction treated them with much more respect.'[42] From target to brand name, the association of breastplates with the right to shoot Aborigines is displaced onto the use of the plates for target practice and displaced again onto collectors' benign curiosity. The shift from bullets to bidding implies not only a canny reverence for market values but also, perhaps, a sense of an end to ill will directed at indigenous people. These displacements enable one of those characteristically modern historiographic conceits: a separation of past from present that enables the here and now to be a place always so much better. Breastplates are now 'treated ... with much more respect'; they are 'symbols of reconciliation'. In this sense, breastplates become objects of the past that represent the distance between a violent past and a respectful present. This is the flip side of my emotional response to breastplates as shocking objects because the cold brass is so clean and yet so encrusted with a patina of colonial relationships that endures in the present. Both of these perspectives grant different but extraordinary powers to history as either progress or problem; the present is either no longer encumbered by the past or it is still burdened by the past. It's difficult to think in other than historicist ways about past–present relationships, but I've already suggested some options in insisting that breastplates clearly had various historical uses for indigenous and non-indigenous people, and that they have been remembered in productive ways by some indigenous people. But I want to push this further and consider whether, for some non-indigenous people, breastplates were proleptic objects, directed towards, or involving a calculation about the future. Rather than thinking about breastplates as representations that fixed meaning or brought relationships into existence, I want to consider them as attempts to remember for the future; objects that anticipate successful genocide.

Some breastplates are memorial in the sense of commemorating an event. This is particularly the case with plates distributed as 'rewards' or in recognition of service, bearing inscriptions such as:

Woondu
of
Amity Point
Rewarded by the Governor,
for the assistance he afforded with five of his countrymen,
to the survivors of the wreck of the Steamer 'Sovereign'
or:
A reward for merit to
Charley
of Tullungunnully

These plates record, acknowledge or memorialise existing relation-

'Coomee – Last of her Tribe'. Photo: George Serras © National Museum of Australia. (With the permission of the National Museum of Australia)

ships and can be said to be already archival, producing as much as recording an event.[43] But in naming or identifying a 'king' or a 'queen' the vast majority of plates were future-oriented. Rather than accounting for or producing a (past) event, they sought to bring into existence relationships that would be of use in the future, whereby the recipients would function as the inscription named them. The most extreme example of this mimetic magic and an example that takes us to the postcolonial remembrance of breastplates is the plate given to Coomee Nullanga in the first decade of the 20th century.

> A nice brass shield, suitably inscribed, has been sent to
> old 'Coomie' (Maria) who is the only survivor of the old
> Murramarang Aboriginal tribe. It has been given to her by
> Mr Milne, Railway Inspector of Orange, who was in Milton a
> short time back on holiday. Mr Milne takes a deep interest in
> the Aboriginal races and is supposed to have the best collection
> of Aboriginal weapons in New South Wales. The stipulation is
> that 'Coomie' must not part with her shield til death.[44]

The breastplate given to Coomee Nullanga was inscribed:

> Coomee
> Last of her Tribe
> Murramarang

The notion that a particular indigenous person was 'the last of his or her tribe' is a recurring motif, specific 'proof' of the characterisation of indigenous people as a 'doomed race'. It can be found in poetry (Henry Kendall's 'The last of his tribe') and fiction (Henry Lawson's 'Black Joe'), in painting and photography, settler narratives and anthropological texts, local and national histories.[45] The inscription on Coomee's breastplate is, if not unique, certainly rare. Very few of the breastplates recorded in the available inventories are in fact 'plates given ... to the last living member of a tribe'. Yet accounts of breastplates are strongly associated with 'the last of'. From Cora Gooseberry (a wife of Bungaree), who died at the Sydney Arms Hotel in 1852, to 'King Billy ... last of the Ballarat tribe', who died in 1897, their breastplates are remembered as marking them as 'the last of'. Frederick McCarthy, a curator of anthropology at the Australian Museum, made the association explicit in 1952 when he wrote:

> A tragic aspect of the contact between the whites and the natives in Australia is revealed by the plates given, as many of them were, to the last living member of a tribe – thus they represent the final act in the struggle of our native tribes in those localities.[46]

Why does McCarthy, a trained anthropologist and experienced curator, remember breastplates as things they were not? What does McCarthy mean when he writes that the plates 'represent the final act'?

Coomee was, predictably enough, not the 'last of her tribe' as her breastplate (pro)claimed. Even as Coomee was imagined as 'passing', in Daisy Bates's ambiguous term, or 'fading' as the 1990 local history imagined the matter, nearby the Bomaderry Infants Home was being established for a predominantly indigenous 'clientele' by Miss Thompson, 'a missionary to the Aborigines'. Today, we would describe Miss Thompson's 'mission' as one institution involved in the systematic removal of Aboriginal children from their families in order that they be raised white and, it was hoped, then assimilated through the virtuous eradication of all signs of their indigeneity. So, if the inscription on Coomee's breastplate was not a statement of fact, what was it? It was mimetic and proleptic. The plate was inscribed not only with the words I've already quoted but with three parallel lines on either side of the inscription about which the accession notes comment: 'The three parallel gashes with raised edges either side of the breastplate inscription are similar to the initiation scars described by Milne on Coomee's shoulders'.[47] In other words, these marks on the plate literally reproduced what are said to be Coomee's bodily scars, while the inscription names her status – the last. The breastplate, given with the instruction that '"Coomie" must not part with her shield til death', was intended to stand in for Coomee once she was dead. A photograph of Coomee wearing the plate would be obscene because the photograph would actually perform what the breastplates are remembered as recording; it is a photograph of a woman who is of value because she (will be) dead. Such an image is shocking to contemplate because it looks forward to death of the person being photographed, both pre-empting and performing the prophesy of the death of the last. The plate announces that event before it occurs and, in the absence of a body, becomes the proof of local extermination. The camera operates as the hands of a clock moving forwards in time, to the imagined future. Such photographs, like the breastplates themselves, are not representations but evidential artefacts of *methexis* – the performance of a seemingly successful genocide that could then be melancholically recalled.

I think of the light that emanates from the breastplates, as the critic Roland Barthes would have it, locking our gaze onto a body. I think of the wax cylinder recordings of Fanny Cochrane Smith, once believed to be the last person able to sing indigenous songs in Tasmania. Seated across the table from her as she was about to be recorded were men who spoke about how wonderful it would be to study these songs after Fanny had died. Even before her last breath expired, they were looking forward to studying the physical reproduction of her bodily voice. I think of the body casts made of Khoisan in South Africa, another people imagined as dying whose body traces were collected in anticipation. A vacuum opened up before the colonisers, in their erasure of alterity, that they were desperate to fill, to replace bodily absences with body traces that could be studied – sounds, casts and signs on plates. One last colonial performance, that of dying for the record, just had to be recorded. And so the postcolonial remembrance of breastplates began by calling them headstones worn by 'the last of the tribe'. How they were remembered denies not only indigenous survival but also the 'antagonistic intimacy' of the world in which they were produced and the 'unexpected moves of mimesis and alterity across quivering terrain', both historical and still present.

BREASTPLATES TODAY

For just as nature abhors a vacuum, so the vertiginous
cultural interspace effected by the reflection makes many
of us desperate to fill it with meaning, thereby defusing
disconcertion. To resist this desperation is no easy task. After
all, this is how cultural convention is maintained. But let us
try. Let us try to uncover the wish within such desperation
and be a little more malleable, ready to entertain unexpected
moves of mimesis and alterity across quivering terrain, even
if they lead at the outermost horizon to an all-consuming
nothingness.

Michael Taussig[48]

Unless you know a collector of breastplates or chance upon one at an auction viewing, the only place you're likely to see one is in a museum. That many breastplates have ended up in museums is, perhaps, not such a long journey. If, for collectors from Cook and Joseph Banks onwards, Australia was a kind of open-air museum, then breastplates *in situ* might be thought of as labels on living exhibits. Then, after the demise of their owners, they would be remembered *in context* through displays in the museum.[49] The contexts within which visitors to the Melbourne Museum and the National Museum of Australia can see breastplates on display are very different. In the Melbourne Museum, breastplates are part of a small display at the entrance to the 'Australian Gallery', a gallery concerned with Australia post-1788. There is only a single breastplate on display in Bunjilaka, the indigenous gallery. By contrast, at the National Museum of Australia (NMA), visitors can see a display of breastplates in First Australians: Gallery of Aboriginal and Torres Strait Islander Peoples. In both cases, it seems to me that the choices about how and in what museum locations to exhibit involve (different) kinds of forgetting which do not adequately recognise the 'two-sidedness' of breastplates. But the question I want to explore here is not whether curators have made 'mistakes' in choosing how and where to display breastplates. Instead, I want to examine the display of breastplates in relation to the transformations of heritage discussed in the previous chapter. My argument there was that notions of heritage in Australia were opened up by the recognition and authorisation of indigenous memory in the bicentennial year, government inquiries and judicial rulings. Here I want to suggest that Aboriginality has taken new and distinctive cultural and spatial forms in some recent museum developments. These developments have shifted the capacity of the museum to resocialise objects such as breastplates. So, in concluding this chapter, I want to consider how the Melbourne Museum and the NMA have, in different ways, produced spaces within which non-indigenous people might make a different kind of relationship to Aboriginality.

Over the last few decades, indigenous people have made a place for themselves in, and sometimes been invited, and sometimes been accepted, into museums through convoluted journeys. There is no doubt that indigenous people are playing increasingly significant roles in constructing new relationships between museums and indigenous communities, transforming the public programs of museums, establishing new priorities for collection and so on. One of the key aspects of this kind of work has been the re-working of existing collections in ways that demonstrate how indigenous property in museums can provide more than a mirror for the colonising gaze. As it's turned out, museum collections have been, and are being, used as resources in more dynamic processes of remembering. It's clear that some of the remnants of colonial encounters and Western historical imagination can provide opportunities for supplanting the 'original' appropriation of materials, for remaking connections, meaning and memory between objects, culture and history.[50]

During the same period, many Australian museums have renovated existing, or created new, galleries and exhibitions in relation to indigenous people and things.[51] The former Curator of Indigenous Studies at the Melbourne Museum, Gaye Sculthorpe has argued that these same museums have, to varying degrees, increased the number of indigenous staff, established consultative processes and broadened their use of specialist professional knowledge in relation to Aboriginality.[52] Here, however, I'm concerned not with celebrating the successes of indigenous people in Australian museums – important though those achievements certainly are – but with some of the consequences of these successes for non-indigenous social memory. I want to focus on Bunjilaka and First Australians as exemplifying a number of broad tendencies in relation to museums, Aboriginality and memory. First, I argue that these indigenous galleries have developed distinctive programs that, in important ways, set them apart from ordinary routines and logics of the museum. Functioning more as cultural centres, these initiatives supplement and perhaps open new directions for 'the traditional museum'. Second, I explore the significance of the separateness of these indigenous galleries/centres. I want to suggest that these distinct and to varying degrees, autonomous, indigenous-controlled galleries/centres both concentrate attention on indigenous knowledge, culture and history and separate Aboriginality off from the rest of the museum. These initiatives have yet to be matched, intellectually or practically, by a comparable non-indigenous reconsideration of the postcolonial inheritance of remembering Aborigines in the museum.

> The set of objects the Museum displays is sustained only
> by the fiction that they somehow constitute a coherent
> representational universe. The fiction is that a repeated
> metonymic displacement of fragment for totality, object to
> label, series of objects to series of labels, can still produce a
> representation which is somehow adequate to a nonlinguistic
> universe. Such a fiction is the result of an uncritical belief
> in the notion that ordering and classifying, that is to say,
> the spatial juxtaposition of fragments, can produce a
> representational understanding of the world.[53]

This provocative characterisation of the museum is used by the critic Susan Stewart as one way to begin to think about the cultural work performed by the museum collection. Her argument is that the representational work of a collection consists of two moves by which the collection comes to stand for the world:

> the first in the metonymic displacement of part for whole,
> item for context; and second, the invention of a classification
> scheme which will define space and time in such a way that
> the world is accounted for by the elements of the collection.[54]

For Stewart, the archetypal collection is Noah's Ark, a world that, by containing 'two of every sort', literally comes to stand in for a world that is to be destroyed, a catastrophe that will erase the context of origin so that the collection is a bounded and knowable 'whole' journeying into the future.[55] While this model of collection and display is obviously recognisable in both historical and contemporary displays, it does not, in fact, underpin the development of an indigenous 'gallery' such as Bunjilaka.

In the first place, the program of Bunjilaka is not founded solely or even primarily on the 'world-making' of the object, the label and the exhibition. John Morton, who worked on the development of the initial exhibitions at Bunjilaka, comments that:

> The Aboriginal Centre, Bunjilaka, is as much an Aboriginal community space as it is an exhibition area. There is a welcome area (Wominjeka); a performance space (Kalaya); a community meeting place used by leading members of the Indigenous community in Victoria (Wilim liwik); a special gallery that mimics the Yarra River (Birrarung); an outdoor courtyard and garden containing Indigenous themes (Milarri); and the main exhibition gallery itself (Jumbunna) which, significantly enough in this context, comes from the Woiwurrung (Wurundjeri) word for telling stories. As a whole, this mix reflects the Museum's desire to make the centre as user-friendly as possible to Aboriginal visitors and in relation to Aboriginal aspirations.[56]

In the case of Bunjilaka, the issue is not whether the vast collection of indigenous objects now housed in the Melbourne Museum could have been used, as fragments, to create the fiction of an Aboriginal totality. The project of Bunjilaka is quite different. Here is how it is articulated by the objectives of the Indigenous Cultures Program: 'improving the recognition of contemporary Indigenous cultures, enhancing awareness of Indigenous peoples' right to self-determination; and improving understanding of indigenous knowledge systems and intellectual property rights.'[57] Notably, these objectives do not derive from the logic of the museum. There is not a word about displays, representations, objects, labels, collections and so on. I should add immediately that Bunjilaka is deeply concerned with all of the professional protocols and practices of museum practice. My point is that the museum work of Bunjilaka is not guided by museum-like objectives. John Morton puts it this way; that 'the Bunjilaka exhibitions in general were designed as a contribution to ... the political process known as Reconciliation [which] occurs through a general moral questioning of colonial history in a highly politicised climate'.[58] In other words, Bunjilaka is not a place for displays of indigenous cultures but a space where ideas about indigenous cultures are produced as interventions in the world of the museum and beyond.

These are not abstract aspirations. On the contrary, programmatic aspects of Bunjilaka were built into the centre:

> The Aboriginal community provided clear directions for the architectural designs. They identified the need for exhibitions, information services, education programmes, performances, fire-making, story-telling, a resources centre, meeting facilities, and changing rooms.[59]

In architectural terms, Bunjilaka is both integrated into the overall design of the Melbourne Museum and clearly separate. The Denton Corker Marshall design works with a series of what we can think of as shipping containers, stacked and sequenced to produce strong and definite patterns of connection and circulation. The roof that holds the containers together is broken by a huge north-projecting mantle enclosing an exhibition of a temperate rainforest in the Forest Gallery. Separated from this unifying roof are the cube-form Children's Museum to the west and the 'shelter' that is Bunjilaka to the east. The design of the Melbourne Museum is fundamentally modular (hence my shipping container metaphor) and structured so as to enable visitors to choose to visit particular parts of the museum. At the NMA, First Australians is also discrete within the design and circulatory logic of the Ashton Raggatt McDougall building, but for very different reasons. The NMA is fundamentally holistic and integrated. Despite the metaphors of 'tangled destinies' and the invocation of mathematician George Boole, the visitor's route through the museum is like a walk through a terrace house, down a corridor and into the backyard. In a typical first-shall-be-last reversal, if we include the Torres Strait Islander Gallery, First Australians is the final gallery in the NMA. Although there is access to First Australians from the Garden of Australian Dreams (via the back gate), there is really only one way in. So, if it is not a literal centre or node like Bunjlaka, it is certainly separate, and although it is definitely a key part of the normative journey through the NMA, in important respects the design separates First Australians from the rest of the museum.

Other commentators do not share this perspective. The American architectural critic Charles Jenks has argued an entirely opposite point of view, comparing the NMA with those US and UK museums that ghettoise minority histories and cultures:

> Where [US and UK museums] ... disperse the pluralism into
> safely separate components, the Australian museums pull
> together history into one messy and conflicting whole ... The
> curators and the Director of the NMA, Dawn Casey, have
> even taken clues from the architects; one of their permanent
> installations makes use of the metaphor 'tangled destiny' and,
> it appears, the architects conceived of much of the content of
> the museum before there was even a program.[60]

Here Jenks is confusing architectural and museological programs, and the rhetoric of designers with the actual buildings they have helped make. Melbourne Museum and the NMA are certainly singular museums. In this sense, they are unlike, say, the suite of museums on the Washington Mall, where the National Museum of the American Indian might be regarded as an example of safely dispersed pluralism. (Although it is equally possible to assert that such a major new institution as the National Museum of the American Indian actually centralises the place and role of indigenous Americans in a significant fashion.) Jenks has not recognised the ways in which First Australians produces the separate and distinct spatial ordering of an indigenous presence. He privileges the architectural rhetoric, 'tangled destinies', as if that architectural instruction has shaped not only the actual design – which is predominantly linear and processual rather than entangled – but also the program and the content of the NMA itself; mystical powers indeed. Similarly, in discussing the development of Melbourne Museum, curator Richard Gillespie insists: 'We have tried to blur the boundaries between the galleries: there are several elements of Aboriginal history within the exhibition on Melbourne and Victoria'.[61] That may be the case, but such blurring only needs to happen where spatial boundaries are already firmly in place. Sculthorpe seems much closer to the mark when she writes: 'Indigenous content in Australian museums remains largely self-contained within an Indigenous gallery and is not integrated across the whole institution as part of an overall conceptual framework.'[62]

The establishment of Bunjilaka and First Australians as organisationally and architecturally distinct elements within two significant new museum buildings marks a major development in the history of these museums, and resonates with similar international developments in New Zealand and the Pacific and with recent examples in North America. I have suggested that their significance lies in the production of spaces and institutional structures that provide some measure of indigenous autonomy. As new cultural assemblages, these initiatives are literally remaking (parts of) the museum as a host of indigenous spaces. As W Richard West, the founding Director of the National Museum of the American Indian, said of his institution, 'We also hope that Native people will look upon the museum as a truly Native place, where they are welcomed and honoured guests.'[63] I'm certainly not claiming that these are utopian places of pure indigenous autonomy and indigenous 'self-realisation'. These museums are public cultural institutions shaped in important ways by intellectual, bureaucratic, political and economic imperatives, both internal and external. Bunjilaka and First Australians are special places that are both constrained and enabled by their separateness. It is a predicament that, while offering real opportunities for indigenous curators, is not without costs.

The responses of non-indigenous critics to these developments have been mixed. I do not want to forget the overwhelmingly positive endorsements provided by museum visitors through surveys.[64] Nor do I want to discount the many thoughtful and generally positive appraisals of both Bunjilaka and First Australians produced by critics, including, to the surprise of some, the Carroll Report.[65] But in addition to these responses, there have been a raft of more negative critiques.[66] These seem to me to fall into two categories: those with intellectual objections to the spaces and exhibitions, and those who interpret these spaces as metaphors for the 'problem' of indigenous separateness and difference. In the first case are those who want to reform these revisionist galleries in order to reinstate disinterested scholarship and resanitise 'Aboriginal propaganda' by eliminating the 'slur of hindsight' and 'voguish ... didacticism'.[67] It's remarkable how many of these critiques, particularly in the case of Bunjilaka, focus on how Baldwin Spencer is dealt with at Bunjilaka. Spencer was a professor at the University of Melbourne, director of, what was then, the National Museum of Victoria for over 20 years from 1899, an administrator of Aboriginal Affairs and the author of a number of significant works of anthropology on Northern Australia. He features in Bunjilaka in two forms: as a figure in a glass case, collected next to the object which he collected and in a brief video that stages a dialogue between actors playing Spencer and Irrapmwe, an Arrernte man who was one of Spencer's key 'informants'. The video is, from an academic point of view, heavy-handed and didactic, but it's also effective in highlighting the survival of indigenous knowledge and underlining how Spencer conceived of indigenous people. But, to some critics, the figure of Spencer in the vitrine is a disrespectful curatorial gesture. Tony

Bennett has a different position, arguing, 'the collector of Aboriginal culture is collected alongside his collection in an Aboriginal framing of both – these artefacts are wrenched from the evolutionary time, in which they had originally been installed, to open up a new indigenously marked time'.[68] Morton puts the same case differently when he argues that many of the more scholarly criticisms have mis-recognised exhibitions in Bunjilaka as being versions of or representations of history or culture as opposed to being exhibitions about cultural and historical relationships.[69]

The other tendency of some critical responses to both Bunjilaka and First Australians resonates with reactions against indigenous autonomy, a position that gained ground in Australia in the wake of Mabo and Wik. This is a politics that's fixated with special treatment, including a belief that there are forms of special sentencing for indigenous offenders or demands for the end of special education in indigenous communities. It relies on the well-established tradition of identifying indigenous people as bearing the responsibility for 'the Aboriginal problem'. Things would be better, for instance, if indigenous people took personal responsibility for observing common norms rather than choosing to be unemployed, drink too much alcohol, eat poorly, commit crimes and neglect their children. But there is a more recent twist: indigenous people have been enabled in the exercise of irresponsibility and criminality by the special treatment afforded to them by their non-indigenous supporters. So, much of the post-1972 policy framework in support of indigenous self-determination becomes culpable because the only alternative is mainstreaming state policy and service delivery for indigenous people. In terms of the cultural politics of the museum, it connects Bunjilaka and First Australians to a whole range of examples of indigenous autonomy, from control of land to copyright.

These initiatives in museums can be thought about more persuasively as connected to a much broader politics; what Dipesh Chakrabarty, in a brief account, has described as '[museums] opening themselves up to the politics of experience ... to questions of the embodied and the lived'.[70] For me, one of the most powerful examples of this is the Koori Voices exhibition at the Melbourne Museum. It's a very simple display of six large two-sided and gently curved partitions, each hung with about 100 photographs. The black-and-white photographs are predominately portraits of individuals, but there are also shots of two and three people and some of larger groups. A small video screen on each partition cycles through brief dialogues to camera. Because the images date from the mid-19th century through to the 1990s, the most obvious effect of the exhibition is that of walking along the pages of a giant family photo album as names and places recur. There's a studio shot from Coranderrk, another Briggs, a group shot from Cummeragunja, a Mullett at Lake Tyers, a Clarke at Framlingham and so on. In this sense, the photographs give form to what historian Tony Birch identifies as Bunjilaka's central question: 'the relationship between communities and museums'.[71] Earlier in this chapter, I suggested that some photographs of indigenous people wearing breastplates seem to look forward to the death of the subject. By contrast, Koori Voices is a form of living memory. Like any family album, it's a document that looks backwards to previous generations. For a local Koori person or their friends, it might also work to connect contemporary people with their forebears and perhaps prompt storytelling. And it seems to look forward to indigenous vitality. Koori Voices is a generous offering to a non-indigenous viewer. Far from being didactic or separatist, the portraits invite an emotional connection in the domain of Aboriginality because, as historian Jane Lydon has written, 'photographs still speak eloquently of oppression, but also of collaboration and intimacy'.[72] It's to questions of intimacy and Aboriginality that I turn in the next chapter.

6 WALKING LURUJARRI

Everyone is now on the move, and they have been for
centuries: dwelling-in-travel.

James Clifford[1]

In 2002, *Time Australia* produced a special issue with the tag 'Australian Journeys. Tracks: Ancient and modern pathways through
the heart and history of the continent'. The cover image was of
sand completely covered by car, bicycle and foot tracks. Inside, the
map that introduced the 'Australian Journeys' section named and
marked state boundaries, identified 'Aboriginal Land' (in a beige
brown), and six routes. The map is uncannily like those 'empty'
maps of the continent in my school geography books, the only difference being the inclusion of one 'indigenous' journey: 'Arnhem
Land Dreaming (from c. 50 000 B.C.)'. In strict equal opportunity
terms, one in six is an over-representation, but indigenity plays
other roles in the textual introduction to the section:

Nobody knows when the first human foot marked the soil
of Australia. We can be confident that nomads arrived here

at least 50,000 years ago, crossing the shallow seas between the islands of Indonesia and the fledgling continent ... For Australia's Aborigines, the country was born of the sacred Dreamtime, which exists beyond modern concepts of time. An intricate web of trails, left by ancestral beings and recorded only in song, art and ceremony, were sufficient to guide the planet's oldest continuous culture through some of its least hospitable terrain.

The first European settlers two centuries ago found no roads, no maps, and knew no way to read the ancient Aboriginal compass, so set about inscribing their own paths ...

The passage of humans across Australia tells tales of myth, of adventure, of progress, and we celebrate them in these pages; but we should reflect, too, that tracks lie on the surface, are of their essence superficial. Stand at night in the silent outback as stars crowd the darkness, and the scale of human achievement can seem suddenly tiny, our impact on the land as slight as that first bare footprint in the northern sand.[2]

This homily seems to encapsulate some of the key incoherence of contemporary non-indigenous claims around Aboriginality. Indigeneity is recognised and claimed for the nation and yet disappears with the arrival of settlers only to reappear, incongruously, as Aboriginal property rights and remote places where 'Aboriginal people follow an ancient cycle, singing and dancing the creation journeys of the Morning Star, the Yabby and the Wagilag Sisters'. To think about Aboriginality and remembering in terms of journeys runs the risk of reproducing these clichés. Yet whitefella travelling is also one way to approach questions of Aboriginal, intimacy and experience.

In her book *Destination Culture*, Barbara Kirshenblatt-Gimblett has argued that tourism and its ancillary industries such as museums and heritage are central to how experience is produced in late modernity; it's actually through mobility that first world citizens arrive at and occupy 'culture'.[3] There's certainly plenty of support for this argument in how metaphors of travel in contemporary cultural criticism seem to have proliferated exponentially, so that the postmodern subject is inevitably in-between or in-transit, constantly mobile and surfing waves of data. She is constituted by global flows, a border-crosser, a nomad, a wanderer, diasporic, an exile on permanent detour, a migrant returning, a trekker, a drifter, an itinerant, a road-runner, an (involuntary) vagrant. On the other hand, when it comes to actual travel, and particularly the intersections of travel theory and postcolonialism, the scholarly analytic repertoire often seems inadequate, moralistically clichéd or stuck in ideological critique.[4] Travel metaphors, actual travel and the problematically postcolonial intersect in a myriad of ways. Take, for example, *Millennium: Wisdom of the Elders*, the Body Shop–funded, PBS broadcast series narrated by David Maybury-Lewis, which included one episode on Paddy Roe, a lawman and guardian of the Lurujarri Trail in Broome, Western Australia. In one scene, Paddy draws two parallel lines in the dirt as his spatial mapping of indigenous/non-indigenous relations during his long lifetime. He assigns white people to the top line, to a position not touching the land, and black people on the bottom, with the earth. Roe is concerned with what happened in the space between the two lines, the contact zone. He says that his people moved half way to meet white people and is very matter-of-fact about the refusal of white people to make a commensurate move towards his people. But what happened next is, for Roe, clearly disappointing; his people kept moving towards the white people. The result: the worst of possible outcomes – his people haven't come back. The problem, I'm sure, is not with the mobility that Roe describes but with how movement was truncated, how it became fixed and naturalised as the outcome of a history that has colonised the past more effectively than it has colonised the land. Paddy Roe wanted his people to come back to the land and his involvement with the Lurujarri Trail was one major way in which he sought to do that.

The Lurujarri Trail exists in its current form by virtue of a number of organisational and discursive coincidences. A product of indigenous survival and creativity, it is part Paddy Roe's vision for his family and his country. The trail is also of the international leisure market and the Broome regional economy; it is a product of government funding, Aboriginality, the tourist industry and the powerful magic of its advertising wing. It has intersected with global television, travel writing, landscape architecture and the textual collaborations between cultural critic Stephen Muecke and Paddy Roe. In this sense, Lurujarri is a site of convergence, a place where vectors of cultural force and mobility meet and disperse, a place of dwelling and travelling and memory.

The Lurujarri Trail is one of many ventures in Aboriginal cultural tourism that, over the last decade or so, have brought significant numbers of non-indigenous people onto indigenous land and into contact with indigenous people in new and creative ways. But before I get to walking, we need to be aware of other ways of imagining journeys.

'AUSTRALIAN ABORIGINAL TOURS' WITH AFRICAN STYLE SAFARI CAMPS AND INSECT PROOF CABINS'

Although Australia has a culture and a certain tradition, this culture and tradition can only be experienced behind closed doors. Are you going to go to the Aboriginal people and ask them: please show me how you live? This would be ridiculous.

German male, aged 30–35 years[5]

A proper history of 'Aboriginal tourism' would refuse the moment in *Time Australia* when white feet hit the sand of Australia and Aborigines disappear. Such a history would be concerned to continue the project historian Paul Carter began in *The Road to Botany Bay*, of thinking of place-making in this country as involving indigenous and non-indigenous people from the beginning. It would take seriously how indigenous roads and maps and compasses actually oriented explorers and settlers through and in country. It might be interested in how, in the 20th century, travel and Aboriginality were central to the public education performed by newsreels, popular publishing and television. Such an account would revisit some places we've already encountered in this book. Both Coranderrk (in the 19th century) and Lake Tyers (in the 20th century) were significant sites of tourism. Similarly, there are long and complicated relationships between 20th-century indigenous art and tourism, and Bill Onus's business Aboriginal Enterprises was, in part, selling to tourists. A longer history would be interested in the 1964 report commissioned by the Australian National Travel Association.[6] That report identified Aboriginal culture as 'one of Australia's important visitor attractions'. It made five fascinating recommendations calling, among other things, for 'competent and sympathetic presentation of Aborigines' life and history in museums of natural history' and the 're-establishment of Aboriginal art and artefacts to their natural, former level'.[7] The report also endorsed the view of anthropologist AP Elkin, that 'Aborigines could well be an integral part of tourism as producers, performers, and workers – not just as curios.'[8]

Aboriginal cultural tourism refers to a heterogeneous set of businesses and cultural practices that have emerged across Australia over the last couple of decades.[9] This includes ventures such as the Brambuk Aboriginal Cultural Centre at Gariwerd in the heavily 'settled' south-east of the continent, Monkey Mia Dolphin Resort in Western Australia, Tjapukai Aboriginal Cultural Park in Queensland, Gab Titui Cultural Centre in the Torres Strait, Kooljaman at Cape Leveque and Umorrduk Safaris Arnhem Land on 'remote' lands now owned by indigenous people in the far north.[10] It's an ambivalent field of frontier holidays and sunset cruises, art shops and rock – art tours, safari camps and walking trails, corroboree performances, wilderness experiences, trekking adventures, bush tucker and craft tours, cultural centres and museum displays. Aboriginal cultural tourism is one element of a massive global industry. While estimates of the size of the global tourism industry vary considerably, Andrew Ross provides a broadly accurate snapshot in his assertion that 'tourism is *the* modern medium of neo colonial relations between First and Third Worlds, the uneasy passport to development for many countries, the single largest item in world trade at 8 per cent, and one of the biggest providers of inter cultural knowledge today'.[11] In Australia, the tourism industry accounts for approximately 10 per cent of GNP. Not only is the scale of the tourism industry significant but it's an expanding sector with growth in so-called cultural tourism and eco-tourism currently running at 25 per cent per annum. Although a tiny component of a global industry and, indeed, a relatively small sector of the Australian tourism market, Aboriginal cultural tourism in Australia is also big business. Tourism Research Australia reported in June 2005 that 'In 2004 there were 552,000 international visitors (12 per cent of total international visitors) and 475,000 domestic overnight visitors (0.6 per cent of total domestic overnight visitors) who participated in Indigenous tourism activities.'[12]

This data refers to a variety of activities. The 2005 Tourism Australia survey used the category 'Indigenous based visitor', which it defined as a visitor 'who participated in either of the two activities while travelling in Australia: "experiencing indigenous art or craft and cultural display" or "visiting an indigenous site or community"'.[13] The 2007 Tourism Australia data refers to an 'indigenous cultural experience'.[14] The Australian Tourist Commission formerly defined Aboriginal tourism as 'a tourism experience or service, which is majority owned or operated by Aboriginal people and/or owned or operated in partnership with non-Aboriginal people'.[15] The kinds of ventures to which these designations refer vary in form, embracing cultural. institutions, performances, display, exhibitions and service provision. They vary in scale, ranging from an indigenous park ranger conducting tiny tours to the mass tourism of Uluru-Kata Tjuta. They also vary in terms of actual indigenous involvement, ownership and control. As I'm not concerned here with quantitative data, I'm using Aboriginal cultural tourism as a broad designation that allows me to consider a field stretching from ventures in which indigenous involvement is perhaps purely nominal, grossly exploitative and culturally destructive to instances in which complete indigenous control may be productively linked to cultural and economic autonomy. In this sense, I want to defer, as I've done elsewhere in *Forgetting Aborigines*, any in-principle ideological condemnation of Aboriginal cultural tourism as ongoing colonialism, expropriation and non-indigenous hegemony. In order to begin a detour, let us agree that the term can stand (for the moment) as designating tourism ventures centred on indigenous people and Aboriginality that are designed for non-indigenous touristic use.

As with any kind of tourism, nobody gets anywhere these days without tourist experiences having been, at least to some extent, already organised, imaged, narrated, timetabled and valued. Like most forms of travel, the leisure cultures around Aboriginal cultural tourism are available in the first place not in acts of travel but in the work of cultural institutions and the circulation of travelling texts. Non-indigenous people imagine, understand, encounter or consume Aboriginal cultural tourism first in the storytelling of advertising, guidebooks, and newspaper and magazine travel writing; in the images of postcards, photographs and luscious advertisements; in the moving images of television travel shows, documentaries and film; in the websites of travel agencies, Tourism Australia or the remarkable portal created by Indigenous Tourism Australia[16]; and certainly in the diffuse circulation of travel-talk among friends and acquaintances. To suggest that these signs are important in organising and interpreting travel before the event is merely to state a truism. This is obvious in the Pacific, a place first constituted for Europe in those bestselling accounts of voyages, which, as I've argued elsewhere, inaugurated a project of bringing 'a region and its peoples under the gaze of Europe ... etching new networks of power ... enacting coasting journeys which explored metaphors on new horizons'.[17] This truism is instantly persuasive in the world of cultural analyses of tourism that have grappled with the stories and images of tourism in their attention to sites and signs, spectacle and semiotics, glancing gazes, and their photographic and written records.[18] And these representations are also where we can find strong examples of memory contributing to contemporary spaces of Aboriginality.

The largest number of ventures in Aboriginal cultural tourism are to be found in the Northern Territory and are promoted through two publications. One brochure, *Come Share Our Culture*, features an artful cover image of bush tucker and 'traditional' craft objects. The text welcomes tourists to 'Aboriginal country' – 'Pukulpa pitjama Ananguku ngurakuta' – and invites the prospective tourist on 'a variety of tours that have dared to be different. By putting yourself in Aboriginal hands you will experience the traditional way of life unique to the Northern Territory.' This booklet describes the 8-day Top End Dreamtime Safari, the 3-hour Springvale Corroboree and some 47 other tours, walks, festivals and adventures. An accompanying brochure, *Aboriginal People of the Northern Territory*, aims to orient the potential visitors with a brief introduction to Aboriginal history, culture, land rights, politics, health and economics. Already at this level of promotion, Aboriginal cultural tourism (and more vaguely, a version of Aboriginality) is being put to use for non-indigenous purposes, in this case those of the Northern Territory Tourist Commission. This is not an isolated instance because Aboriginality has become an important component in the marketing of Australia as a tourist destination. As one recent government-commissioned study put it:

> Australian Aborigines, their culture and art are an
> important asset, which is strongly promoted to domestic and
> international tourists as a unique cultural tourism experience
> in which they can participate. In the context of cultural
> tourism, Aboriginals and their culture are most relevant.[19]

This kind of rhetoric is driven by the imperative of differentiating Australian tourism in a global market. So Aboriginal cultural tourism is both an attempt to establish a particular market niche – it is another commodity that a tourist might choose, and a mobile marker that can be deployed to establish a national distinctiveness for Australia. As the tourist industry claims Aboriginality for the nation, there are both implicit and explicit exhortations that Stephen Muecke has perceptively rendered:

> 'Tell us what you are really like', say the white institutions,
> 'Dance for us once more and sing your songs. We will say to
> the world that this too is our *Australian* heritage: this is the
> nation which can stand proud amongst others because it has a
> timeless history in the Aboriginal peoples'.[20]

But it's not just a question of semiotics. Tourism studies have discovered a desire on the part of both domestic and international tourists to 'experience contact with Aboriginal people and learn about their culture on a visit to the Northern Territory'. The research has calibrated degrees of contact desired as ranging from a mere passing interest, which can be gratified primarily through buying curios, through more extended contact in half-day or short tours, to 'cultural immersion', intense and intimate experiences such as those offered by the tour Desert Tracks (eight days with Pitjantjatjara people).

Predictably enough, much of the tourism promotional and policy material, although not all of it, is greatly enamoured with racist discourses of authenticity and primitivism. It is easy to find examples that figure indigenous people and the land as fused and timeless, as in the case of a regional report from Broome, which gushes breathlessly on the market share possibilities that might follow in the wake of Aboriginal cultural tourism:

> Naturally, Australia with the oldest culture and landmass on
> earth and its vast tracts of pristine bush and coast is ideally
> placed to take advantage of this [expanding interest in eco
> and cultural tourism]. Broome in particular, with the recent
> extension to its airport, enabling direct flights to and from
> Asia (the first 'packaged' tourists arrive from Singapore 15
> December, 1992 in flights of less than two hours duration) is
> superbly placed to benefit.[21]

Prospective tourists are lured by replaying the permanent emergency of authenticity. In a recent two-part series, one travel writer put it this way:

> [G]rowing Aboriginal involvement in the management
> and control of Aboriginal prehistoric heritage is a nascent
> Aboriginal tourist industry, offering a growing range of
> opportunities to view the land and its mythic and prehistoric

components through the eyes of the first Australians ...
there will never be a better time than now to start seeing
what you can. For one thing, much of Australia's rock art is
deteriorating at an alarming rate through natural agency.[22]

Here 'rock art' functions as a metaphor for authentic indigeneity.
The tropes are not new. The melancholy wish for the imminent
disappearance of real Aborigines has been a persistent theme in
the long and uneven history of the repetitive rediscovery and re-
erasure of indigenous people from popular imagination in Australia. It also meshes smoothly with the contradictory taste regimes of
savvy cultural tourists who pride themselves on picking the trends
before the marauding hordes: those who boast of having been to
Ubud when it was really a village of artists, those who trekked the
hills of Thailand before they were packaged. Yet the tropes also
swerve wildly across an incoherent spectrum. A flyer for the company Australian Aboriginal Tours, purveyors of 'real outback eco-
tourism', describes Putjamirra on Melville Island as an 'African
style Safari Camp', at which you 'join in and share with Aboriginal people a lifestyle unlike your own and one that has never been
offered'. In '[i]nsect proof cabins', with 'the feeling of safety and
isolation – which are of paramount importance', you can experience 'the opportunity of a lifetime'.

It is impossible to make in-general claims about the results of
these variously incoherent representational strategies or to predict
the outcomes for indigenous people of the substantial move into
tourist ventures. Many of the examples I've offered here are, perhaps, more representative of an older mould of marketing Aboriginal cultural tourism. Certainly, the material coming out of Tourism
Australia has changed substantially over the last three years. Also,
Aden Ridgeway, a former Democrats Senator recently appointed
as executive chairman of Indigenous Tourism Australia, has been
associated with much more nuanced indigenous self-presentation
in a number of tourist publications. Yet there are many Aboriginal
cultural tourism ventures that are simply and crudely interested in

commodifying and hence controlling indigenous culture so as to make it available to a market. As historian Tony Birch has argued, the logic of the industry consigns indigenous people to the status of fourth world image and service workers. Academic studies of tourism often couch these issues in terms of impact, studies in which scholars implicitly take responsibility for indigenous culture in the manner of patrician preservationists. There are times when such studies read as if indigenous people need to be 'saved', not only from tourists and a rapacious industry but also from themselves. Despite the importance of appropriation, the extraction of 'ethnic' value and straight out exploitation, here I want to defer these questions in order to consider the actions and stories of those who consume Aboriginal cultural tourism.

In a sense, I am following in the footsteps of Meaghan Morris's wonderful essay 'At Henry Parkes Motel', which develops a general argument towards understanding tourism as a practice of place.[23] Her point of departure is the way in which a number of strands of writing about tourism reproduce patriarchal assumptions about travel as being constituted by an escape from or an erasure of *domus* (home), which is figured as a feminised place of confinement and enclosure. The Henry Parkes Motel becomes interesting and useful for Morris because it is linked to the idea of home, both literally in its semiotics and design and as a space of memory-work linked to Morris's personal history. In her study, the Henry Parkes Motel is unlike the nowhere transit spaces of intercontinental hotels where, in Paul Virilio's vision, 'speed undoes place'; it is different from the sign-filled world of Las Vegas as characterised by Robert Venturi and Denise Scott Brown; it is unsuited to Ian Chambers's distracted methodology. Instead, one motel becomes a place where the fixed and mobile meet. Neither voyage nor home, it is a place of strategic installation, a place of lodgment in which different times coexist. Here these (and other) suggestions are explored in relation to non-indigenous responses to and uses of indigenous-controlled tourism. And, just so as not to ambush the reader, my route is ordered by a search for distinctive and potential transformative modes of intercultural exchanges taking place in Aboriginal cultural tourism. My suggestion is that it's not existing travelling texts that provide a useful guide to post-colonial spatial practices present but in fact those texts still under construction. In the conclusion, I return explicitly to the question of remembering and Aboriginality.

LURUJARRI: WALKING ON BUGARRIGARRA

> In Aboriginal practice following is 'tracking up', hunting, discovering a singularity. In the Aboriginal science of tracking, following someone's footsteps means to 'know' the person. To walk exactly in their footsteps means that there is an imitation – not a reproduction – of the whole movement of their bodies. And for this reason Aboriginal groups know how to walk together, their bodies have the same movement, a technique which will assure that they stay together over long distances. The walking eccentricities of city people are adapted for short displacements, individual journeys (they can't walk together because of their different styles), they are mostly sitting.
>
> Krim Benterrak, Stephen Muecke & Paddy Roe[24]

The Lurujarri Heritage Trail stretches about 130 kilometres from Minyirr to Minarriny along the coast north of Broome. The route traces a part of a song cycle of the Jabirrjabirr, Jukun and Ngumbarl peoples. This heritage trail or Dreaming trail, as it is sometimes called now, has been in operation for well over ten years. It is wholly managed, promoted and run as a venture in cultural tourism by members of the Lurujarri Council and Goolarabooloo Co-op. Members of the co-op and the Roe family guide groups of up to 30 people, who traverse the trail in a variety of walks from day trips to the trek along the entire length of the route.

On the day I began to walk the Lurujarri Trail, a motley crew

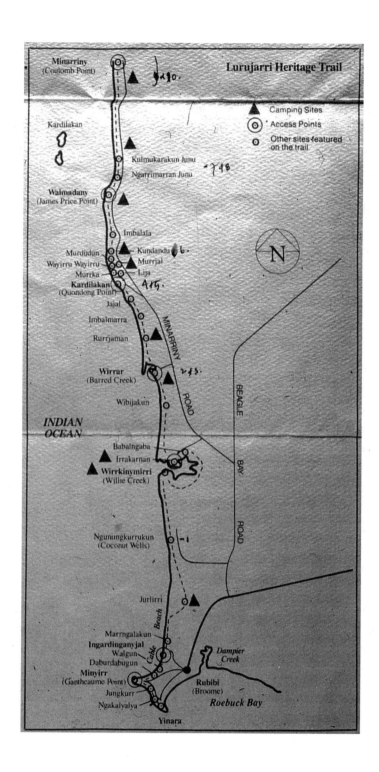

were milling around, cautious, hesitant and perhaps a little equivocal. The group comprised mainly staff and students from the Department of Landscape Architecture at the RMIT University in Melbourne, who were there in large part because of the relationships built between the university and the Goolarabooloo Co-op by Jim Sinatra, a landscape architecture professor.[25] After some preliminaries the truck, which would carry our belongings from one camp site to the next, was loaded and our walking began. Past the cemetery and behind the hostel we skirted a ceremony ground and then tramped through a series of cul-de-sac developments where new steel-framed shells awaited cladding and every house was fringed with a simulated tropical garden and impossibly green neo-regional-colonial lawns over porous, red earth. We emerged quite suddenly from the small cluster of rural-Broome suburbs at an ocean beach. The group spread out as people tried to find a comfortable pace, rhythm and gait, tried to get used to what would be our mode of transport for the next ten days. As the indigenous kids handballed and kicked a football, they kept up a seemingly endless stream of commentary, a football Creole that featured Aboriginal stars kicking impossible goals.

I'd already seen this beach, pristine and full of promises in Broome tourist advertising: but now this was Jurlirri, the route of creation beings, a line marked by songs and stories, a track in ceremony networks, a place both outside of and in my historical temporality, the place of Bugarrigarra. It was also littered with four-wheel drive vehicles and their tyre tracks. A little wagon train of these cars clustered on the sand below Cable Beach Club Resort, an exclusive hotel development built by Lord Alistair McAlpine, the millionaire former secretary of the British Conservative Party. Many of the cars seemed to be on the beach for no other purpose than to provide a seat from which to watch the camel train as it left at sunset. Others just zoomed up and down this tidal highway while we walked on towards the sand dune and pindan country. The car drivers and resort guests were recreational tourists, as I had been the night before. It seemed clear at that moment that

Walking on Bugarrigarra.

resort tourism – luxurious and lavish in the manner of the Cable Beach Club Resort – was distinct from the Lurujarri Trail, which was small-scaled and human rather than capital-intensive, an exercise in indigenous control of indigenous lands. Yet both tourist sites are marketed as an experience of otherness, in terms of place, climate and the semiotics of culture. Both are produced and integrated into circuits of cultural and economic production in which an authentic and different experience is what is sought and prized. Both are stop-over spaces, and although one is imaged as a space in which to worship the temple of the body and the other as a space to worship the land, both are, nevertheless, places to be practised. Yet these distinctions played only a small part in producing the three most obviously available modes of walking Lurujarri.

AESTHETIC LEISURE

The first mode of walking the Lurujarri Trail was a strategy of aesthetic consumption. It was an orientation to the trail as an idyllic holiday site, a holiday site that could have been anywhere, or at least anywhere warm and beautiful. It involved no notion of 'contact' with indigenous people beyond partaking of the services they provided in transport, guidance, food and a schedule of entertainment. When I asked one couple how they'd come there, both described how they had originally booked a package holiday on Bali but had changed their minds after a friend of a friend told them about Lurujarri and they'd read some beautiful Western Australian Government tourist brochures. More interestingly, such aesthetic conventions associated with nature or landscape tourism also appear in a document produced for the Lurujarri Council itself by an American New Age enthusiast who reads like an adherent to the global culture of (white) crystal shamanism. In this document, the trail becomes a kind of spiritual health farm in that indigenous customary law and belief is promoted as enabling an experience of communion with the land to manage the stress of modernity:

> The Goolarabooloo community has always known the great
> power in literally walking on Bugarrigarra. In recent years
> this has been confirmed by the numerous tourists who have
> participated. The lightness and joy which re-enters previously
> stressed and troubled faces is a sure sign of the great healing
> power of this land. It would be difficult to over estimate this
> radically different experience.[26]

This sentiment is no mere aberration. Similar notions are promoted on the trail through an ethic that privileges getting to know the land simply by looking and seeing and feeling the place rather than by 'showing', reading, Socratic dialogue or the routines of investigation that are the staple of intellectual, scientific and juridical inquiry. These putatively 'non-Western' modes may be available and possible for some tourists, or perhaps even many, under the right conditions. Nevertheless, they arise from an orientation to the trail that actually produces the possibility of cultural disinterest; in its extreme version, it would replicate practices of nature tourism and resort-based ecotourism as libertarian consumption. In other words, cultural indifference on the Lurujarri Trail excludes precisely the cultural negotiations and recognitions that are in many ways central to the trail's existence. Indigenous people become what anthropologist Eric Michaels feared in his work on Yuendumu video-making: condemned to inhabit an impossible space of providers of lifestyle culture, just like Bali, just like the Inuit, just like the Kyapo, only unique.[27]

The temporality of this mode of travel is militantly that of the present, but this can involve a number of orientations to remembering. In its purest form, aesthetic tourism at Lurujarri is profoundly forgetful of both the colonising that produced the space and the postcolonial relationships that enable its existence because it is concerned with surfaces. It's not necessary to know about how indigenous knowledge sustains Ngumbarl any more than it's necessary know about the water that sustains the beautiful putting surfaces of a golf course on Bali. In this sense, there is no space for Aboriginality in aesthetic tourism, there is only the moment and the temporal machinery of the camera producing artefacts for the future. Aesthetic tourism that includes spiritual aspects, however, has a different orientation to remembering. It is similarly forgetful of colonial and postcolonial processes but very attentive to the temporality of Bugarrigarra. Frans Hoogland, a Dutchman who has lived at Millinbinyarri for many years and to whom we'll return, puts it this way:

> Our culture, Europeans, Anglo-Saxon culture, we not living with the land. We living from it ... Indigenous people are the land, the land is in their bodies ... We have to learn to see again, learn to walk, to feel all these things again ... When you're here in the land, it fills you up all the time, it will

always give you energy, it always makes you feel all right. It gives you life. But if you kill this country, you kill the people. We all go down together. No matter what colour we are.[28]

In his account of walking the trail, Hoogland is offering an account of memory culture that's very close to the highly influential work of the French historian Pierre Nora. Hoogland is arguing that Europeans no longer have memory; they only possess *lieux de mémoire*, alienated and fossilised memory that has been formalised by history. Aboriginal people, on the other hand, have *milieux de mémoire*, living memory in place. The space of Aboriginality for Hoogland is, quite literally, the experience of country. Thus the presence of nature is what produces the 'presence of the Other'.[29] Hoogland himself is certainly not forgetful of indigenous people, but his orientation to the trail as principally a direct experience of country is forgetful not just of indigenous moderns and Aboriginality but, in its extreme versions, of indigenous people themselves who disappear into country.

There is something about the cultural indifference of aesthetic consumption which appeals to me as a counterpoint to the relentless curiosity and claiming that has driven so much of the interrogation of indigenous peoples and cultures. Such cultural indifference may, in fact, be one way of avoiding some of the consequences of the intensification of indigenous involvement in the tourist industry because, as policy researcher Jon Altman has argued, 'from an Aboriginal perspective, cultural impacts can rarely be neatly separated from economic, social and environmental impacts'.[30] Perhaps the cultural indifference of aesthetic consumption and a willingness to part with cash for Aboriginal guidance through the beauties of nature might produce some interesting and non-intrusive effects. While the sentiments and the articulated rationality underpinning the aesthetic consumption of the trail rely on clichéd and stereotypical versions of Aboriginality, the actual effects of the cultural practice make few demands on indigenous people, and do not intrude on, indeed may contribute to, the means by which indigenous people exercise autonomy.

BOOMERANGS

After a morning's work, Philip Roe was keen to get some wood (gilli girri, I think) to make boomerangs. He found a beautiful elbow, the perfect shape, cut one end and told me to finish the rest. After lunch, many of those who had wood from that outing started to make boomerangs. The first thing you do with an elbow is split the timber. The method Frans had been showing everyone was to use two tomahawks as a wedge and hammer. Once the timber is split in two, you pare back the pale sapwood until the darker heartwood is exposed, roughly shape the blank with the tomahawk and then finish the detailing with a rasp. Frans loved this part of the process. He'd hold one end of the split timber, rest the other end on the ground and with great ferocity and skill send the wood flying.

Meanwhile, I was sitting with the indigenous contingent of the group listening to a football game, sitting in the dirt looking at the boomerang timber I'd got and wondering if there was any chance of my team making a second-half recovery. Frans came over and urged me to get started on the boomerang, offering to show me how to split the timber. I was wondering if I'd show the wood to Paddy, perhaps talk to him about it, perhaps give it to him to make a boomerang. I didn't mention this to Frans but said, just like an equivocating academic, that I was just thinking. Frans replied, reasonably enough and quite sensibly, that thinking about it was useless and that nothing would happen unless I did something. But I wanted to wait. Paddy showed up, not long afterwards. I snuck away from the football and showed him the timber. Paddy liked the timber, but when I suggested that I'd get started with the tomahawk he put up his hand to stop me. He wandered over to one of the utes, pulled out a chainsaw and said along the lines of, 'More better this one. We get four outta 'im.'

So, while a mob of non-indigenous people played at being modern primitives, chopping away in the heat and a mob of indigenous people in the shade were listening to Aboriginal stars kicking impossible goals 3000 miles away, Paddy Roe took a chainsaw to a piece of timber and cut four boomerang blanks. I was casting Paddy as someone who could commune with the spirit of the boomerang wood and he was replying with rational and mechanised efficiency.

HUNTIN' AND FISHIN'

The second mode of walking the trail could be described as a sporting mode – the strategy taken up with a vengeance mainly by young men who rushed to answer the call of the wild. They couldn't wait to get their hands on tomahawks, spears and knives and from then on went about with their shirts off in search of huntin' and fishin'. As most of the landscape architecture students were young men, this manner of walking Lurujarri was as popular as it was ambivalent. It was a kind of mimetic primitivism, but it's crucial to note that this was second or maybe third generation mimesis. They were not copying the indigenous leaders of the walk. Nor do I think they were reproducing a culturally available version of Aboriginality. The model for this mimesis was neither an indigenous man nor Aboriginal men-in-general but a 'white man' born in Holland, Frans Hoogland.

Frans had lived in and around Broome with various indigenous communities for about 30 years. For the last two decades or so, he has lived with Paddy Roe's family near Millinbinyarri. He describes himself as having been initiated into Paddy's way and he has clearly been integrated (in complex and uneven ways) into kinship networks, language, law and country. Paddy Roe describes Frans in this way:

> The first man I found to help us is this man, Frans. Well that's what I was thinking. I can't look after this country with my people, so I bring this man and I been teach him to look after the country, because I want to save country ... It's the law, you know, this song cycle is on the coast. That's why I want to teach my young fellas.[31]

Frans acts both as a mediator for the Goolarabooloo community and, along with Paddy's great-grandson Daniel, he is one of the main day-to-day leaders of walks along the trail. But Frans is also a man of tremendous energy and enthusiasm for getting the things of the land. At every available chance, he would take people on expeditions to cut down saplings for spears and then head off to skewer mud crabs in the mangrove swamps or he'd go in search of wild honey, which can be found by cutting deep into acacia and paperbark trees.

Here I don't want to dwell on Frans himself, although I will return later to him as one of the group of people with more long-term connections with the trail. It is worth noting however that, like Paddy, Frans too has been put into circulation within media cultures with important results for my argument here. It's no accident that the episode of the *Millennium: Wisdom of the Elders* series that features Paddy Roe is not structured around Paddy's wisdom. Certainly Paddy is made both visible and audible as the bearer of wisdom, but it's the coming together of Frans and Paddy, and then the scripting of Frans as becoming Aboriginal, that the viewer is offered. In this sense, Frans stands in for the pedagogic project of the television series as a whole. Predominantly non-indigenous people are ostensibly brought into proximity with tribal wisdom in the hope that these encounters might incite a desire for more proximity. The metaphysics is transubstantiative – the viewer takes in the wisdom in order that they might become that which they ingest. The quest for the other becomes not only extractive but wholly cannibalistic, with Maybury-Lewis functioning as chief masticator for the viewer. A different figuring of the relationship occurs in *Listen to the People, Listen to the Land*. In that book, Paddy features briefly about his relationship to country in ways that substantiate sovereignty, but this functions mostly as an introduction for the long essay by Frans that I quoted from earlier. In that essay, Frans is given the role of explaining his 'indigenous' relationship to country in which the land has will and energy in the form of *le-an*, in which fish and birds and rocks have roles just like those of people and in which a turtle in need of rescue can call Frans from the shore.

But when I walked Lurujarri, I ate turtle. Textual versions of Frans don't capture the ways in which he is an attractive homosocial figure for those who are keen on mimetic primitivism. He is particularly appealing because his primitivism was true to white fantasies of purity. Unlike the indigenous men who, when they considered getting turtle or dugong, would take the car to pick up a motorboat and hunt with a rifle, Frans would stand by the ocean, put a knife between his teeth and dive in to hunt in the old way – or so it seemed to the young men. The anthropologist Lisa Palmer has written about an analogous but different situation in her study of non-indigenous bushwalkers in Kakadu. She writes very eloquently about the conflicts that have emerged in Kakadu where the Bininj/Mungguy have attempted to limit bushwalker access to the stone country in particular. This has produced an interesting conflict. Many of the bushwalkers think of themselves as possessed of ecological consciousness:

> Many bushwalkers in Kakadu National Park assume that
> they, like Aboriginal people, share an affinity for the land,
> a relationship that cares and nurtures the environment and
> fosters a better human relationship with it ... To hear that
> Aboriginal people in Kakadu have concerns about their
> bushwalking activity in the Park is personally confronting
> for many bushwalkers, who might otherwise have thought
> that Aborigines would share their perspectives on nature ...
> 'If only we could get the Aboriginal people to understand
> bushwalking', they imply.[32]

Writing in a critical register, it would be easy to dismiss both the underpinnings and practices of this male mimetic primitivism as at best banal and at worst dangerously romantic. I could argue convincingly that this mode of consuming Aboriginal cultural tourism essentialises indigenous men as 'natives', that it not only makes place, space and identity interchangeable but also assumes that transitory non-indigenous tourists have immediate access to the Aboriginality of all three categories. I would assert its forgetfulness of white colonising. I could point out that at some moments this sporting mode seemed perversely close to the redneck adage 'if it moves shoot it, if it doesn't chop it down'. I could ascribe its valency to an excess of adolescent male testosterone or read it as a tragic men's movement version of hairy-Johns banging drums in the bush, with all its exclusionist and supremacist implications. But such characterisations would be inadequate without mentioning the attendant ways in which mimetic primitivism also produced significant spaces of connection and affect for some young men on the walk. Particularly in its recognition of hunting and fishing as customary practices of great significance to some indigenous men it involved forms of deferral and subservience that were not only respectful but actually generated opportunities for exchange and dialogue beyond the routines of respectable racism.

WHITE BLACKFELLAS

Apart from the tourists who come to Lurujarri to walk the trail there are a number of non-indigenous people who have lived and are living with various indigenous communities on a more long-term basis. For my purposes, these people fall into two groups, the first of which would include Frans Hoogland. These people understand themselves as, what in 19th-century Australia were imagined as, 'white blackfellas' – men and women living 'as if' they were Aborigines. Today they might be better described as 'white nomads', but only in a highly restrictive sense, not in the kind of in-general adoption that has found its way into some cultural criticism. They are nomads in the sense that they are performing what Eric Michaels, borrowing from Deleuze, understood as 'unbecoming' and 'becoming'; they are un-becoming their cultural whiteness and becoming minor. In most cases, these people described themselves as rejecting or shedding their European-derived culture, as leaving behind possessions or the pace of the city, as refusing to work as wage-slaves, refusing to believe in the illusions of cities, wealth and success – self-descriptions that are common within a whole range of youth and alternative cultural formations. But what makes these utterances distinctive are their moves beyond a strategy of refusal. At the same time, they are performing a becoming-minor in place expressed through their use of indigenous languages, through their position in kinship networks, through their knowledge of the country, plants, animals, weather and so on. My point is that they are nomadic only in terms of place: their unbecoming and becoming minor exists only in relation to Lurujarri, so that they are simultaneously on the move – moving away from their own cultural histories as well as walking, and always there because their becoming minor requires that place.[33] It may even be that these white nomads are returning to the moment in Paddy Roe's history of indigenous–non-indigenous relations: that lost moment when indigenous people might have been European-becoming, and Europeans might have been Aboriginal-becoming while both becoming minor.

Whatever the merits of these cultural strategies, they certainly do not provide a model available to the Lurujarri Trail's transient touristic visitors. There are, however, interesting and important possibilities between tourists and the second group of more long-term non-indigenous residents at and around Millinbinyarri – the students and ex-students of landscape architecture who were involved in establishing the trail and have stayed on in various ways. These people have been involved in planning and metric mapping the trail and in writing management plans for local and state governments. They have been part of planning an out-camp and visitor education centre, at which, according to the draft management proposal prepared by one student, Chris Hand:

Visitors will be introduced to the country through Aboriginal · eyes [on] guided walks through the country, focusing on living country, seasonal bushtucker, medicinal trees, middens and other aspects central to Aboriginal culture. Other activities would include traditional shelter building, fishing, carving and tree awareness.[34]

Some of these students and their friends became involved in helping to mount a case under land rights legislation post-Wik, others have prepared a transcultural study of botany along the Lurujarri Trail, and another produced a seasonal calendar of Lurujarri charting the relationships between weather, land, animals and plants across the six Jukun seasons for the areas. They and their professor, Jim Sinatra, have constructed a pedagogic practice that now links Melbourne and Lurujarri in a complex series of personal, teaching, professional and political articulations. Theirs is an uneasy situation to be in, making links based on in-betweenness and mobility with all its attendant uncomfortableness. These landscape architecture students and ex-students are enacting an affirmative strategy; they are building ongoing relationships not based on fixed difference and what we sometimes imagine as identities but practices of deterritorialisation and reterritorialisation.

ALLO-FASCINATION

The third obviously available mode that was adopted by non-indigenous people on the walk could be described as allo-fascination. That was a mode appropriative (in all senses of the term) of Aboriginal culture, particularly Aboriginal culture as personified by Paddy Roe as a source, a voice and a body that was radically other. It could also be applied to the interactions between those non-indigenous women who worked with Teresa Roe (Paddy's daughter) preparing meals and line-fishing – the walk was organised around definite gendered and racialised divisions of labour. Allo-fascination placed Aboriginality at the centre of the experience of the trail. The land became significant through the stories told about it by Paddy or other indigenous people. Cultural practices were important for the meaning attributed to them by indigenous people. Plants, animals, history, weather, travel routes, camp sites and patterns of sociability became important in the language and registers provided by indigenous people.

Paddy Roe is, of course, radically other to most of those who walked the trail; he is initiated in two language groups, he has significant regional stature in indigenous law and is the custodian of an immense body of arcane and practical knowledge. But as literary theorist Eve Sedgwick might remind us, we should not invest too much in otherness so simply racialised. To constitute Paddy as a repository of knowledge and difference is to reify him as a living archive, and so elide what he does, and especially undervalue his translational and transactional skills. Besides, more pragmatically, Paddy Roe was the first indigenous child of a white father in that region. He worked for much of his life in the cattle industry and he was a skilled communicator, a sophisticated user of media technologies and long-term negotiator across the perceptions of cultural difference. Paddy Roe was well used to operating in the terrain of Aboriginality.

So much for the 'allo' part of allo-fascination, what about fascination? Is there anything significant in the kind of rapt attention, enchantment or wonder that greets some indigenous people before certain non-indigenous audiences? I'm thinking of the kind of reception accorded to a disparate group of indigenous political and cultural leaders, a list that might include Mandawuy Yunupingu, David Gulpilil, Pat Dodson or (the late) Oodgeroo Noonuccal among others. Is it possible to mark out this kind of fascinated spectatorship from the longer history of the popularity of Aborigines as 'live ethnological displays', circus performers and pageant artists? Certainly, among the Lurujarri walkers who sat at the feet of Paddy and Teresa Roe there were both varied motivations in and varied responses to the experience. For some, Paddy was tribal wisdom on display; for others, it was too much like hard work to get to the end of his sometimes long and circuitous stories. Some described it in relatively value-free terms as learning, while others felt as if their mode of comportment was meant to communicate respect and deference to a man of great erudition who holds positions of significance in his community and in relation to the trail. Others felt they were witness to an embodied version of the (soon to vanish) simplicity, uniqueness and authenticity that circulate around Aboriginality. In visual terms, some responses called forth gazes of connection, others produced averted gazes of non-recognition.

In setting out these three modes of walking – aesthetic consumption, mimetic primitivism and allo-fascination – I'm really doing no more than suggesting starting points for analysing the practice of walking, or in a more structural inflection outlining some of the available options. The only definite location that most walkers occupied was that of consumers of leisure and learning. The modes of walking I've described do not adequately communicate actual walking practices but merely indicate some available modes of comportment and initial orientations to the knowledges and practices of being on the walk. For most people, the practice of walking and dwelling actually involved negotiating these possible modes, moving between these modes, proliferating possibilities of exchange, and disorganising the comfortable security that these modes presuppose, recognising and being moved around by the shapes and contours of the experience of walking on the land. Before I connect this analysis to my concern with forgetting Aborigines, one last detour.

TRAVELLING AND DWELLING

Somehow it doesn't seem possible to specify a beginning, to mark off when my becoming a tourist on the Lurujarri Heritage Trail commenced. The letter that we received in response to our booking and deposit read, in part:

> We will meet under the Tamarind Tree at the home (in
> the township) of Paddy Roe and Teresa, his daughter, at

3pm on Monday afternoon ... This is also the site of the
Goolarabooloo Hostel ... We will spend some time talking to
Paddy about what is ahead, before setting off on foot to the
Dunes of the coast to head north towards Nurlungurugarr
ck ...

So, after we'd wandered around Broome, explored a museum
devoted to the Japanese and Chinese workers in the pearling industry and discovered air-conditioning in one of the local supermar-
kets, we were at the 'home' of Paddy Roe, a house on an ordinary
street in the Broome township. I don't know if Paddy was under
the Tamarind Tree and I will never know because by now I have
collected at least five published references and six descriptions
from interviews, of Paddy Roe under the Tamarind Tree – the
seer in communion is a popular image for my white informants.
So I can't claim that moment as a beginning. But the homeness of
that place was a beginning of sorts and a very clever one for two
reasons – it was the home of Paddy and Teresa Roe, not a man's
castle or a place of feminised confinement, and it was only one
kind of home qualified by the bracketed phrase (in the township),
a phrase that gestured towards both other places of dwelling and
a travelling imaginary.

Every second day, and sometimes at night, we walked between
8 and 25 kilometres from one camp site to the next. I'm not sure
whether writing on cultural studies are much help in thinking
about this kind of walking – it doesn't call for a typology that
could be borrowed from anthropologist Marcel Mauss, nor is
'Walking in the City' much help. Walking the Lurujarri Trail was,
of course, poetic. It was not a route determined by a metric map,
but it was not walking as ludic resistance to the spatial program
of the city. On the contrary, it was goal-driven (getting to the
next camp site) and regimented (in terms of direction, pace and so
on) under the auspice of a very particular logic, much of which I
didn't understand. I am not a romantic when it comes to walking
long distances; even so, walking and dwelling in these ways was a

Building at Joe's place.

remarkable discipline in terms of how it created a time-space for the body, haptic spaces built around certain kinds of rhythms and relationships to the country. It was at the camp site at Wirrar that I first began to notice the ways in which camp sites were oriented, how cars were positioned, how trees were used, how sleeping and cooking areas were demarcated. That night, Teresa Roe was by a cooking fire and after a while got sick of children bothering her, so she started shooing them away saying, 'Get out of the Kitchen. Outside. Go on, you kids go and play outside.' I began to see the homes we were making under the sky, how we were being trained in everyday ways to fabricate a chronotope to live in.

A more obviously material moment came when we were camping at Joe's Place. Here a number of us were making a shelter for a ceremony and a meeting involving WA parliamentarians, which was to be held in a week or so. The site and orientation of the shelter had been decided by the indigenous men, but the design for the shelter was not fixed and so became the subject of vigorous and playful argument between Philip Roe, Paddy's grandson, and the two non-indigenous architects who were on the walk – an argument full of blustering about practicality versus design, and lots of jokes about white professional incompetence and native aesthetics. Yet, after a few false starts, a hybrid place was built by all of us in the sandy ground. This place was less about a fixed ontology of race than a constitutive performance and made a motel of sorts where white state representatives and black elders would later negotiate. In this shelter, the practical training of bodies in walking and dwelling was being joined to pragmatic questions of producing a space adequate to the open-ended process of emerging forms of cultural practice and their effects. Here, without the metropolitan certainties of nomads, detective or prophets, travelling and dwelling became translational, making a place from which to tell stories: 'I went to Lurujarri once too ...'

GARMA AND GANMA

Ganma is firstly a place; it is an area within the mangroves where the salt water coming in from the sea meets the stream of fresh water coming down from the land. Ganma is a still lagoon. The water circulates silently underneath, and there are lines of foam circulating across the surface. The swelling and retreating of the tides and the wet season floods can be seen in the two bodies of the water. Water is often taken to represent knowledge in Yolngu philosophy. What we see happening in the school is a process of knowledge production where we have two different cultures, Balanda and Yolngu, working together. Both cultures need to be presented in a way where each one is preserved and respected. This theory is Yirrija.

Raymattja Marika[35]

Aboriginal cultural tourism produces complex intercultural spaces for remembering and forgetting Aboriginality and whiteness. They may well be dangerous ventures connected as they are to obscure histories of Aborigines 'holding' utopian promise for non-indigenous people. A bizarre apotheosis of this trajectory can be found in novelist Marlo Morgan's international bestselling book, *Mutant Message Down Under* (1994), in which Aboriginal people are cast as the saviours of Western culture, willing to sacrifice themselves in order to sustain a future for others. Another fantasy of disappearing Aborigines. Few examples of actual Aboriginal cultural tourism share in that fantasy. For some indigenous people, involvement in tourism offers a way to remain connected to or reconnect to country; part of Paddy Roe's vision of Lurujarri was to 'teach my young fellas'. Remembering seems to be a crucial part of enacting this: remembering stories, language, cosmological relationships, skills, family, plants, animals, and so on. Might not this be a lesson in remembering, not as a contemplative process but closer to how the critic Homi Bhabha describes Frantz Fanon's evocation of memory in *Black Skin, White Masks*: 'never a quiet act of introspection or retrospection. It is a painful re-membering, a putting together of the dismembered past to make sense of the trauma of the present.'[36] Perhaps non-indigenous tourists too can reconnect to other travelling modes. In a wonderful essay, 'Origins of sightseeing', Judith Adler has argued that modern tourism comes into existence as part of a whole series of cultural technologies which privilege the visual and turned older regimes of travel into site-seeing. She also recalls an earlier order of travelling, which consisted of 'discourse with the living and the dead – learning foreign tongues, obtaining access to foreign courts, and conversing gracefully with eminent men, assimilating classical texts appropriate to particular sites, and, not least, speaking eloquently upon return'.[37]

The most famous contemporary venture in Aboriginal cultural tourism is the Garma Festival that's been held by Yolngu at Gulku-la in Arnhem Land each year since 1999. Garma is organised by the Yothu Yindi Foundation, which describes it as 'one of Australia's most significant cultural exchange events, a key educational forum, and an award-winning model for authentic, insightful Indigenous tourism'.[38]

I've not been to Garma, nor have I studied Garma in detail – unlike those such as musicologist Aaron Corn, who has a long association with Yolngu and the festival – so I won't discuss it in the same register as I discussed Lurujarri. What interests me here is a specific aspect of Yolngu theory, *garna*. Corn identifies Mandawuy Yunupingu as theorising *garna* in the song 'Mainstream', which was composed while Yunupingu was working as an assistant principal and attempting to formulate a vision of bicultural education for Yolngu. In the first verse of the song:

> The same-moiety meeting of fresh and salt waters at this site
> [*garna*] and the *djinkungun* [yellow foam] that they produce
> represents the fruitful interaction of two similar and equal

socio-political entities that do not assimilate each other and produce something entirely new through their co-operation.

The second verse deals with relations across moieties, while in the final verse 'the two models for equitable cooperation between separate socio-political entities ... are transposed onto the broader arena of cross-cultural relations within Australia to propose a better model for equitable and balanced relationships between Indigenous and other Australians'.[39] In this sense, *garna* is a Yolngu theorisation of the intercultural domain that I've been calling Aboriginality. It is, as Marcia Langton described it, the space of interaction, 'generated when Aboriginal and non-Aboriginal people engage in actual dialogue ... [in which] the individuals involved will test imagined models of the other ... to find some satisfactory way of comprehending the other.'[40] This Yolngu theory of negotiating otherness is a philosophy of memory in place, which Mandawuy Yunupingu has generalised so as to underpin both bicultural learning and a successful festival that brings together Yolngu and other Australians.

The final chapter moves from these particular examples of indigenous cultural tourism to consider whether there might be alternatives to an endless dance of remembering and forgetting. As well as remembering the historical complexity of Aboriginality, non-indigenous people might also have to learn to forget Aborigines in order to remember *garna* and Garma.

7 FORGET ABORIGINES

> Traumas we are not ready or able to remember haunt us all
> the more forcefully. We should therefore accept the paradox
> that, in order to forget an event, we must first summon up
> the strength to remember it properly.
>
> Slavoj Žižek[1]

This minor history has been concerned with the appearance of Aboriginal people and things in public culture. I've argued that, in the recent past, tides of remembering and forgetting seem to rise and fall so that in one moment Aboriginality seems to be enormously significant and in the next, of historical interest only. Often these ebbs and falls coincide with the force of political cycles. Non-indigenous Australians imagine again and again that they have only just learned about indigenous disadvantage – mortality rates, poverty, poor health, housing and educational opportunities, high imprisonment rates, substance abuse or sexual assault, take your pick – as if for the first time.[2] These endless (re)discoveries of, and about, Aborigines are only possible because non-indigenous Australians forget their own forgetting. People such as me have forgotten the long history of the intimate and immediate relations between European and indigenous cultures in Australia. The historian Stephen Turner has argued, in his essay 'Settlement as forgetting', that this predicament is foundational for settler societies because of the overwhelming evidence that 'The will to forget is stronger than the wish to know.'[3] In enumerating 'the will to forget' in Australia, *Forgetting Aborigines* has been implicitly calling forth an ethical and political response – the will to remember. Rather than repressing and hence repeating the past, I've been concerned to remember the continuing presence of indigenous people and the many postcolonial inheritances of dispossession, to remember the present past as, in part, a trauma and to remember white forgetting. At this point, however, the question is whether or not it's enough to simply incite more memories.

In some respects, my argument against forgetting echoes WEH Stanner's 40-year-old condemnation of a cult of forgetfulness, but there are also important differences. Stanner, like Henry Reynolds, thought that knowledge about Aborigines would solve the problem. We can see this clearly in the record of a 1961 academic conference he convened in Canberra. The aim of the symposium was, in the words of the then Prime Minister Robert Menzies, to review the 'present state of our knowledge in the field of Aboriginal studies'.[4] It was an important moment in the processes that led to the foundation of what was initially the Australian Institute of Aboriginal Studies and is today the Australian Institute for Aboriginal and Torres Strait Islander Studies. Papers presented include: AA Abbie, 'Physical Characteristics of Australian Aborigines'; Catherine H Berndt, 'Art and Aesthetic Experience'; OA Oeser and DW McElwain, 'Notes on Psychological Research'; Norman B Tindale, 'Tribal Distribution and Population'; and JH Bell on the 'contemporary scene' in Sydney. Unsurprisingly, not one indigenous scholar was in the room. There were a variety of orientations to 'Australian Aboriginal Studies', but the 'salvage paradigm' was dominant with the anthropologist TGH Strehlow reporting, 'In many areas probably only another ten years or less remain for the gathering of first-class anthropological, ethnological, sociological and linguistic data ... *We are the last white generation which has these opportunities.*[5]

Alongside these interests Stanner, however, had another agenda. He wrote of 'an immense intellectual struggle to bring the native Australians within a perspective that is at one and the same time detached, informed and respectful'.[6] Crucially, this struggle was not simply about academic knowledge. He was also interested in much broader questions of Aboriginality and public culture:

> The masquerade of preconceptions, fiction and half-truth
> as demonstrated fact was well under way before empirical
> anthropology began within Australia. Some of the products
> are still with us. Public opinion, never well informed on
> the true nature and quality of Aboriginal life, draws on an
> old, deep well of misinformation. Schools and universities
> still use texts containing extraordinary misconceptions
> about Aboriginal mentality and custom, and citing the
> misconceptions as proof of fanciful notions concerning the
> origin, history and character of such universal institutions
> as marriage, the family, property, law, government and
> religion. If the full record of our empirical knowledge of the
> Aborigines could only be made available it would force a
> radical revision of many fundamental teachings about man
> and society.[7]

Stanner's respect for indigenous people was genuine and in the 1970s he welcomed and supported indigenous activism; however, here 'learning about Aborigines' is important so that anthropology can make pronouncements about Man. The production of this kind of knowledge about Aborigines seems to require the disappearance of indigenous moderns. After more than four decades, the 'full record of empirical knowledge' is fuller still and yet the material needs, human rights, civic entitlements and political aspirations of 'their' communities are so often forgotten. Part of the reason is that the 'Europeanality' of the full record is also forgotten.

In his recent book *Bad Dreaming: Aboriginal men's violence against women and children*, the novelist and playwright Louis Nowra writes:

> Indigenous communities have to recognise that they are
> part of Australian society and integrate into their cultural
> sensibility the idea of personal and individual responsibility
> for their actions. Furthermore, they need to accept that
> certain aspects of their traditional culture and customs – such
> as promised marriages, polygamy, violence towards women
> and male aggression – are best forgotten.[8]

Bad Dreaming is without doubt well intentioned. Like *Little Children are Sacred*, the report of the Northern Territory Board of Inquiry into the Protection of Aboriginal Children from Sex Abuse, which was the immediate impetus for the dramatic intervention by the federal government in June 2007, *Bad Dreaming* was motivated by raw experience of the levels of violence directed at indigenous women and children. *Little Children are Sacred* was a serious report that went to great lengths to defuse sensationalism, to refuse to demonise indigenous men and to make it abundantly clear that abuse was perpetrated by both indigenous and non-indigenous men. It also had a strong sense of institutional memory, heading one section of the overview 'It's all been said before' and referring to a judge having provided a very similar analysis 30 years earlier.[9] All to no avail. *The Australian* editorialised:

> FINALLY, we can hear them screaming … Aboriginal children
> are being abused in every indigenous community in the Northern
> Territory … Here is the evidence. It can no longer be denied. It is
> not confined to a few bad communities. It is culture-wide.[10]

The 'crisis' was quickly crystallised in the ambiguous phrase 'Aboriginal child abuse'.

Like Nowra's diagnosis, the problem becomes either 'traditional Aboriginal culture' or 'Aboriginal culture' as it has been deformed by insidious government policies. Such analyses, influenced significantly by the work of Noel Pearson, have been developed as alternatives to so-called 'leftist' accounts, which, it's argued, have produced forms of regulation focused on 'white' responsibility that's been reconciled by the guilt money of passive welfare. These debates, ostensibly about public policy formation, are a product of our contemporary moment when forms of race-thinking have gained a new legitimacy as if they were ideology-free. The new authority of such views has been fused with neoliberal notions of personal responsibility so as to be able to confidently locate culpability in the pathology of the primitive. These are important debates to which scholars such as Ian Anderson, Larissa Behrendt, Peter Sutton, Tim Rowse and others have made major and challenging contributions.[11] I do not have the expertise to make such contributions, but I think questions of memory are part of what's at issue in these debates. Nowra's proposition that they need to forget seems particularly deficient, not least in the absence of any reflection as to non-indigenous forgetting. I'm interested in exactly the opposite proposition. I want to think about how non-indigenous people might forget the cultural assemblage that is 'the Aborigine'.

I shouldn't have needed Louis Nowra as a foil to help me figure this out because periodically while I've been working on this book, my friend Tony Birch would find second-hand publications that he thought might interest me. They were things such as Dymphna Cusack's *Black Lightning* and the 'Schools' Edition' of *On Aboriginal Affairs* (1965). He'd give them to me saying, 'Here's something for your book on Ab-bor-idg-in-ees.' I think that in saying this he wasn't mocking my interests but he was telling me something of the ambiguity of the term 'Aborigine' for a Koori man born and bred in Fitzroy in the second half of the 20th century. Tony has strong family connections with a generation of men and women who were and are centrally involved in the political work of organisations such as the Aboriginal Advancement League. Decades of political activism have resulted in the suburb – his 'country' and where I now live – being scattered with the headquarters of many Koori organisations, from the Aboriginal Health Service to the Aboriginal Legal Service. All of them created by models that arose from long struggles for self-determination. For Tony, I think that the term 'Aborigine' is unrelentingly white, a product of colonialism that is both irredeemably tied to its colonial history and almost entirely unconnected to his life experiences as a Koori. 'Aborigine' in this sense is a term that performs a particular version of indigenous presence (or absence), a term that colonial culture required for its own purposes, whether in *Alcheringa* or Abo art, the culture wars, museums or tourism.

The historiography of the term 'Aborigine' has been explored in historian Bain Attwood's pioneering work *The Making of the Aborigines*.[12] Using south-eastern Australia as a case study, Attwood argues that the category 'Aborigine' comes into existence 'only in the context of colonisation'.[13] There is no doubt that for the colonisers, indigenous people became Aborigines and much of *Forgetting Aborigines* has been concerned with some of the consequences of that becoming. But it's another thing entirely to assume that this process was simply mirrored by indigenous people, that they became Aborigines in relation to themselves. That Attwood implicitly and explicitly makes this argument is, in part, the result of him mapping onto colonial processes Edward Thompson's famous account of the English working class becoming a class for itself in *The Making of the English Working Class*. Thompson did not have to consider the fundamentally asymmetrical relationship between coloniser and colonised. Indigenous people certainly made themselves Aborigines in a number of ways. These instances are, however, overwhelmingly cases in which this kind of subjectification was required by colonial agencies. For example, in considering the political campaigns mounted by indigenous people in the 1880s, Attwood writes that 'they increasingly developed a different consciousness of themselves, as "Coranderrk Aborigines"'.[14] This is hardly surprising. These people were, after all, trying to make a case to the Board for the Protection of Aborigines. They had to be Aborigines in order to have standing before this government agency. That process of becoming is no different to any one of us becoming a plaintiff or a defendant, the accused or a witness in judicial proceedings.

We do not have to follow Attwood when, after the phrase, 'they increasingly developed a different consciousness of themselves, as "Coranderrk Aborigines"', he writes, 'rather than "the Kulin"'. The question simply doesn't have to be posed as either 'Coranderrk Aborigines' or 'the Kulin'. On the evidence, it could equally be 'Coranderrk Aborigines' and 'the Kulin', or 'Coranderrk Aborigines' (for the purposes of appearing before the Board for the Protection of Aborigines) and 'the Kulin' (for a range of other purposes). Even if one did want to make a case for 'Coranderrk Aborigines' 'rather than "the Kulin"', it's extremely difficult in any historical study, let alone one of colonial entanglement, to make a case for the absence of identity categories. If we were less interested in thinking about such identity categories in either/or terms, we might recall that in *The Lamb Enters the Dreaming*, Robert Kenny – certainly no anti-empirical relativist – produced a rich ethnographic account of indigenous people becoming Christian *and* being Aborigines *and* being Wotjobaluk.[15] Despite its many virtues, *The Making of the Aborigines* directs us towards processes that were of ontological significance to settlers – they were about the nature of 'different' kinds of people – but were of tactical significance to indigenous people enduring in a ruptured world. Attwood is entirely right to argue that indigenous people 'were named and have named themselves "Aborigines", "blacks", "Kooris" or "Murris" etc. only in the context of colonisation and of their ensuing relationship with Europeans'.[16] All of these names and their production took place in the domain of Aboriginality. But these names were not fashioned from the same typeface. 'Aborigines' and 'black' were, in the first place, names bestowed by settlers in colonial worlds. 'Koori' and 'Murri' were names produced by indigenous moderns in postcolonial worlds. All of these terms are a product of various kinds of race-thinking. There is no outside of this predicament, no magic words beyond 'race'. However, in some instances, terms such as 'Koori', 'Palawa' or 'Waanyi' are preferable because at least they are both specific and historicised. On the other hand, 'Aborigine' is so general, so tied to hierarchies of race and history, so fundamentally concerned with the primitive other, so much a term tethered to dispossession and repressive governance that it seems at a deep level that it might best be forgotten.

In the 1980s, Eric Michaels was inventing ways of forgetting Aborigines. He asked: 'What might television look like if it had been invented by Warlpiri Aborigines?'[17] His answer was that Warlpiri television was documentary; it was true television made and authorised by and through social networks, 'preserving knowledge over time by encoding it as true stories collectively authored'.[18] Michaels's question arose out of his involvement with the actual Aboriginal invention of television, particularly at Yuendumu, and the notion that new histories of image-making and media policy were being enabled by these practices. He took it as axiomatic that 'Aborigines and Aboriginality have always been subject to appropriation by European Australians'.[19] But what seemed different in the 1980s was this:

> What may be new is who Australia now regards as having
> the rights to make this appropriation. By identifying a class
> of people as Aborigines and providing some of these [people
> with] the right to authorize programs about each other
> of these [people], we may risk not only inhibiting unique
> indigenous expression, we risk employing media's vast
> transmission range to usurp local autonomy and to attack the
> base of traditional life.[20]

Part of the problem for Michaels was that:

The dominant filmic and documentary conventions (not to mention the ethics) applied to imaging Aborigines are rarely more recent than the 1950s; we engage a vulgar and ill-considered realism in the treatment of Aborigines. But do the few specialist readers we now position politically (both professional students of Aborigines and professional Aborigines themselves) to evaluate any text offer any improved insights? In the polemics that emerge here, these students and Aborigines seem to ask, as do remote people, whether an image is 'truthful.' But unlike truth in the Dreaming Law, this truth is based on public relations law: Is the text sympathetic to an image certain Aborigines think useful to project when based on essentially public relations notions of the persuasive function of film and TV?[21]

For Michaels, this 'law' was a means of furthering 'culturecide', the destruction of the very 'communication process' that sustains locally based indigenous communities. His prescription: 'If we take "community" rather than "Aboriginality" to be the subject, and make "local" the qualifier, only then do we avoid the traps of racism and paternalism in our rhetoric and practice.'[22]

Conventional intellectual histories of the idea of race insist that in the years after the Second World War, 'race', as a concept that organised categories of people in an intra-species hierarchy, was no longer viable. The impact of anti-colonial movements, the rise of new paradigms in anthropology, reactions against the consequences of Nazi racism and changing scientific understanding in genetics are among the factors that historians refer to as undoing the legitimacy of humanity as divided by race. This intellectual history neither accounts for the enduring force of racism nor for the many economic, cultural and political manifestations of race-thinking which persist despite 'race' being an intellectually discredited term. Against this general backdrop, 'race' in Australia has its own many histories. One of the most peculiar and decisive moments in those histories came in the referendum of 1967 when it was thought that indigenous Australians became full political subjects with these words: 'People of the Aboriginal Race'. The use of this phrase enabled the peculiar synonymy of the terms 'Australian' and 'white' to be reaffirmed.[23] The widespread and persistent use of the term 'Aborigine' into the late 20th century drags with it 200 years of baggage, most of it heavy with (various inflections of) race-thinking. To object to the term 'Aborigine' is not to image that alternatives – Blak, First Australians, indigenous or Koori – are necessarily 'free' of racism. But that objection does draw attention to race-base heritage and race-based homogenising of the term. It draws attention to the many attachments of 'white' Australia to its Aborigines.

ONE RED BLOOD

If the legitimacy of liberal democracy depends on certain narratives and foundational presuppositions, including progress, rights, and sovereignty, what happens when those narratives and assumptions are challenged, or indeed simply exposed in their legitimating function? What kinds of political cultures are produced by this destabilization of founding narratives and signal terms? ... How do we live in these broken narratives, when nothing has taken their place?

Wendy Brown[24]

If not Aborigines, then what might be the subject of remembering? Surely there are many possibilities. Eric Michaels suggested local community, the photographer Ricky Maynard suggests place. These untitled images are from the series *In Response to Place*. They are all taken along the north bank of the Yarra River in central Melbourne and all but one juxtapose sculptural elements in the landscape with what might be loosely described as the 'built environment'. It's important to be clear that Maynard is not capturing a historical indigenous presence in his images. The Yarra

Ricky Maynard, untitled, from In Response to Place, *City Gallery, 2007.*
(Courtesy of the artist and the City of Melbourne Art and Heritage Collection)

and its surrounds were completely transformed by major engineering interventions in the 19th and 20th centuries. The sculptures are recent works, most of them produced as part of the construction of a new riverside park, Birrarung Marr, which includes Birrarung Wilam ('River Camp'), described as:

> [an] installation that celebrates the diversity of Victoria's indigenous culture by interpreting stories from local communities through public artworks, marked by a tall, intricately carved message stick standing at either end. A textured, twisting pathway acknowledges the significance

of the eel as a traditional food source for groups camped by the river. Large rocks incised with animal drawings enclose a performance space and, closer to the river, a semi-circle of metal shields represents each of the five groups that comprised the Kulin Nation.[25]

Tony Birch writes of the photographs: 'In Maynard's work there is no self-conscious attempt to reclaim an indigenous attachment to place. Equally there appears no anxiety to recover a "lost" indigenous past or to justify an indigenous presence in the city of Melbourne in 2006.' Birch observes the exact opposite: 'The Indigenous loss of place as an outcome of colonialism appears as an absence in Ricky Maynard's photographs of Melbourne. But without contradiction, a continued and unbroken presence is also a constant vibration throughout.'[26] And Birch hears these vibrations in the voices of artist, intellectual and elder William Barak and the poet and photographer Lisa Bellear, as he walks through the places of loss and presence.

Forgetting Aborigines has been concerned with the 'task of revisiting, remembering and, crucially, interrogating the colonial past.'[27] I've tried to demonstrate that, in the recent past, across a number of cultural fields, patterns of forgetting Aborigines can be mapped in the appearance and disappearance of indigenous people and things. In this cultural history, I've wanted to recall the persistence of indigenous presence and to draw attention to non-indigenous forgetting. In search of a more useable past, my antidote for forgetting Aborigines has been the resources of memory and history. I've also argued that the forgetting of indigenous presence seems tightly bound to the category 'Aborigine'. Aborigines are forgotten because that's what they are there for, they are anachronisms belonging to the past, not the pasts of indigenous moderns in the present. There may be real ethical and cultural gains to be had by summoning up the strength to both properly remember forgetting Aborigines and produce the conditions in which to properly forget Aborigines. In the meantime, indige-

Ricky Maynard, untitled, from In Response to Place, *City Gallery, 2007.*
(Courtesy of the artist and the City of Melbourne Art and Heritage Collection)

nous people will bear the burden of working through bad feelings
as non-indigenous people make Aboriginal policy and buy Aboriginal art, learn about Aboriginal culture and bemoan Aboriginal disadvantage, fly Aboriginal flags and dissect an Aboriginal
body to learn how a liver was cleaved in two on the steps of a
Palm Island watch-house. Warlpiri and Koori, Murri, Yolngu and
Nyungar, will do what they do as indigenous moderns, but not in
conditions of their choosing. The sooner 'white' Australia learns
to forget the race-thinking of the term 'Aborigine' the better, for
everyone.

CODA: 'SORRY 2008' – ON FEELING GOOD AND BAD

> To the Stolen Generations, I say the following: as Prime
> Minister of Australia, I am sorry. On behalf of the
> Government of Australia, I am sorry. On behalf of the
> Parliament of Australia, I am sorry. I offer you this apology
> without qualification.
>
> Kevin Rudd, 13 February 2008

In February 2008, after the manuscript of this book was completed, I went to a public place to watch and hear Prime Minister Kevin Rudd deliver a speech at the opening of the first parliamentary sitting of his new government. Melbourne's Federation Square was full to near capacity and most of the diverse crowd were focused on the large-screen broadcast of the event. Rudd is not a charismatic orator, but his speech on that day was clear, unambiguous and sincere. As the elected representative of the Australian people, he said sorry to the stolen generations.

There is no doubt that the apology meant a great deal to many indigenous men and women touched by the state-sanctioned violence of the removal of children organised on the basis of 'race'. If there was a single emotion that seemed to join a great many indigenous and non-indigenous people on that day, it was relief; relief that 'their/our' story was at last accepted, and relief that 'our' leaders were no longer in denial. That speech certainly brought to an end the political conjuncture in relation to indigenous affairs that has dominated the writing of this book. Beyond these simple observations, there seem to me a number of more ambiguous aspects of 'Sorry 2008'. On the one hand Rudd's speech was tightly focused on the stolen generations, while on the other he seemed to be making reference to a broader process of reconciliation. In the long run, in terms of shifting notions of sovereignty it may be more important that, for the first time, the opening of a new parliamentary sitting was preceded by what's commonly called a welcome to country. That this apology was broadcast in places like Federation Square, broadcast live on television, watched in schools and workplaces, and broadcast on radio is significant. Parliamentary speeches often seem an archaic form of performance as besuited men address 'the Honourable Member' and punctuate bombastic banality with repetitive entreaties to 'Mr Speaker!' But this speech was anticipated as a historic event and was staged so that it became just that. Rudd's speech brought into existence a new public truth built on the persistence of indigenous memory, the *Bringing Them Home* report and the work of thousands who campaigned in support of the stolen generations. Rudd authorised what Emilio Crenzel, writing about the disappeared in Argentina, calls an emblematic memory.[28] In this sense, the apology to the stolen generations is a particular assemblage which integrates personal memories and experiences, evokes the past and provides a framework of interpreting that past, and articulates this in the public sphere in ways which authorise and popularise a new sense of the past. But Rudd's apology also raises questions of feeling good and feeling bad.

A few years ago, over dinner, I took part in a discussion about Aboriginality that produced bad feelings. I was talking with a legal scholar about why the stolen generations report, *Bringing Them Home*, had proved so difficult for the Howard government, about public pain and recognition, and about restorative justice. This discussion upset my hosts, an elderly couple of comfortable circumstances who, although politically conservative and racist, on the surface at least did not seem to be people who lacked compassion. What had been a civil conversation became heated, although just what was generating the heat was unclear until one of them, obviously both upset and furious, turned to me and said, 'Why do you keep going on about Aborigines? It just makes us feel bad.' At the time, I gave no answer to the question and opted to keep a smoker company outside. Now I think the question is much less important than the statement about feeling bad.

Sara Ahmed has observed that 'bad feeling' can orient non-indigenous Australians towards both support for and opposition to ideas of reconciliation.[29] Her reading of the 'Sorry Books' notes that many entries speak of the shame people feel, of disgrace, and of how the lack of recognition of a 'brutal past' has taken away the capacity to feel truly proud of Australia. Ahmed argues that such sentiments are in search of redemption, about reclaiming pride in whiteness and that 'to transform bad feeling into good feeling ... is not necessarily to repair the costs of injustice'. Paradoxically, in both cases – of saying sorry and not saying sorry – bad feelings are something to be resolved, overcome and be done with.

What's striking in these examples of 'feeling bad' is a narcissist shift from Aboriginality as a space of potential negotiation to a focus on 'we' who have won and are the model for all people.[30] This is less forgetting Aborigines than a complete displacement of Aboriginality. The feelings of the 'white' Australia are what matter. One of the (many) problems of narcissism is that it operates in an economy of all blame and no responsibility; the narcissistic subject can never be the source of bad feelings. But, in a similar fashion to Ahmed's argument about 'sorry', the anthropologist Gillian Cowlishaw has argued that a mirror of this configuration can be identified in those who profess nothing but good will towards Aborigines through 'a widespread narcissistic desire, often muted and pressed into unconsciousness, to improve the Indigenous population. The apparent difficulty of helping Indigenous people, evidenced by their persistent, statistically measured marginality, invigorates the desire to understand, intervene, and remedy.'[31]

In February 2008, Kevin Rudd spoke of 'a new beginning for Australia'; of a parliament that 'has come together to right a great wrong'; of bringing two centuries 'to a close, as we begin a new chapter'. He urged 'us to turn this page together ... and write this new chapter'. Rudd also invoked the spirit of 1967. In that year the prodigious author Patsy Adam-Smith, who was for many years a manuscript field officer for the State Library of Victoria, began an article in *Walkabout* on 'New Deal for the Aborigines':

When I was a child no one had thought to educate the aborigines. Those of us who lived on the edges of the inland deserts and shared our lives with them believed what we were told: 'The aborigines will disappear.' It was sad but to an extent true. Learned men wrote: 'All we can do is to smooth their dying pillow.'

In our corner of the continent on the edge of the Hattah Desert my family had no reason to doubt the scientist as we watched the Kulkyne tribe die out. Mary Woollong, who nursed me as a baby, had, by the time I was a young woman, died as 'the last of the Kulkyne tribe'. Daisy Bates, whom I later camped with, herself said that we could only ease their passing; in fact she wrote a book on her experiences, *The Passing of the Aborigines*.

... The past 10 years have seen such liberalisation of thought as to make nearly two centuries of misunderstandings not worth the time that many people waste in discussing them. There is so much excitement and challenge in the aboriginal world today that the more enlightened say: 'Let's stop talking about the past. Where does it get us to go on about the errors of the white man and the faults of the black? Let's start out afresh.'[32]

Like many 'friends of the Aborigines' both then and now, Adam-Smith wanted to be forward-looking. In 1967 there was a widespread sense that the future was likely to be a much happier place for indigenous people. But this orientation did not require her to forget that her family 'watched the Kulkyne tribe die out' some time in the 1930s. Adam-Smith is prepared to remember, to take ownership of her past by writing about it. In an important sense, that makes it impossible to believe in starting out afresh or turning new pages. Aboriginality is always there for settler and indigenous Australians. It haunts both those who are prepared to disinter unpalatable memories and those enamoured with amnesia, repression or denial. But Aborigines we can forget. In their place we might imagine friends, neighbours and strangers who live near and far; citizens marked by difference and sameness; people of varying predicaments, capacities and desires; people who, like all of us, live with the possibilities and constraints of being in history.

NOTES

1   Forgetting Aborigines

1   Andreas Huyssen, 'Present pasts: Media, politics, amnesia', *Public Culture*, vol. 12, no. 1, 2000, p. 28.

2   Nicholas Thomas, *Possessions: Indigenous art/colonial culture*, Thames & Hudson, London, 1999, p. 10, describes these entanglements as 'antagonistic intimacy'.

3   Andrew McGahan, *The White Earth*, Allen & Unwin, London, 2004.

4   Klaus Neumann, 'Among historians', *Cultural Studies Review*, vol. 9, no. 2, 2003, p. 185.

5   Marcia Langton, *Well, I heard it on the radio and I saw it on the television...* (An essay for the Australian Film Commission on the politics and aesthetics of filmmaking by and about Aboriginal people and things), Australian Film Commission, Sydney, 1993. Langton was certainly not the first person to use the expression 'Aboriginality' – the *Bulletin* magazine used the term extensively and scholars such as Jeremy Beckett have used it in different ways to Langton.

6   Langton, *Well, I heard it on the radio*, p. 81.

7   Langton, *Well, I heard it on the radio*, p. 34.

8   Langton, *Well, I heard it on the radio*, pp. 33–35.

9   Langton, *Well, I heard it on the radio*, pp. 34–35.

10   Carolyn Stachan & Alessandro Cavadini, *Two Laws*, Australian Film Commission, 1981; Rolf de Heer, *Ten Canoes*, Film Finance Corporation Australia, 2006.

11   Langton, *Well, I heard it on the radio*, p. 31.

12   See *The Members of the Yorta Yorta Aboriginal Community v The State of Victoria*, Federal Court of Australia, 1998, 1606, in which Justice Olney used

Edward Curr's, *Recollections of Squatting in Victoria*, (1883) as a foundation for his judgment.

13 Fred R Myers, *Painting Culture: The making of an Aboriginal high art*, Duke University Press, Durham, 2002.

14 Mary Louise Pratt, *Imperial Eyes: Travel writing and transculturation*, Routledge, London, 1992, pp. 6–7.

15 See James Clifford, *Routes: Travel and translation in the late twentieth century*, Harvard University Press, Cambridge, Mass., 1997, especially the chapter 'Museums as contact zones'.

16 Walter Benjamin, *Selected Writings. Vol. 2, Part 2, 1927–34*, eds Michael Jennings, Gary Smith & Howard Eiland, Belknap Press, Cambridge, 2005, p. 597.

17 The two collections, Susannah Radstone & Katharine Hodgkin (eds), *Regimes of Memory*, Routledge, New York, 2003 and Susannah Radstone & Kate Hodgkin (eds), *Contested Pasts: The politics of memory*, Routledge, London, 2003, provide a strong introduction to contemporary memory studies.

18 Maurice Halbwachs, *On Collective Memory*, ed. LA Coser, Chicago University Press, Chicago, 1992.

19 Philip Morrissey, 'Dancing with shadows: Erasing Aboriginal self and sovereignty', in Aileen Moreton-Robinson (ed.), *Sovereign Subjects: Indigenous sovereignty matters*, Allen & Unwin, Sydney, 2007, p. 65.

20 Thomas, *Possessions*, p. 38.

21 Introduction to Cathy Caruth (ed.), *Trauma: Explorations in memory*, Johns Hopkins Press, Baltimore, 1995, p. 5.

22 See Heather Goodall, '"The Whole Truth and Nothing But ...": Some intersections of Western law, Aboriginal history and community memory', *Journal of Australian Studies* (Special Issue 'Power, Knowledge and Aborigines'), no. 35, 1992, p. 112.

23 Ann Curthoys, 'Mythologies', in Richard Nile (ed.), *The Australian Legend and its Discontents*, University of Queensland Press, 2000. See also Henry Reynolds, *The Breaking of the Great Australian Silence*, Trevor Reese Memorial Lecture 1984, Australian Studies Centre, London; Ann McGrath (ed.), *Contested Ground*, Allen & Unwin, Sydney, 1995.

24 Ann McGrath, 'History', in Sylvia Kleinert & Margo Neale (eds), *The Oxford Companion to Aboriginal Art and Culture*, Oxford University Press, Melbourne, 2000, p. 604.

25 Mark McKenna, *Looking for Blackfellas' Point: An Australian history of place*, UNSW Press, Sydney, 2002.

26 McKenna, *Looking for Blackfellas' Point*, p. 68.

27 Meaghan Morris, *Identity Anecdotes: Translation and mass culture*, Sage, London, 2006, p. 120.

28 Anna Haebich, *Broken Circles: Fragmenting indigenous families 1800–2000*, Fremantle Arts Centre Press, Perth, 2000.

29 For Blair, see S Thomas & M Crooke, *Harold*, ABC Television video recording, 1993. For Namatjira, see N Amadio (ed.), *Albert Namatjira: The life and work of an Australian painter*, Melbourne, 1986; J Hardy et al. (eds), *The Heritage of Namatjira*, Melbourne, 1992. For boxers and other sports stars, see Bret Harris, *The Proud Champions: Australian Aboriginal sporting heroes*, Little Hills Press, Sydney, 1989.

30 WEH Stanner, *After the Dreaming*, 1968.

31 Reynolds, *The Breaking of the Great Australian Silence*, p. 20.

32 Henry Reynolds, *Why Weren't We Told?: A personal search for the truth*

about our history, Penguin, Melbourne, 1999, p. 1.

33 See Bain Attwood, *Rights for Aborigines*, Allen & Unwin, Sydney, 2003, especially Part III 'Citizenship'.

34 John Hartley & Alan McKee, *The Indigenous Public Sphere: The reporting and reception of Aboriginal issues in the Australian media*, Oxford University Press, Oxford, 2000. See also John Hartley, 'Television, nation and indigenous media', *Television and New Media*, vol. 5, no. 1, 2004, pp. 7–25.

35 Morris, *Identity Anecdotes*, p. 107.

36 WEH Stanner, in Helen Sheils (ed.), *Australian Aboriginal Studies: A symposium of papers presented at the 1961 research conference*, WEH Stanner, Convenor and Chairman of the Conference, OUP, Melbourne, 1962, for the Australian Institute of Aboriginal Studies. Foreword by RG Menzies, p. xv.

37 Peter Howson, 'Death of symbolic reconciliation', *The Australian*, 26 November 2004.

38 See Patricia Karvelas, 'Convert saw light around the fire', *The Australian*, 13–14 October 2007, pp. 1 and 4.

39 Murray Goot & Tim Rowse, *Divided Nation: Indigenous affairs and the imagined public*, University of Melbourne Press, Melbourne, 2007.

40 Keith Windschuttle, *The Fabrication of Aboriginal History. Volume one: Van Diemen's Land 1803–1847*, 2nd rev. edn, Macleay Press, Sydney, 2003.

41 Neumann, 'Among historians', p. 177.

42 Windschuttle, *The Fabrication of Aboriginal History*, p. 3.

43 Windschuttle, *The Fabrication of Aboriginal History*, p. 377.

44 Neumann, 'Among historians', p. 181.

45 Neumann, 'Among historians', p. 182.

46 Leela Gandhi, *Postcolonial Theory: A critical introduction*, Allen & Unwin, Sydney 1998, p. 5.

47 Morrissey, 'Dancing with shadows', p. 70.

48 See, for example, Michele Grossman (ed.), *Blacklines: Contemporary critical writing by indigenous Australians*, Melbourne University Press, Melbourne, 2003; Moreton-Robinson, *Sovereign Subjects* (2007).

49 Morris, *Identity Anecdotes*, p. 111.

50 Thomas, *Possessions*, pp. 8–11.

51 Gandhi, *Postcolonial Theory*, p. 4.

52 Stephen Muecke, 'Lonely representations: Aboriginality and cultural studies', in Bain Attwood & John Arnold (eds), *Power, Knowledge and Aborigines*, La Trobe University Press, Melbourne, 1992, p. 43.

53 Quoted in Attwood, *Rights for Aborigines*, pp. 162–63.

54 Leonard Joel catalogue of 20 March 1970, p. 22.

2 Aborigines on television

1 Mungo MacCallum, *Mungo: The man who laughs*, Duffy & Snellgrove, Sydney, 2001, pp. 50–52. Earlier versions of this work were presented at the Settlers, Creoles, and the Re-Enactment of History Conference, Vanderbilt University, 11–12 November 2005 and the History of Australian Television Conference, University of Technology Sydney and the Powerhouse Museum, 8–10 December 2005. Thanks to Jonathan Lamb and Liz Jacka for those invitations. A shorter version of this chapter appeared in *Australian Cultural History*, 27, 2007, pp. 69–90. I thank AIATSIS for supplying me with a copy

of *Alcheringa*, Wendy Borchers for generously passing on to me her earlier unpublished research on *Alcheringa* and John Murray and Betty Few for agreeing to be interviewed.

2   Germaine Greer, *Whitefella Jump Up: The shortest way to nationhood*, Quarterly Essays, 11, Black Inc., Melbourne, 2003, pp. 21–22.

3   Ann Curthoys, *Freedom Ride: A freedom rider remembers*, Allen & Unwin, Sydney, 2002. See especially chapter 10, 'Meaning and memory'.

4   Sally Morgan, *My Place*, Fremantle Arts Centre Press, Perth, 1987.

5   Vivien Johnson, *Clifford Possum Tjapaltjarri*, Art Gallery of South Australia, Adelaide, 2003, p. 47.

6   Mary & Elizabeth Durack, *The Way of the Whirlwind*, Angus & Robertson, Sydney, 1941.

7   James Hill, *Born Free*, Columbia Pictures, 1966.

8   The series is available from ABC Enterprises <http://www.abc.net.au/programsales/s1122598.htm> and from the Australian Institute of Aboriginal and Torres Strait Islander Studies. The term *alcheringa* is Aranda. In Baldwin Spencer & Frank Gillen, *Native Tribes of Central Australia*, Macmillan, London, 1899, the term is 'translated' as 'Dreamtime'. Any sense in which I might suggest a straightforward translation is complicated by the fact that the meaning attributed to the term is central to debates between Spencer and Gillen, on the one hand, and Carl and TGH Strehlow about 'dreamtime' as an Aranda concept. Carl Strehlow writes, for example, 'The word "*alcheringa*", which according to Spencer and Gillen is supposed to mean "dreamtime" is obviously a corruption of *altjirrinja*. The natives know nothing of "dreamtime" as a designation of a certain period of their history.' Quoted in Barry Hill, *Broken Song: T.G.H. Strehlow and Aboriginal possession*, Knopf, Sydney, 2002, p. 141. See also pp. 140–41, 164, 174–75, 388, 531 and 629, where Hill explores differing interpretations of *alcheringa* and related terms. More generally, see Patrick Wolfe, 'On being woken up: The Dreamtime in anthropology and in Australian settler culture', *Comparative Studies in Society and History*, vol. 33, no. 2 (Apr. 1991), pp. 197–224.

9   My memories of the film were probably consolidated by the fact that I also owned two of the three books that were spin-offs from the series: *The Boomerang Maker* and *The Stone-axe Maker*; the third book in the series was *The Fire Maker*. (Frank Few & Betty Few, *The Boomerang Maker*, Rigby, Adelaide, 1963; Frank Few & Betty Few, *The Stone-axe Maker*, Rigby, Adelaide, 1966; and Frank Few & Betty Few, *The Fire Maker*, Rigby, Adelaide, 1969.) Each of these books tells the story of a father making things through a relatively simple narrative on the verso pages, accompanied by very beautiful black-and-white photographs.

10   There are two further characters who make an appearance: a member of another tribe who the father figure meets very briefly in 'Trading' (episode 2) and an older man who is both a comic figure and an instructor in hunting expeditions (episodes 4, 7, 8 and 9).

11   Episode 2.

12   Stephen Atkinson, 'A rumble in the great Australian silence: *Whiplash* and the telling of the Australian frontier', *ACH: The Journal of the History of Culture in Australia*, vol. 26, 2007, pp. 37–57.

13   Marianna Torgovnick, *Gone Primitive: Savage intellects and modern lives*, University of Chicago Press, Chicago, 1990, p. 9.

14   Johannes Fabian, *Time and the Other: How anthropology makes its object*, Columbia University Press, New York, 1983.

15 Episodes 2, 5 and 7.

16 It is interesting that this filmic tradition seems to draw on conventions in 19th-century painting, that can be seen in the work of artists such as William Barak. See *Remembering Barak*, [Exhibition catalogue], National Gallery of Victoria, Melbourne, 2003.

17 For Eugène von Guérard, see Nicholas Thomas, *Possessions: Indigenous art/colonial culture*, Thames & Hudson, London, 1999, pp. 71–87. On the complex question of Aboriginal 'presence' in Namatjira, see Alison French, *Seeing the Centre: The art of Albert Namatjira 1902–1959*, National Gallery of Australia, Canberra, 2002.

18 Interview with John B Murray, 4 May 2004, Melbourne.

19 Torgovnick, *Gone Primitive*, p. 20.

20 Betty Few is adamant that it was a program made for children. Interview with Betty Few, 29 June 2004, Melbourne.

21 Similarly, *The Boomerang Maker* begins: 'Kirri and his sister Jeenga lived in eastern Australia. One day when they were walking through the bush, their father, Nambruk, decided it was time to teach Kirri how to make a boomerang and how to throw it.' (n.p.).

22 Atkinson, 'A rumble in the great Australian silence'.

23 *Shorter Oxford English Dictionary on Historical Principles*, Oxford University Press, Oxford, 2002, vol. 1.

24 Dipesh Chakrabarty, *Provincializing Europe: Postcolonial thought and historical difference*, Princeton University Press, Princeton, 2000, p. 28.

25 Chakrabarty, *Provincializing Europe*, p. 8.

26 Chakrabarty, *Provincializing Europe*, p. 238.

27 Chakrabarty, *Provincializing Europe*, p. 238.

28 Chakrabarty, *Provincializing Europe*, p. 254.

29 Chakrabarty, *Provincializing Europe*, p. 11.

30 Stephen Muecke, *Ancient & Modern: Time, culture and indigenous philosophy*, UNSW Press, Sydney, 2004.

31 Murray interview, 2004.

32 Few interview, 2004.

33 Murray interview, 2004.

34 Entry for Onus, Bill (William) Townsend (1906–68), in Sylvia Kleinert & Margo Neale (eds), *The Oxford Companion to Aboriginal Art and Culture*, Oxford University Press, Melbourne, 2000.

35 Murray interview, 2004.

36 Lake Tyers was established as a Church of England mission in 1861. In 1908, it became a Government Station under the control of the Board for the Protection of Aborigines and then, from 1957 until 1969 under the Aborigines Welfare Board. Originally 'home' to Kurnai people, other Aboriginal people from across the state were moved to Lake Tyers over a long period as other stations, such as those at Lake Condah and Coranderrk, were closed following the *Aborigines Protection Law Amendment Act 1886*. In Haebich's judgment, 'The 1886 Act set out to sweep Aboriginal identity away with the stroke of a pen and to negate the government's special responsibilities to its indigenous people'. Anna Haebich, *Broken Circles: Fragmenting indigenous families 1800–2000*, Fremantle Arts Centre Press, Perth, 2000, p. 166. While the results were extremely destructive, Aboriginal families and communities survived at Lake Tyers, and at many other sites of former stations across the state, in fringe and town camps, and in the larger cities where their Aboriginality was officially denied but often assiduously policed. In 1971, the Victorian Government

returned Lake Tyers Reserve, including 4000 acres, to the local Koorie community under the *Aboriginal Lands Act (1970)*.
37 Haebich, *Broken Circles*, pp. 498–99.
38 Haebich, *Broken Circles*, p. 500.
39 See the ABC Radio series, 'Mission Voices', available from: <http://www.abc. net.au/missionvoices/lake_tyers/default.htm>.
40 Murray interview, 2004.
41 Murray interview, 2004.
42 Murray interview, 2004.
43 *Gippsland Times*, 17 March 1961.
44 David Batty & Francis Jupurrula Kelly, *Bush Mechanics: The series*, Film Australia and Warlpiri Media Association, 2001. See also <http://www. bushmechanics.com>. Kelly was Eric Michaels's collaborator and the subject of his book, *For a Cultural Future: Francis Jupurrurla makes TV at Yuendumu*, Arts & Criticism Monography Series, vol. 3, Artspace, Sydney, 1987.
45 For a brief overview, see Ken Gelder, 'Aborigines and cars', in Kleinart & Neale, *Aboriginal Art and Culture*, pp. 447–53.
46 In his discussion of ethnographic film, Peter Sutton has argued that it's naive to think that 'doing ethnographic films is a one-way exploitation by the film-maker of Aboriginal film objects.' He insists, 'In a great many cases, film is being actively used.' Peter Sutton, 'Some observations on Aboriginal use of filming at Cape Keerweer', a paper presented at the Ethnographic Film Conference, AIAS [AIATSIS], 1977.
47 <http://www.bushmechanics.com>.

3   Old and new Aboriginal art

1 Phillip Adams, 'The art of saying sorry', *The Weekend Australian Magazine*, 3–4 April 2004, p. 11. An early version of this paper was presented at the University of Auckland in 2006. Thanks to Alex Calder for the kind invitation to present.
2 Jon Altman, 'Brokering Aboriginal art: A critical perspective on marketing, institutions, and the state', Kenneth Myer Lecture in Arts and Entertainment Management, Deakin University, Melbourne, 2005, p. 8, estimates the size of the market in these terms: 'In 1980 it was estimated to be worth $2.5 million (Pascoe 1981); in 1987–88, $18.5 million (Altman 1989); and most recently somewhere around $100 million per annum (Altman 2003)'.
3 Vivien Johnson, '8.5 Desert art', in Kleinert & Neale, *Aboriginal Art and Culture*, p. 214.
4 Fred R Myers, *Painting Culture: The making of an Aboriginal high art*, Duke University Press, Durham, 2002, p. 342. It's worth being clear that it's not my intention here to assess this work as art – I'm no art critic – nor judge its cultural significance for indigenous people, a project that would, at the very least, need to consider the economic and cultural impacts on the creative communities, how that art represents different local communities to each other and how the use of that art has placed indigenous people differently in relation to the nation.
5 Paul Carter, 'Introduction: The interpretation of dreams', in Geoffrey Bardon & James Bardon, *Papunya: A place made after the story: The beginnings of the Western Desert Painting Movement*, The Miegunyah Press, Melbourne, 2004, p. xiv.

6   Dennis Dugan, review in *Herald*, 20 January 1968.

7   Howard Morphy, *Aboriginal Art*, Phaidon, London, 1998, pp. 282–83.

8   Fred Myers, *Pintupi Country, Pintupi Self: Sentiment, place, and politics among Western Desert Aborigines*, Smithsonian Institution Press, Washington, 1986, pp. 40–44. It's important to note in passing that the Pintupi efforts to establish separate communities begin in 1968 at Waruwiya; that is, before the invention of painting at Papunya.

9   Fred Myers, 'We are not alone: Anthropology in a world of others', *Ethnos*, vol. 71, no. 2, June 2006, p. 254.

10 Ian Gerard, 'Six months after picking up a brush, Sally, 83, a top seller', *The Australian*, 5 September 2005, p. 6. This story is about Sally Gabori, who is identified as a Kayardild and Kaiadilt woman living on Mornington Island. She is described as both having 'gone from being a no one to an established artist in less than six months' and, paradoxically, as having been a 'weaver for most of her life'.

11 Bardon, *Papunya: A place made after the story*, p. xxiii.

12 Geoffrey Bardon, *Art Report* to the Australia Council, Sydney, 1972.

13 Geoffrey Bardon, *Aboriginal Art of the Western Desert*, Rigby, Adelaide, 1979; Geoffrey Bardon, *Papunya Tula: Art of the Western Desert*, McPhee Gribble, Melbourne, 1991.

14 See Bardon, *Papunya: A place made after the story* for an extensive bibliography.

15 See James Bardon's comments at the launch of the book; 'Speech at Bonham and Goodman Art Gallery – 17/11/04 for the launch of *Papunya: A place made after the story*', unpublished.

16 Hetti Perkins & Hannah Fink (eds), *Papunya Tula: Genesis and genius*, The Art Gallery of New South Wales, Sydney, 2000, p. 174.

17 Bardon, *Papunya: A place made after the story* p. 3.

18 Bardon, *Papunya: A place made after the story*, p. 16.

19 Bardon, *Papunya: A place made after the story*, p. 3. Bardon writes that he applied to work at Papunya after teaching in the Tennant Creek Area School because 'working with tribal Aboriginals had a real interest for me'.

20 Bardon, *Papunya: A place made after the story*, p. 8.

21 Bardon, *Papunya: A place made after the story*, p. 3.

22 Bardon, *Papunya: A place made after the story*, p. 5.

23 Bardon, *Papunya: A place made after the story*, pp. 140–46.

24 Bardon, *Papunya: A place made after the story* p. xvii.

25 Bardon, *Papunya: A place made after the story*, Dedication, below which is printed: 'Given to the innocent that which is their due.'

26 Bardon, *Papunya: A place made after the story*, p. xv.

27 Bardon, *Papunya: A place made after the story*, p. xxii.

28 Perkins & Fink, *Papunya Tula: Genesis and genius*, p. 247.

29 See, for example, the differentiations he makes in relation to different historical experiences: 'The Aranda at Papunya were few, the merest human residue of that tribal group from the Central Macdonnell Ranges … and they were not during my time a tribal group as such for they had no tribal lands or place of affirmation and were I suppose, lost … the Anmatjira Aranda … had a very strong tribal knowledge and interest, although they had for a long time been connected with cattle stations.' Bardon, *Papunya: A place made after the story*, p. 7.

30 Bardon, *Papunya: A place made after the story*, p. 82.

31 Vivien Johnson, *Clifford Possum Tjapaltjarri*, Art Gallery of South Australia,

Adelaide, 2003, p. 54.

32 Fred Myers, cited in Johnson, *Clifford Possum*, p. 50.

33 Johnson, *Clifford Possum*, p. 53. *Galgardi*, a 'pre-Bardon' work of Kaapa was entered into the Caltex Art Award in August 1971 by Jack Cooke, District Welfare Officer from the Northern Territory Welfare Branch, who had seen Kaapa's paintings in the Papunya canteen.

34 She argues, Johnson, *Clifford Possum*, p. 53, that there are structural similarities between the work of the second generation of Hermannsburg painters and what came into existence at Papunya: 'Their experimentation with effects of simplification, schematisation and repetition were dismissed as formulaic by watercolour landscape enthusiasts of their day, but have since been hailed as a daring counter-appropriation of the traditions of European landscape painting to their own expressive ends. The Papunya painters employed their same strategies in the invention of the painting language of Western Desert art. In some ways, these second-generation Hermannsburg artists portrayed their totemic landscape just as starkly as later generations of Papunya painters would theirs. In the meantime, the works of the "School of Kaapa", depicting actual ceremonial performances in which the artists' connections to country and Dreaming were celebrated, were taking Central Australian Aboriginal art into wholly new ground.'

35 Johnson, *Clifford Possum*, p. 52.

36 Johnson, *Clifford Possum*, p. 53.

37 Bardon, *Papunya: A place made after the story*, p. 147.

38 Roman Black, *Old and New Australian Aboriginal Art*, Angus & Robertson, Sydney, 1964.

39 Examples are drawn from all states, except Tasmania and from the Northern Territory. Nor is this art given short shrift; it's carefully located and discussed over 100 pages featuring 95 illustrations.

40 Black, *Old and New Australian Aboriginal Art*, pp. 4–5.

41 This was the response of Margaret Preston to one of Black's works that he showed her. Black, *Old and New Australian Aboriginal Art*.

42 Richard Bell, <http://www.kooriweb.org/foley/great/art/bell.html>.

43 Nicholas Thomas, *Possessions: Indigenous art/colonial culture*, Thames & Hudson, London, 1999.

44 Thomas, *Possessions*, pp. 93 and 92.

45 Thomas, *Possessions*, p. 96.

46 Spencer, quoted in Thomas, *Possessions*, p. 115.

47 See John Mulvaney on McCarthy in *Records of the Australian Museum*, May, 1993, Sup. 17, pp. 17–23.

48 Thirty years later, Geoffrey Bardon, with Tim Leura Tjapaltjarri, exhibited paintings by Papunya artists in David Jones's George St store in 1972; see Hetti Perkins & Margie West, *One Sun, One Moon: Aboriginal art in Australia*, Art Gallery of New South Wales, Sydney, 2007, p. 336.

49 Jennifer Isaacs, 'Indigenous designs on Australia' in *Art and Australia*, vol. 37, no. 1, 1999, p. 71.

50 Thomas, *Possessions*, p. 109.

51 Thomas, *Possessions*, p. 110.

52 Robert Hughes, 'Iron and bark', *Nation*, 10 September 1960.

53 Thomas, *Possessions*, p. 110.

54 The dominant attitude to this is described in Judith O'Callaghan, *The Australian Dream: Design in the fifties*, Powerhouse Publishing, Sydney, 1993; 'In the fifties there was a tension between the sophistication and

skill of craftspeople, their numbers having been boosted by migration from Europe, and the amateurism and commercialism of the souvenir trade. Both extremes ransacked Aboriginal cultures for motifs, elite culture in works such as John Antill's ballet *Corroboree*, popular culture in tea-towels and garden ornaments.', p. 23.

55 See, for example, Margaret Lawrence, 'Aboriginal art has inspired Australian design', *South West Pacific*, no. 18, 1948, pp. 46–50.

56 Robin Boyd, cited in Geoffrey Serle, *Robin Boyd: A life*, Miegunyah Press, Melbourne, 1995, p. 136.

57 Thomas, *Possessions*, p. 125.

58 Thomas, *Possessions*, p. 140.

59 Thomas, *Possessions*, p. 143.

60 Carolyn Lovitt, 'Aboriginal art as décor: The politics of assimilation in white Australian homes 1930–1970', MA thesis, University of Melbourne, Dept of Fine Arts, 2001, p. 3.

61 Frederick McCarthy (1939), p. 62; quoted in Lovitt, 'Aboriginal art as décor', p. 20.

62 Lovitt, 'Aboriginal art as décor', p. 2.

63 Lovitt, 'Aboriginal art as décor', p. 25.

64 Lovitt, 'Aboriginal art as décor', p. 39.

65 Lovitt, 'Aboriginal art as décor', p. 63.

66 Anna Haebich, 'Assimilation and hybrid art: Reflections on the politics of Aboriginal art', in Fiona Foley (ed.), *The Art of Politics. The Politics of Art: The place of indigenous contemporary art*, Keeaira Press, Queensland, 2006, pp. 52–53.

67 Beth Dean & Victor Carell (1955), quoted in Haebich, 'Assimilation and hybrid art', p. 54.

68 Haebich, 'Assimilation and hybrid art', p. 55.

69 Haebich, 'Assimilation and hybrid art', p. 55. On copyright more generally, see Vivien Johnson, *Copyrites: Aboriginal art in the age of reproductive technologies*, National Indigenous Arts Advocacy Association and Macquarie University, Sydney, 1996; see also Vivien Johnson, 'Cultural brokerage: Commodification and intellectual copyright', in Kleinert & Neale, *Aboriginal Art and Culture*, pp. 471–81.

70 Haebich, 'Assimilation and hybrid art', p. 54.

71 Haebich, 'Assimilation and hybrid art', p. 55.

72 Haebich, 'Assimilation and hybrid art', p. 56.

73 Lovitt, 'Aboriginal art as décor', p. 14.

74 In a sense, this is exactly how some of the costumes from *Corroboree* and a sample of other examples of Abo art are exhibited at the National Museum of Australia, as the last display in the 'Nation' gallery before the visitor enters the Gallery of First Australians.

75 Bardon, *Papunya: A place made after the story*, p. 10.

76 Perkins & Fink, *Papunya Tula: Genesis and genius*, p. 256.

77 *Destiny Deacon: Walk & don't look blak*, exhibition catalogue, Museum of Contemporary Art, Sydney, 2004, p. 110. The subtitle of this section is borrowed from the title of a show by Destiny Deacon.

78 Barry Humphries, *Barry Humphries' Treasury of Australian Kitsch*, Macmillan, Melbourne, 1980. The images are at pp. 35 and 89 respectively.

79 Lovitt, 'Aboriginal art as décor', p. 71.

80 Thanks to Phillip Jackson for the details of his soundtrack sources and to Lisa Bellair for a copy of an interview between Lisa Bellair and Ross Moore, *Not*

Another Koori Show, 4 November 1994, Radio 3CR (Melbourne).
81 Ian Anderson, 'Post-colonial Dreaming at the end of the whitefella's millennium', in Kleinert & Neale, *Aboriginal Art and Culture*, pp. 433–34.
82 Anderson, 'Post-colonial Dreaming', p. 427.
83 Jennifer Isaacs, *Spirit Country: Contemporary Australian Aboriginal art*, Hardie Grant, Melbourne, 1999, p. xi.

4   The spectre of heritage

1   Gillian Cowlishaw, *Blackfellas, Whitefellas, and the Hidden Injuries of Race*, Blackwell, 2004, p. 243. An earlier version of this chapter appeared as Chris Healy, '"Race portraits" and vernacular possibilities: Heritage and culture", in Tony Bennett & David Carter (eds), *Culture in Australia: Policies, publics and programs*, Cambridge University Press, Melbourne, 2001, pp. 278–98.
2   *Becoming an Australian citizen*, Commonwealth of Australia, 2007, p. 43.
3   *Becoming an Australian citizen*, pp. 1, 5, 7, 9, 11, 13.
4   Graeme Davison et al. (eds), *The Oxford Companion to Australian History*, Oxford University Press, Melbourne, 1998, p. 308.
5   Benedict Anderson, *Imagined Communities: Reflections on the origin and spread of nationalism*, rev. edn, Verso, London, 1991, p. 11.
6   Robert Hope, *The National Estate: Report of the Committee of Inquiry into the National Estate*, Australian Government Publishing Service, Canberra, 1974.
7   Cited in Davison, *The Oxford Companion to Australian History*, p. 308.
8   Robert Hewison, *The Heritage Industry: Britain in a climate of decline*, Methuen, London, 1987.
9   Meaghan Morris & Ian McCalman, 'Public culture', in *Knowing Ourselves and Others: The Humanities into the 21st century*, vol. 3, *Reflective Essays*, Department of Employment Education, Training and Youth Affairs, Canberra, 1998, p. 7.
10 Elizabeth Jelin, *State Repression and the Labors of Memory*, trans. Judy Rein & Marial Godoy-Anativia, University of Minnesota Press, Minneapolis, 2003, p. 10.
11 Jelin, *State Repression and the Labors of Memory*, p. 23.
12 *Becoming an Australian citizen*, pp. 8–33.
13 *Becoming an Australian citizen*, p. 33.
14 Tim Rowse, *Indigenous Futures: Choice and development for Aboriginal and Islander Australia*, UNSW Press, Sydney, 2002.
15 See David Goodman, 'Postscript 1991 – explicating openness', in Tony Bennett et al. (eds), *Celebrating the Nation: A critical study of Australia's Bicentenary*, Allen & Unwin, Sydney, 1992, p. 193.
16 John Howard, *Future Directions*, Liberal Party of Australia, Melbourne, 1988, p. 7.
17 See Graeme Davison, *The Uses and Abuse of Australian History*, Allen & Unwin, Sydney, 2000.
18 See generally Susan Janson & Stuart Macintyre (eds), *Making the Bicentenary*, a special issue of *Australian Historical Studies*, vol. 23, no. 91; Bennett, *Celebrating the Nation*.
19 David Burchell, 'The Bicentennial dilemma', *Australian Society*, 6, 1987, p. 22.
20 Peter Cochrane & David Goodman, 'The Great Australian Journey: Cultural logic and nationalism in the postmodern era', in Janson & Macintyre, *Making*

the Bicentenary, p. 33.

21 Quotations from Cochrane & Goodman, 'The Great Australian Journey', p. 33 and Goodman, 'Postscript 1991 – explicating openness', p. 198.

22 John Murphy, 'Conscripting the past: The Bicentenary and everyday life', in Janson & Macintyre, Making the Bicentenary, p. 54.

23 Meaghan Morris, 'Panorama: The live, the dead and the living', in Paul Foss (ed.), Islands in the Stream: Myths of place in Australian culture, Pluto Press, Sydney, 1988, pp. 160–87.

24 Meaghan Morris, Too Soon Too Late: History in popular culture, Indiana University Press, Minneapolis, 1998, p. 12.

25 Morris, 'Panorama', p. 181.

26 Morris, 'Panorama', p. 181.

27 Richard White, Inventing Australia: Images and identities 1688–1980, Allen & Unwin, Sydney, 1981.

28 Richard White, 'Inventing Australia revisited', in Wayne Hudson & Geoffrey Bolton (eds), Creating Australia: Changing Australian history, Allen & Unwin, Sydney, 1997, p. 15.

29 See Bennett, Celebrating the Nation and David Carter, 'Future pasts', in David Headon et. al. (eds), The Abundant Culture: Meaning and significance in everyday Australia, Allen & Unwin, Sydney, 1994, pp. 3–15.

30 See Bain Attwood, Rights for Aborigines, Allen & Unwin, Sydney, 2003, especially chapter 3 'A memorial of death' and pp. 335–39.

31 Terry Smith, 'Public art between cultures: The "Aboriginal Memorial", Aboriginality and nationality in Australia', Critical Inquiry, vol. 27, no. 4, Summer 2001, p. 636.

32 Michael Taussig, Defacement: Public secrecy and the labor of the negative, Stanford University Press, Stanford, 1999.

33 An Aboriginal Petition to the King, 1937.

34 Royal Commission into Aboriginal Deaths in Custody, National Report Overview and Recommendations (Commissioner Elliott Johnston), Australian Government Publishing Service, Canberra, 1991, p. 7.

35 I'm borrowing this sense of stories and listening from John Frow, 'The politics of stolen time', Australian Humanities Review, February, 1998; 'Listening is a form of ethical responsiveness which recognizes a duty to the story of the other'. <http://www.lib.latrobe.edu.au/AHR/archive/Issue-February-1998/frow2. html>.

36 Richard Bartlett, The Mabo decision, and the full text of the decision in Mabo and others v State of Queensland, Butterworths, Sydney, 1993, p. 42.

37 Council for Aboriginal Reconciliation, Making Things Right: Reconciliation after the High Court's decision on native title, Council for Aboriginal Reconciliation, Canberra, 1993, p. 7.

38 Royal Commission into Aboriginal Deaths in Custody, National Report Overview, pp. 9–10.

39 Royal Commission into Aboriginal Deaths in Custody, National Report Overview, p. 11.

40 Henry Reynolds, 'After Mabo, what about Aboriginal sovereignty?', Australian Humanities Review, 1, April 1996. <http://www.lib.latrobe.edu.au/AHR/ archive/Issue- April-1996/Reynolds.html>.

41 Katrina Alford, 'White-washing away native title rights: The Yorta Yorta land claim', Arena, 13, 1999, pp. 67–83.

42 Fiona Paisley, 'Race and remembrance: Contesting Aboriginal child removal in the inter-war years', Australian Humanities Review, November, 1997. <http://

www.lib.latrobe.edu.au/AHR/archive/Issue-November-1997/paisley.html>.

43 Bringing Them Home: Report of the National Inquiry into the Separation of Aboriginal and Torres Strait Islander Children from the Families, Human Rights and Equal Opportunity Commission, Sydney, 1997, p. 3.

44 Frow, 'The politics of stolen time'.

45 Philip Morrissey, 'Aboriginal children', *Australian Humanities Review*, August 2007 <http://www.lib.latrobe.edu.au/AHR/archive/Issue-August-September%202007/Morrissey.html>, notes something similar when he writes that he, 'has the feeling when reading some of the transcripts of testimonies of members of the Stolen Generation that under the words there are hardly any memories'.

46 Grayson Cooke, 'Let's We Forget: Responsibility and the Archive Under Howard', Refereed Proceedings of UNAUSTRALIA: The Cultural Studies Association of Australasia's Annual Conference, December 2006 <http: unaustralia.com/proceedings.php>.

47 Judith Brett, 'Why Howard can't say sorry', *Arena Magazine*, 50, Dec. 2000–Jan. 2001, p. 39.

48 Cooke,' 'Let's We Forget'.

49 Paul Patton, 'Justice and difference: The Mabo Case', in Paul Patton & Diane Austin-Broos (eds), *Transformations in Australian Society*, Research Institute for Humanities and Social Sciences, University of Sydney, 1997, p. 88.

50 Reynolds, 'After Mabo'.

51 Cited in Patton, 'Justice and difference', p. 84.

52 Nicos Poulantzas, *State, Power and Socialism*, Verso, London, 1980, p. 114.

53 Richard Mulgan, 'Citizenship and legitimacy in post-colonial Australia', in Nicolas Peterson & Will Sanders (eds), *Citizenship and Indigenous Australians: Changing conceptions and possibilities*, Cambridge University Press, Melbourne, 1998, p. 185.

54 Ann Curthoys & Stephen Muecke, 'Australia for example', in Wayne Hudson & David Carter (eds), *The Republican Debate*, UNSW Press, Sydney, 1993, p. 190.

55 Morris, *Too Soon Too Late*, p. 182.

56 Don Watson, 'Birth of a post-modern nation', *Weekend Australian*, 24–25 July, 1993, p. 21.

57 Sean Brawley, '"A comfortable and relaxed past": John Howard and the "Battle of History", *Electronic Journal of Australian and New Zealand History*, 1997 <http://www.jcu.edu.au/aff/history/articles/brawley.htm>.

58 Geoffrey Bolton, 1994, 'Beating up Keating: British media and the republic', in Don Grant & Graham Seal (eds), *Australia in the World: Perceptions and possibilities*, Black Swan Press, Perth, 1994, p. 149.

59 Morris, *Too Soon Too Late*, p. 222.

60 John Howard, 'Sir Robert Menzies Lecture, 18 November 1996', reported in *The Australian*, 19 November 1996.

61 Tony Birch, '"Black armbands and white veils": John Howard's moral amnesia', *Melbourne Historical Journal*, 25, 1997, pp. 8–16, and Geoffrey Gray & Christine Winter (eds), *The Resurgence of Racism*, Monash Publications in History 24, Department of History, Monash University, Melbourne, 1997.

62 Janet McCalman, 'Two Nations arise to threaten a peaceful land', *The Age*, 10 June 1998.

63 McCalman, 'Two Nations'.

64 Janet McCalman, 'In the heartland of the poor, One Nation still fails to appeal', *Age*, 24 June 1998.

65 McCalman, 'In the heartland of the poor'.

66 Bartlett, *The Mabo Decision*, p. 50.

67 Ranajit Guha, 'The authority of vernacular pasts', *Meanjin*, vol. 51, no. 2, 1992, pp. 299–302.

68 Louis Mink, *Historical Understanding*, Cornell University Press, Ithaca, 1987.

69 Guha, 'The authority of vernacular pasts'.

70 Richard Rorty, *Achieving Our Country: Leftist thought in twentieth-century America*, Harvard University Press, Cambridge, Mass., 1998, p. 121, quoted in Robert Kenny, *The Lamb Enters the Dreaming: Nathanael Pepper and the ruptured world*, Scribe, Melbourne, 2007.

71 Kenny, *The Lamb Enters the Dreaming*, p. 166. See also pp. 77–78.

72 Kenny, *The Lamb Enters the Dreaming*, pp. 173–92 and p. 199.

73 Kenny, *The Lamb Enters the Dreaming*, p. 214.

74 Patton, 'Justice and difference', p. 95.

75 Frow, 'The politics of stolen time'.

76 Noel Pearson, 'The concept of Native Title at Common Law', *Australian Humanities Review*, 1996 <http://www.lib.latrobe.edu.au/AHR/archive/Issue-March-1997/pearson.html>.

77 See Peter Read, *Belonging: Australians, place and Aboriginal ownership*, Cambridge University Press, Melbourne, 2000.

78 John Howard, cited in Tony Birch, '"Black armbands and white veils"', p. 9.

5   Objects and the museum

1 Nicholas Rothwell, 'Beyond the Frontier', Exhibition text for 'Beyond the Frontier – Jirrawun Arts' (April 2005), <http://www.shermangalleries.com.au/artists/inartists/mixed.asp?exhibition=92>.
   Some of the work in this chapter has appeared in Chris Healy, 'Chained to their signs: Remembering breastplates', in Barbara Creed & Jeanette Hoorn (eds), *Body Trade: Captivity, cannibalism and colonialism in the Pacific*, Pluto Press, Routledge in association with Pluto Press and University of Otago Press, 2001, pp. 24–35 and Chris Healy, 'Very special black people: Indigenous people and the museum', in Chris Healy & Andrea Witcomb (eds), *New South Pacific Museums: Experiments in culture*, Monash University ePress, Melbourne, 2006, pp. 16.1–16.10.

2 See Donna McAlear, 'Repatriation and cultural politics: Australian and Canadian museum responses to first peoples challenges for cultural property ownership', PhD thesis, Griffith University, 1999.

3 Shelley Ruth Butler, *Contested Representations: Revisiting into the heart of Africa*, Gordon & Breach, Amsterdam, 1999; William Fitzhugh, 'Ambassadors in sealskins: Exhibiting Eskimos at the Smithsonian', in Amy Henderson & Adrienne Kaeppler (eds), *Exhibiting Dilemmas: Issues of representation at the Smithsonian*, Smithsonian Institution Press, Washington, 1997.

4 Bernard Cohen, *Colonialism and its forms of knowledge: The British in India*, Princeton University Press, Princeton, 1996.

5 Strong examples of such work can be found in the early and influential Peter Vergo (ed.), *The New Museology*, Reaktion Books, London, 1989 and Timothy Luke, *Museum Politics: Power plays at the exhibition*, University of Minnesota Press, Minneapolis, 2002.

6 For a succinct account, see Tony Bennett, 'Civic laboratories: Museums, cultural objecthood and the governance of the social', in Healy & Witcomb,

South Pacific Museums, pp. 8.12–8.13.

7   See, for example, those exhibited in the show 'Rusty Peters: Longfella Standing Up', William Mora Galleries in association with Jirrawun Arts, 23 June–17 July 2004.

8   Victoria Lynn, 'Parallel lives', in *Tarrawarra Biennial 2006. Parallel Lives: Australian painting today* (exhibition catalogue), Tarrawarra Museum of Art, Healesville, 2006, p. 7.

9   Rusty Peters in conversation with Frances Kofod <http://www.shermangalleries. com.au/artists/inartists/mixed.asp?exhibition=92>.

10 Jennifer Loureide Biddle, *Breasts, Bodies, Canvas: Central Desert art as experience*, UNSW Press, Sydney, 2007, p. 12. Here I'm drawing on the strong consensus that seems to now be emerging in serious scholars of indigenous art that a model of painting as representation does not adequately account for some indigenous image-making. For example, Christine Watson writes, 'I choose to use the word "present" rather than "represent", as in the Kutjungka view, the icons and indices in their works do more than represent the objects and beings to which they refer: as empowered traces of the being which made them, they index and contain the continuing presence of the Ancestors within the earth.' Christine Watson, *Piercing the Ground: Balgo Women's image making and relationship to country*, Fremantle Arts Centre Press, Fremantle, 2003, p. 29.

11 Peters, in conversation with Frances Kofod.

12 See RHW Reece, 'Feasts and blankets: The history of some early attempts to establish relations with the Aborigines of New South Wales, 1814–1846', *Archaeology and Physical Anthropology in Oceania*, 1, 1967, pp. 190–205; Malcolm Henry Ellis, *Lachlan Macquarie: His life, adventures and times*, Angus & Robertson, Sydney, 1973.

13 Tania Cleary, *Poignant Regalia: 19th century Aboriginal breastplates and images*, The Historic Houses Trust of New South Wales, Sydney, 1993, p. 7, 'The breastplates included in the exhibition reveal the following divisions: 15.2% Chiefs, 57.7% Kings, 4.3% Queens, 3.8% Royal Couples, 2.2% Royalty, 5.4% Rewards, 4.8% In Recognition of Service and 6.5% Unspecified Recognition. These groupings would be broadly representative of the entire range of extant breastplates'. The other major account of breastplates is Jakelin Troy, *King Plates: A history of Aboriginal gorgets*, Aboriginal Studies Press, Canberra, 1993.

14 John Hillcoat, *The Proposition*, Autonomous, 2005.

15 Cleary, *Poignant Regalia*, p. 11.

16 Philip Jones, *Ochre and Rust: Artefacts and encounters on Australian frontiers*, Wakefield Press, Adelaide, 2007, contains some very rich studies of such objects.

17 James Clifford, 'Indigenous articulations', *The Contemporary Pacific*, vol. 13, no. 2, 2001, pp. 468–90.

18 Cleary, *Poignant Regalia*, p. 7.

19 Carolyn Webb, 'Chance find uncovers rare piece of history', *The Age* 10 February 2007.

20 Press release from Hon Jay Weatherill MP, 23 April 2007 <http://www. ministers.sa.gov.au/news 28 April 2007>.

21 Weatherill press release, 23 April 2007.

22 John Frow, *Time and Commodity Culture: Essays on cultural theory and postmodernity*, Oxford University Press, Oxford, 1997, pp. 102–32.

23 'Perhaps the most famous of such photographs is "Native Prisoners in Chains" by Frances Birtles which appeared in *The Lone Hand*, 1 March 1911.' It was

an image like this that appeared on the cover of the Penguin edition of Charles Rowley's *The Destruction of Aboriginal Society* in 1972.

24 Cleary, *Poignant Regalia*, p. 14.

25 Cleary, *Poignant Regalia*, p. 17.

26 Carl Lumholtz, *Among Cannibals: An account of four years travels in Australia, and of camp life with the Aborigines of Queensland*, John Murray, London, 1889, pp. 362–63, cited in Troy, *King Plates*, p. 24.

27 Cleary, *Poignant Regalia*, p. 11.

28 Cleary, *Poignant Regalia*, p. 11. A similar point about 'inappropriate Kings' not being respected by Aboriginal people is made in Jimmie Barker, *The Two Worlds of Jimmie Barker: The life of an Australian Aboriginal 1900–1972*, Australian Institute of Aboriginal Studies, Canberra, 1980, cited in Troy, *King Plates*, pp. 41–42, where Troy also argues that changing Aboriginal responses to breastplates is a reflection of changing Aboriginal social relationships under pressure from colonialism.

29 Cleary, *Poignant Regalia*, p. 44.

30 Cleary, *Poignant Regalia*, p. 37.

31 Cleary, *Poignant Regalia*, p. 35.

32 See letter of E Reid to E Milne, 13 October 1911, which reads in part, 'she [Hopping Molly] died some five or six years later and was buried on the sea shore…Some years afterward…I was informed that there were some human bones on the beach, and upon investigation, I found the skeleton of "Hopping Molly"…the identification rested upon the old residents of the place, who upon being shown the thigh and shin bone…declared it to be the leg of Hopping Molly, the knee joint having become completely ossified, which caused her to hop, and from which she derived her name…This was one of the best curios I ever saw…I finally decided to give it to [Dr Forbes who very much coveted the same]…a matter I have very much regretted ever since, as I should have never separated it from the plate [that of 'Billy Kelly King of Broadwater' the husband of 'Hopping Molly']', Cleary, *Poignant Regalia*, p. 76.

33 Cleary, *Poignant Regalia*, p. 15.

34 Cleary, *Poignant Regalia*, p. 17.

35 The expression comes from Paul Behrendt in Cleary, *Poignant Regalia*, p. 19.

36 For an analysis of comparable objects which takes its analysis in productive directions, see Rodney Harrison, '"The Magical Virtue of these Sharp Things": Colonialism, mimesis and knapped bottle glass artefacts in Australia', *Journal of Material Culture*, vol. 8, no. 3, pp. 311–36.

37 Cited in Cleary, *Poignant Regalia*, p. 107.

38 For a thoughtful discussion of such humour which draws on Greg Dening's notion that this kind of theatre expresses a 'hegemony of laughter', see Jane Lydon, *Eye Contact: Photographing indigenous Australians*, Duke University Press, Durham, 2005, pp. 161–64.

39 Cleary's contention is that these 'badges of distinction' were 'an attempt at social control and domination'; see Cleary, *Poignant Regalia*, p. 9.

40 Ellis, *Lachlan Macquarie*, p. 355.

41 Cleary, *Poignant Regalia*, p. 9.

42 *National Times*, 7 March 1981.

43 Jacques Derrida, *Archive Fever: A Freudian impression*, trans. Eric Prenowitz, University of Chicago Press, Chicago, 1996, p. 17.

44 *Milton and Ulladulla Times*, 6 February 1906. See also National Museum of Australia, Breastplates File, 35/310 f.165. 'The breastplate was presented to Coomee by Edmund O Milne in 1909. He had first become acquainted with

'Coomee' about 1868 when a boy attending school at Ulladulla. In those days it was stated by her that she remembered her grandmother speaking of "the first time the white birds came by", an allusion to the sailing ships of Captain Cook or the First Fleet'.

45 See Russell McGregor, *Imagined Destinies: Aboriginal Australians and the Doomed Race Theory, 1880–1939*, Melbourne University Press, Melbourne, 1997.

46 Frederick McCarthy, 'Breast-plates: The blackfellows reward', *The Australian Museum Magazine*, 10, 1052, pp. 326–31.

47 National Museum of Australia: 1985.59.374 (A-ON-93).

48 Michael Taussig, *Memesis and Alterity: A particular history of the senses*, Routledge, New York, 1993, p. 237.

49 I've borrowed this sense of indigenous people in an 'open-air museum' from C Nadi Seremetakis, 'The memory of the senses: Historical perception, commensal exchange, and modernity', in Lucien Taylor (ed.), *Visualising Theory: Selected essays from V.A.R. 1990–1994*, Routledge, New York, 1994.

50 This passage is adapted from Chris Healy, *From the Ruins of Colonialism: History as social memory*, Cambridge University Press, Melbourne, 1997, pp. 94–95.

51 Gaye Sculthorpe, 'Exhibiting Indigenous histories in Australian museums', in *National Museums: Negotiating histories* (Conference proceedings), Daryl McIntyre & Kirsten Wehner (eds), National Library of Australia, Canberra, 2001, p. 74 notes: 'The current level of activity in developing exhibitions relating to Indigenous peoples across Australia is probably the highest ever in Australian museum history.' Sculthorpe lists these developments, including: the Australian Museum, new Indigenous Australians gallery in (April 1997); the Western Australian Museum, refurbished Aboriginal gallery (April 1999); the South Australian Museum, new Aboriginal gallery (March 2000); Museum Victoria, Bunjilaka, (July 2000); and the National Museum of Australia, the First Australians gallery (2001).

52 Sculthorpe, 'Exhibiting Indigenous histories' provides a detailed overview of these developments. See also Carol Scott, 'Australian museums and indigenous cultures now', in Steve Miller (ed.), *Our Place: Indigenous Australia now* (Australia's contribution to the cultural Olympiad of the Athens 2002 Olympic Games), Powerhouse, Sydney, 2004, pp. 103–106.

53 Eugenio Donato, 'The museum's furnace: Notes towards a contextual reading of *Bouvard and Pécuchet*, in Josue Harari (ed.), *Textual Strategies: Perspective in post-structuralist criticism*, Cornell University Press, Ithaca, 1979, p. 223.

54 Susan Stewart, *On Longing: Narratives of the miniature, the gigantic, the souvenir, the collection*, Duke University Press, Durham, 1993, p. 162.

55 Stewart, *On Longing*, p. 152.

56 John Morton, '"Such a man would find few races hostile": History, fiction and anthropological dialogue in the Melbourne Museum', *Arena Journal*, no. 22, 2004, p. 55.

57 Sculthorpe, 'Exhibiting Indigenous histories', p. 77.

58 Morton, '"Such a man would find few races hostile"', p. 57.

59 Lindy Allen, Bunjilaka: The Aboriginal Centre of the Melbourne Museum, Museum Victoria, Melbourne, 2000, p. 9.

60 Charles Jenks, 'Constructing a national identity', in Dimity Reed (ed.), *Tangled Destinies: National Museum of Australia*, Images Publishing, Melbourne, 2002, p. 69.

61 Richard Gillespie, 'Making an exhibition: One gallery, one thousand objects, one million critics', *Meanjin*, vol. 60, no. 4, 2001, p. 119.

62 Sculthorpe, 'Exhibiting Indigenous histories', p. 80.

63 James Volkert, Map and Guide. National Museum of the American Indian, Smithsonian Institution, Smithsonian Institution, Washington, 2004, p. 7.

64 See the figures cited in Dawn Casey, 'Culture wars: Museums, politics and controversy', *Open Museum Journal*, vol. 6, 2003, <http://amol.org.au/omj/abstract.asp?ID=25>.

65 Commonwealth of Australia, 2003 Review of the National Museum of Australia, its Exhibitions and Public Programs, a report to the Council of the National Museum of Australia, Commonwealth of Australia, Canberra <http://www.dcita.gov.au/Article/0,,0_1-2_2-4_113158,00.html>, p. 20; See also Chris Healy & Kylie Message, 'A symptomatic museum: The new, the NMA and the culture wars' Borderlands, Nov 2004 <http://www.borderlandsejournal. adelaide.edu.au/vol3no3_2004/messagehealy_symptom.htm>.

66 In addition to the references that follow, here I'm drawing particularly on Morton, '"Such a man would find few races hostile"' and a debate between Gaye Sculthorpe and Andrew Bolt, ABC Local Radio 3LO, 29 November 2000. Leo Schofield, 'Object lesson', *The Bulletin*, 122, 2004, p. 36 and Rob Foot, 'The grand narratives of the National Museum', *Quadrant*, March 2004, pp. 37–39.

67 The quotes belong, respectively to Andrew Bolt, 'Museum of spin', *Herald Sun*, 20 November 2000 and Philip Jones, 'Our hidden histories', *The Age*, 23 January 2002.

68 Bennett, 'Civic laboratories', p. 08.15.

69 Morton, '"Such a man would find few races hostile"'.

70 Dipesh Chakrabarty, 'Museums in late democracies', *Humanities Research*, vol. 9, no. 1, 2002, pp. 9 and 11.

71 Tony Birch, '"All things are linked or inter-related in one way or another": The recognition of indigenous rights with the Museum of Victoria', unpublished essay produced for the Museum of Victoria, 1996, p. 39.

72 Lydon, *Eye Contact*, p. 251.

6 Walking Lurujarri

1 James Clifford, 'The transit lounge of culture', *Times Literary Supplement*, 3 May 1991, pp. 7–8. Thanks to Stephen Muecke, Krim Benterrak and Paddy Roe for their textual introductions to Paddy's Country; Jim Sinatra and Chris Hand for additional materials, all those from the Goolarabooloo Co-op for their generosity and my hosts at the Centre for Cultural Studies, University of California, Santa Cruz for their responses. An earlier version of this chapter appeared as Chris Healy, 'White fee and black trails: Travelling cultures at the Lurujarri Trail', *Postcolonial Studies*, vol. 2, no. 1, 1999, pp. 55–73.

2 *Time Australia Magazine*, 2 December 2002, pp. 71–72.

3 Barbara Kirshenblatt-Gimblett, *Destination Culture: Tourism, museums, and heritage*, University of California Press, Berkeley, 1998.

4 For more useful cultural criticism on travel, see Chris Rojek & John Urry (eds), *Touring Cultures: Transformations of travel and theory*, Routledge, London, 1997; Caren Kaplan, *Questions of Travel: Postmodern discourses of displacement*, Duke University Press, Durham, 1996; James Clifford, *Routes: Travel and translation in the late twentieth century*, Harvard University Press,

Cambridge, Mass., 1997.

5 Male, German, aged 30–35 years, never visited Australia, reported in Australian Tourist Commission, *Market Research Intelligence on Aboriginal Tourism*, Australian Tourist Commission, 2003, p. 10.

6 Harris, Kerr, Forster & Co, *Australia's Travel and Tourism Industry, 1965*, Harris, Kerr, Forster & Company and Stanton Robbins, Sydney, 1966.

7 The full recommendations were:
The competent and sympathetic presentation of Aborigines' life and history in museums of natural history';
Performances and ceremonies as an important part of the Aborigines' place in Australia's tourist programme';
Presentation at missions, settlements and stations of the Aborigines' traditional way of life;
Re-establishment of Aboriginal art and artefacts to their natural, former level;
Tourist facilities should be established at certain destinations where there are natural tourist attractions and also Aboriginal settlements; pp. 281–83.

8 Harris, *Australia's Travel and Tourism Industry*, p. 281.

9 The most thorough national survey, although now somewhat out of date, is Jon Altman, *Aborigines, Tourism and Development: The Northern Territory experience*, Australian National University North Australia Research Unit, Darwin, 1988.

10 Each of these examples is explored as a case study on the Indigenous Tourism Australia website: <http://www.indigenoustourism.australia.com>.

11 Andrew Ross, 'Cultural preservationism in the Polynesia of the Latter Day Saints', in David Bennett (ed.), *Cultural Studies: Pluralism and theory*, Melbourne University Literary and Cultural Studies, vol. 2, Melbourne, 1994, p. 9.

12 Tourism Research Australia, 2005, *Snapshot: Indigenous based tourism in Australia*, TRA, Canberra (the major industry research body now amalgamated with Tourism Australia).

13 Tourism Research Australia, 2005.

14 Tourism Research Australia, *Sharing Culture: Indigenous experience and the international visitor*, Tourism Australia, Canberra, 2007.

15 Australian Bureau of Statistics, *Year Book Australia, 2004* <http://www.abs. gov.au/Ausstats/abs>.

16 <http://www.indigenoustourism.australia.com>.

17 Healy, *From the Ruins of Colonialism*, p. 17.

18 See John Frow's essay 'Tourism and the semiotics of nostalgia' in his *Time and Commodity Culture*.

19 Peter Brokensha & Hans Guldberg, *Cultural Tourism in Australia*, Department of Arts, Sport, the Environment and Territories, Canberra, 1992, p. 108.

20 Krim Benterrak, Stephen Muecke & Paddy Roe, *Reading the Country: Introduction to nomadology*, Fremantle Arts Centre Press, Fremantle, 1984, p. 126. See also Stephen Muecke, *No Road (bitumen all the way)*, Fremantle Arts Centre Press, Fremantle, 1997.

21 Department of Planning and Urban Development, *Cable Beach/Riddle Point, Broome Development Concept Plan*, Department of Planning and Urban Development, Perth, 1990.

22 AN Maiden, 'A traveller's guide to Aboriginal civilisation' and 'The hidden treasures of Aboriginal Australia', in *The Independent Monthly*, August and September 1994.

23   Meaghan Morris, 'At Henry Parkes Motel', *Cultural Studies*, vol. 2, no. 1, Jan. 1988, pp. 1–47.
24   Benterrak, Muecke & Roe, *Reading the Country*, p. 248.
25   Some of the results of this association are documented in Jim Sinatra & Phin Murphy, *Landscape for Health: Settlement planning and development for better health in rural and remote indigenous Australia: Visual story and documentation*, RMIT OutReach Australia Program, Melbourne, 1997 and Jim Sinatra & Phin Murphy, *Listen to the People, Listen to the Land*, Melbourne University Press, Melbourne, 1999.
26   *The Land of the Waterbank Pastoral Station*, Goolarabooloo Association, Broome, 1992, p. 10.
27   Michaels, *For a Cultural Future*.
28   Frans Hoogland, in Sinatra & Murphy, *Listen to the People, Listen to the Land*, pp. 22–28.
29   Val Plumwood, 'Wilderness scepticism and wilderness dualism', in J Baird Callicott & Michael Nelson (eds), *The Great New Wilderness Debate*, University of Georgia Press, Athens, 1998, p. 682.
30   Jon Altman, 'Indigenous Australians in the National Tourism Strategy: Impact, sustainability and policy issues', CAEPR Discussion paper 37, 1993, p. 7. It's interesting that Philip Morrissey makes a related point in comparing Paddy and Kevin Gilbert; 'Roe taking pains to emphasise Aboriginal sovereignty and the power of the *maban* (clever man) and by implication pre-contact forms of Aboriginal culture; and Gilbert working to emphasise Aboriginal dispossession and settler brutality and hypocrisy.' Philip Morrissey, 'Aboriginal writing' in Kleinert & Neale, *Aboriginal Art and Culture*, p. 318.
31   Sinatra & Murphy, *Listen to the People, Listen to the Land*, p. 18.
32   Lisa Palmer, 'Bushwalking in Kakadu: A study of cultural borderlands', *Social & Cultural Geography*, vol. 5, no. 1, 2004, pp. 119–20.
33   As the dedication of Benterrak, Muecke & Roe, *Reading the Country* reads: 'To the nomads of Broome, always there and always on the move.'
34   Chris Hand, *Draft Management Plan for the Lurujarri Heritage Trail, Broome, Western Australia*, Lurujarri Council in collaboration with RMIT University, Broome, 1993, p. 69.
35   Raymattja Marika, 'The 1998 Wentworth Lecture', *Australian Aboriginal Studies*, 1999, no. 1, p. 7.
36   Homi Bhabha, *The Location of Culture*, Routledge, London, 1994, p. 63.
37   Judith Adler, 'Origins of sightseeing', *Annals of Tourism Research*, vol. 16, no. 1, p. 9.
38   <http://www.garma.telstra.com/aboutgarma.htm>.
39   Aaron Corn, 'When the waters will be one: Hereditary performance traditions and the Yolngu re-invention of post-*Barunga* intercultural discourses', *Journal of Australian Studies*, 84, 2005, p. 30.
40   Langton, *Well, I heard it on the radio*, pp. 34–35.

7   Forget Aborigines

1   Slavoj Žižek, *Welcome to the Desert of the Real: Five essays on Sept 11 and related dates*, Verso, London, 2002, p. 22.
2   And so, in her Director's statement about *Vote Yes for Aborigines*, Frances Peters-Little can write, '[This] is a film about a time when Australians were yet to discover themselves and learn about Aborigines for the first time, and when

Aborigines were still able to shock whites into recognition and compassion', *The Age*, 24 May 2007.

3   Stephen Turner, 'Settlement as forgetting', in Klaus Neumann, Nicholas Thomas & Hilary Ericksen (eds), *Quicksands: Foundational histories in Australia and Aotearoa New Zealand*, UNSW Press, Canberra, 1999, p. 20.

4   Helen Sheils (ed.), *Australian Aboriginal Studies: A symposium of papers presented at the 1961 research conference*, WEH Stanner, Convenor and Chairman of the Conference, OUP, Melbourne, 1962, for the Australian Institute of Aboriginal Studies. Foreword by RG Menzies.

5   Sheils, *Australian Aboriginal Studies*, pp. 455–57. As Ronald M Berndt put the matter: 'in my view Aboriginal traditional life as a functioning reality and as a major emphasis will have virtually disappeared from the face of the continent within the next ten years or so.', p. 397. See also John Mulvaney's account, '"A sense of marking history": Australian Aboriginal Studies 1961–1985', DJ Mulvaney, Wentworth Lecture, 1986, <http://www1.aiatsis.gov.au/exhibitions/wentworth/m0032866_a.rtf>.

6   Sheils, *Australian Aboriginal Studies*, p. xvii.

7   Sheils, *Australian Aboriginal Studies*, pp. xiv–xv.

8   Louis Nowra, *Bad Dreaming: Aboriginal men's violence against women and children*, Pluto Press, Melbourne, 2007, p. 92.

9   Rex Wild & Pat Anderson, Ampe Akelyernemane Meke Mekarle: 'Little Children are Sacred' Report of the Northern Territory Board of Inquiry into the Protection of Aboriginal Children from Sexual Abuse, Northern Territory Government, Darwin, 2007, p. 13.

10 *The Australian*, 16 June 2007.

11 See, for example, Ian Anderson, *National Strategy in Aboriginal and Torres Strait Islander Health : A framework for health gain*, VicHealth Koori Health Research and Community Development Unit, 2002; Larissa Behrendt, *Achieving Social Justice: Indigenous rights and Australia's future*, Federation Press, Sydney, 2003; Peter Sutton, 'The politics of suffering: Indigenous policy in Australia since the 1970s', *Anthropological Forum*, vol. 11, 2001, pp. 125–73 and the subsequent debates in *Australian Aboriginal Studies*; Tim Rowse, *Indigenous Futures: Choice and development for Aboriginal and Islander Australia*, UNSW Press, Sydney, 2002.

12 Bain Attwood, *The Making of the Aborigines*, Allen & Unwin, Sydney, 1989, p. 95.

13 A process that, he argues, 'was determined more by Europeans than by Aborigines, because they had the power to shape the indigenous peoples as "Aboriginal"' (Attwood, *The Making of the Aborigines*, p. x). 'Out of the exchange or dialectic between the dominant and the dominated there came a transformed consciousness for the indigenes, one shaped by both European culture and by their own – and so their part in *becoming* Aborigines was both determined and determining. In other words, they played an important part in their own making.' (p. xi).

14 Attwood, *The Making of the Aborigines*, p. 95.

15 Kenny, *The Lamb Enters the Dreaming*.

16 Attwood, *The Making of the Aborigines*, p. x.

17 Eric Michaels, *Bad Aboriginal Art*, The University of Minnesota Press, Minneapolis, 1994, p. 29.

18 Michaels, *Bad Aboriginal Art*, p. 30.

19 Michaels, *Bad Aboriginal Art*, p. 41.

20 Michaels, *Bad Aboriginal Art*, p. 41.

21 Michaels, *Bad Aboriginal Art*, pp. 40–41.

22 Michaels, *Bad Aboriginal Art*, p. 42.

23 Here I'm adapting Paul Gilroy's formulation: 'It is also necessary to affirm that the peculiar synonymy of the terms "European" and "white" cannot continue.' Paul Gilroy, *Against Race: Imagining political culture beyond the color line*, The Belkap Press of the Harvard University Press, Cambridge, Mass., p. 141.

24 Wendy Brown, *Politics Out of History*, Princeton University Press, Princeton, 2001, p. 14. One Red Blood is an allusion to Darlene Johnson and David Gulpilil, *Gulpilil: One Red Blood*, Australian Film Commission, Sydney, 2000.

25 See Birrarung Marr at <http://www.melbourne.vic.gov.au/info.cfm?top=25&pg=2286>.

26 Tony Birch, '"Private Property" Responses to place in the work of Ricky Maynard', in *In Response to Place: Recent photographs from Ricky Maynard*, Exhibition Catalogue, 2007, n.p.

27 Leela Gandhi, *Postcolonial Theory: A critical introduction*, Allen & Unwin, Sydney, 1998, p. 4.

28 Emilio Crenzel, 'The voice of the State and memories of the disappeared in Argentina', unpublished paper, 2008.

29 Sara Ahmed, 'The politics of bad feelings', *Australian Critical Race and Whiteness Studies Association Journal*, vol. 1, 2005, pp. 72–85.

30 Here I'm paraphrasing Isabelle Stengers: 'For me, as a daughter to Western traditions, it is very important to say that we are unable to produce a conclusion to our history, because it means resisting the most obvious conclusion – we have won, we are the model for all people.' Isabelle Stengers, 'A "cosmo-politics": Risk, hope, change', in Mary Zournazi (ed.), *Hope: New philosophies for change*, Pluto Press, Sydney, 2002, p. 250.

31 Cowlishaw, *Blackfellas, Whitefellas*, p. 244.

32 Patsy Adam-Smith, 'Winds of change in the Territory', *Walkabout*, vol. 33, no. 8, August 1967, p. 35.

ACKNOWLEDGMENTS

My brother Mark asked often and patiently about this 'difficult second album'. It would not have been done without the support of many people who offered me the academic equivalents of occasional gigs and residencies, the chance to do a single or have a track on a compilation, invitations to collaborate, to put on a concert, produce a record, have a guest slot on radio or the space to try something out. It's meant a lot to me to have had these opportunities, most of which are acknowledged in the notes, but thanks again.

All of the institutions, businesses and individuals who granted permission to use images have been extremely helpful. Thank you. I'm also grateful for the assistance of Eddie Butler Bowden and Victoria Lynn in relation to images.

More generally, I'm grateful for the sustenance of collegial support; at the University of Melbourne from John Frow, Audrey Yue, Marion J Campbell, Fran Martin and Brett Farmer, and more broadly in the academic community, particularly from Tony Bennett, Dipesh Chakrabarty, Meaghan Morris and Graeme Turner. I also thank those graduate students from whom I've learnt a great deal, especially Hilary Ericksen, Alison Huber, Brian Morris, Maria Tumarkin and Paul Williams. Thanks to Stephen Muecke for setting me on some of the paths here and Klaus Neumann for reading the manuscript. I was lucky to be able to rely on outstanding research assistants in Isabelle de Solier, Alison Huber and Perrie Ballantyne and copy editing by Penny Johnson and Stephen Roche. Thanks to Phillipa McGuinness and her team at UNSW Press who were tough and staunch.

Special thanks to my long-suffering friends, particularly Dennis, Jeana, Carolyn, Jodi, Andrew and Annamarie, my brothers Paul, Mark, and Matthew, and their partners, Sharyn, Nicole and Lisa, my other brother Anthony Keith Birch, and my son, Finn.

INDEX